PATTON'S 1989 FANTASY
BASEBALL PRICE GUIDE

ALEX PATTON

A FIRESIDE BOOK • PUBLISHED BY SIMON & SCHUSTER INC.
NEW YORK • LONDON • TORONTO • SYDNEY • TOKYO

For Peg, who's next

FIRESIDE

Simon & Schuster Building
Rockefeller Center
1230 Avenue of the Americas
New York, New York 10020

Designed by Kathy Kikkert
Manufactured in the United States of America

10 9 8 7 6 5 4 3 2 1

ISBN 0-671-67444-7

"Rotisserie League Baseball" is a trademark of Rotisserie League Baseball, Inc., and is used by permission. For further information about the Rotisserie League Baseball Association, which provides position eligibility lists, official 24-man rosters mailed on Opening Day, a quarterly newsletter, access to a National Commissioner to interpret rules and settle disputes, a championship certificate for your pennant winner, and a bottle of Yoo-Hoo (if you live outside the Yoo-Hoo belt) to pour over your champion's head, write to the Rotisserie League Baseball Association, 211 West 92nd Street, Box 9, New York, NY 10025, or call 212-496-8098.

C O N T E N T S

Everybody has a system. Everybody. From Nathan Detroit to Jimmy the Greek, from Arnold Rothstein to Charles Goren. Systems are why Las Vegas stays open twenty-four hours a day. Systems are what keeps Donald Trump interested in Atlantic City real estate. Everybody has one.

Take Dan Okrent. (Someone, please. . . .) The Beloved Founder and Former Commissioner-for-Life of Rotisserie League Baseball has systems the way George Steinbrenner has pitching coaches. Serially. One, two, three a season. There is a special revolving door in the Okrent Fenokee clubhouse for the Swampmaster's system-of-the-moment.

One year it was a Relief Pitching System. The BFFCL decided he would buy only bullpen specialists, ranging from $40 closers to $3 setup men. I'll win Saves for sure, he convinced himself in another episode of the never-ending dialogue he carries on with his rich and varied assortment of personae. And I'll finish near the top in ERA and Ratio. So what if I finish last in Wins?

(While Okrent is talking to himself, may I have a few words with you? I haven't bothered to explain what "Ratio" is, much less "Rotisserie League Baseball," because I figure that if you didn't already know, you wouldn't have bought this book. After all, upwards of 500,000 people in America and Canada now play Rotisserie League Baseball, according to *USA Today* estimates, which confirms that it has actually become what we've always said it is—the Greatest Game for Baseball Fans Since Baseball.)

Where were we? Oh, yes—Okrent and his Relief Pitching System. He figured that his Fenokees would build up 28 to 30 pitching points and have enough money left from not buying the Orel Hershisers and Mike Scotts of the world to put together the most powerful offense in Rotissehistory. I'll rack up 34 to 36 offensive points, he said to one of his selves, and take my first ever Yoo-Hoo shower.

News flash: he still uses soap and water. (Though not, alas, as often as his closer friends might wish.) The thing is, it just might have worked. He *coulda* been a contender for the ritual anointment that confirms the new Rotisserie League champion each year. But our BFFCL is a charter member of the world's oldest fraternity, Woulda Coulda Shoulda.

As with his Starting Pitching System and his No Player Over $25 System and his Corner the Market on Speed and Trade the Excess for Power System, the Relief Pitching System never had a chance. One month into the season Okrent swapped a top reliever for speed. That might have been okay, because the Fenokees still had a topflight bull-pen, but the BFFCL got a starter back in the deal, and soon the System began to unwind. Next he jumped on a "great" deal for yet another starter, who promptly went sour and was out of the rotation an ugly month later. And by the All-Star break, our Founding Okie was right back in his ancestral bog, the Fenokee Triangle, a dismal place pop-ulated by teams that don't know whether they're coming or going, much less how to get there.

Why did Okrent's Relief Pitching System go sour? We'll never know for sure, because shortly after the season was over we passed an amend-ment to the Rotisserie League Constitution requiring a team to accu-mulate 1,000 innings pitched in a season or be dropped to the bottom in the ERA and Ratio categories. The amendment was Okrent's idea, of course: he's our Thomas Jefferson and James Madison rolled into one, with a pinch of latakia for depth.

Everyone who knows the BFFCL believes his systems bite the dust because he lacks the patience to test them adequately. The simple truth is you have to have more than good ideas in this world. The main difference between Okrent and Einstein, other than taste in popular music? Perseverance.

I don't want you to think that I'm picking on Brother Dan, singling out him and his much-ballyhooed Systems for special abuse. (No self-respecting Rotisserian would ever do that, unless it gave him a slight edge in a trade negotiation.) As I said before, all God's creatures have systems.

Take Harry Stein. (*Please!*) He has a System: "Lock up two cate-gories, usually Stolen Bases and Saves," he told us at last fall's Award Banquet, in explaining how his loathsome Stein Brenners had just won their third Rotisserie League Pennant. "Two categories, and smart drafting to fill in the gaps."

(Thanks a lot for the scoop, Harry. Let's see how the snerd does this season without Vince Coleman, finally a free agent after anchoring two of the Brenners' three pennant-winning teams.)

Or take Steve Wulf, boss of the Wulfgang and Stevie's Wunders. A pennant-winner in the Rotisserie League (NL players) and the Junior League (AL players), Steve hates starting pitchers. "Hate" may seem too strong a word, but how else can you explain his reluctance to pay more than $1 for a starter? In many seasons, Steve's entire starting rotation has cost no more than five or six bucks. Maybe "despise" is a better word. Whatever, his contempt can sometimes make for some pretty nasty ERA, Ratio, and Wins numbers.

Maybe it's time to take Alex Patton and *his* system.

(As a matter of fact, you already have—unless you're still standing in the bookstore, reading as fast as you can, trying to get as much information as you can without actually springing for the few bucks this priceless volume costs. Not that I want to put pressure on you, but the cashier is right over there, okay?)

If Dan Okrent is the Newton of Rotisserie League Baseball, then Alex Patton may well be its Einstein. Or maybe they're Drs. Frankenstein and Seuss; my memory's fuzzy. There's even a small Chance that they might be its Tinker and Evers.

Anyway, Alex has—are you ready for this?—a system. He calls it Patton Dollars. The $ have to do with how much a player was actually worth in Rotisserie League terms in a particular season, based on his performance compared with league norms. Notice the past tense: Patton $ refer to what a player was worth last year, the year before, two years ago. (Alex has another term for his prognostications about what the players will be worth this coming season: Patton Guesses. But you'd already guessed that, hadn't you?)

You will find out all about his system soon enough, so I will only make this observation: in Patton $, as in $E = mc^2$, the elegant simplicity of the superstructure camouflages an infrastructure of delicious complexity. Of course, Alex goes Einstein one better by adding player commentaries that are delightfully idiosyncratic and provocative.

If Alex Patton really has found the Rosetta stone of Rotisserie League Baseball, you will be washing your hair in Yoo-Hoo come October. But, hey—even if he just turns out *not* to be Dan Okrent, you've got a good shot at the first division.

Glen Waggoner
National Clubhouse Attendant
Rotisserie League Baseball
New York City
November, 1988

At this, which should be my happiest task, I find myself doing just what Satchel Paige advised never to do: looking over my shoulder to see dozens of people I have forgotten shaking their fists at me. Nevertheless, I must try to remember everyone, and they fall into various categories.

First of all, the price guide I self-published last year—which got me just the attention I was hoping for—couldn't possibly have been produced through my efforts alone. I attached myself to a fledgling company called Village Consulting. It had nothing like an organizational chart, but if it had, it would have looked like this: Adam Summers, Peg Summers, Colin Summers, Brett Summers, Alan Silber, Steve Stoneburn, Steve Levy, Henry Patton, and Michael Smith.

In the guide, I invited readers to become my ''consultants,'' sending me material about their leagues. The response overwhelmed me. I examined every item and in each found fascinating story lines; unfortunately, the stories couldn't end until October, and as I started writing, I relied heavily out of necessity on a huge, single source of information, only rarely weaving the names of my other consultants into the story in this book. Thanks to the following people, I had detailed information on twenty-nine leagues: Michael Belsky, Jim Chaffin, Jack Cohen, Barry Cohen, Michael Dean, Chris Dechiario, Dave Disselbret, Al Ettl, F. X. Flinn, Ron Fox, Steve Fox, Doug Garr, Bruce Grabell, Rich Gurnett, Rick Heath, Alan Jacknow, Karl Junkersfield, Frank Kastelic, Tom Leone, James Morgan, A. P. Morgan, Michael Nabi, Roger Neiss, Roy Nelson, Gene Oestreicher, Dave Peregrim, Brad Scharff, Sam Watson, Cary Wolfson.

Two people who helped me in my own Rotisserie campaign last year need to be thanked: Ilya Brook and Adrian Williams.

Two people who have taught me things about baseball which I would never have figured out myself deserve a nod: Eric Lindow and Bruce Buschel.

I very much appreciate the contributions Hollie Manheimer and Larry Zuckerman made to the manuscript.

That still leaves four glaring omissions.

1) Dollar Bill Berensmann, who was my partner, not coincidentally, back in the true glory days of Moose Factory. Such a shame he moved to France and then to the suburbs.

2) Jerry Heath of Heath Research: a prince of a person who provides an utterly reliable statistical service, the address of which is listed in the first Q & A to make sure more people see it.

3) My editor, Jeff Neuman, who shares my love of baseball and nearly killed me with his passion for perfection.

4) Peter Golenbock, who one day arrived at my apartment with a tape recorder to talk about Rotisserie baseball, and after a while clicked it off, saying, "Would you mind writing that down?"

It's about baseball. At least, that's what I told the few people I saw when I was writing this book. But it's not really.

It's about why Rickey Henderson, not Jose Canseco, was the best player in the game last year. Since that's obviously untrue, we must be talking about a different game, and we are.

I did not understand that, or understand it sufficiently, when I started playing fantasy baseball (which is really Rotisserie baseball, and henceforth will be called just that) in 1982. I had a little trouble that year. I knew more about baseball than was good for me, but I only finished fifth. I *knew* I knew more about baseball than the four bozos who finished ahead of me, so what happened?

I spent the winter figuring that out. (I teach, and am afraid I sort of cut down on batting practice, showing up just in time for the games.) I formulated a strategy with my partner that was different from the way other people played, and we squeaked into first in 1983.

The next year, I formulated a strategy that was radically different, and we won by a wide margin.

Facing fire-sale competition and the wrath of an entire league, we refined our method still further for 1985, taking it to its legal limits, and out-foxed everybody again.

Since then, we've been practically outlawed (the legal limits aren't what they used to be); worse, we've been copied. Nevertheless, it took that long for eleven teams in the American Dreams League, composed of many more than eleven extremely bright and absurdly dedicated owners, to catch up to Moose Factory, and they still haven't exactly *overtaken* the Moose. The record, since we figured out what we were doing: three firsts and five times in the money in six years.

That doesn't tell you why Rickey Henderson was worth $56.

Some people couldn't care less why; they take that ipso facto, curious though it may be, and want to rush forward from there.

Others are more skeptical; they don't want a lot of tips and advice when it's all based on prices which (A) they don't understand and (B) disagree sometimes drastically with their own evaluations.

Still other people, reading this introduction, haven't the faintest idea what *any* of this means.

Let's go backwards. If you don't know what Rotisserie baseball is, you'll want a book that will tell you, and this one doesn't. The only book that contains the complete and official rules of Rotisserie ball is *Rotisserie League Baseball,* by Daniel Okrent and Glen Waggoner. (For further information on joining the Rotisserie League Baseball Association, write to the Association at 211 West 92nd Street, Box 9, New York, NY 10025, or call 212-496-8098.) The 1989 edition, published by Bantam, should be in your bookstore right next to this volume. Another book, Peter Golenbock's *How to Win at Rotisserie Baseball,* was published in 1986, but was still on some shelves last year; it can tell you the basics, but doesn't have the complete and official rules. If this is your first year, you'll definitely want to buy one of these two; if that, on top of the price of the book you have in your hand, seems steep, save yourself a lot of money by taking up skiing or scuba diving instead.

Those of you who are skeptical, start reading. I've dealt with you many times; you're my favorites. When you're right, it's easy to take criticism.

Those of you who are impatient—well, you're gone already, I know that. I don't mean I've lost the sale; you're out the door with the book in a paper bag so no one else sees it. You're calling up the Conmen's Cannonballs to offer them Ron Darling at $18 for Ryne Sandberg at $25 before the Cannonballs learn Darling earned $15 last year and Sandberg $33.

You've taken all the other copies of the book on the shelf and put them in the football section, which I really don't appreciate.

So here, briefly, is the way the book proceeds. First, I explain what the prices are (a measurement of players' 1988 statistics in rotisserie terms) and the rationale for arriving at them. Understanding this will help with your single biggest job in the Rotisserie game—setting your own prices for the upcoming season.

Next, the earnings of all important hitters and pitchers for the last three years are given in the player profile section. A wealth of numbers, together with comments and hunches written in the dim light of November. Players are placed in their leagues as of December 10—just after the winter meetings.

Then I start discussing some of the implications of the numbers.

Based on much more data than I've ever had before, I look at how actual Rotisserie teams have fared. I compare the prices they paid for players, the market prices, to what Patton $ say those players earned.

I proceed from there to the minor leagues, which is very interesting, I think; that being so, I slip in the very boring technical stuff, which some people insist on, next.

The book comes to its penultimate end with one more Q & A devoted to some of the finer points of strategy, finally facing the thorny question in established leagues of Patton $ and freeze lists.

Last, an appendix ranking virtually all major leaguers at their positions in 1988 according to the value of their performances.

They are values to the dollar, with two exceptions. Among AL outfielders, the first two players are carried out to two decimals. This was how far I had to go to show which one was better, which one was the best player in Rotisserie baseball last year. Six cents may not seem like much, and it's not, but Patton $, like real baseball games, don't end in ties.

So the idea is that you're going to tell me how much to spend for everybody, right?

Not really. What I'm going to do is tell you what each player was worth last year, and that should help you decide this year's prices.

How do you figure the prices for last year?

Do you mean generally or technically?

Generally, generally. I've got a partner who's into numbers. I just want to know the basic theory.

All right. (Your partner should check out the ''Notes for Masochists'' in the back of the book.) The general idea behind my prices is to figure out what the average hitter and pitcher accomplishes, put a price on it, and spin all actual hitters and pitchers off of that.

Well, I can do that. Twenty-three players, $260 . . . that's 11.3. A little over $11 to spend on each player.

To spend, yes, but that's not what they earn. Hitters earn more than pitchers.

How can that be? Since pitching counts for half of the eight categories, they've got to earn as much. In fact, now that I think of it, since you've got only nine pitchers but fourteen hitters, each one of them should theoretically earn more.

But you know as well as I do that only suckers spend anywhere near half their money on pitching.

Because half the pitchers are bums. Even last year, with the new baseball, you had people like Blyleven and Valenzuela just totally trashing you in both ERA and ratio.

Yes, while even a wretched hitter can only really hurt you in one category.

What we're talking about is the difference between the stats you just total up (homers, RBIs, steals, wins, and saves) and those you calculate (average, ERA, and ratio). By definition, the average hitter is neutral in batting average, the average pitcher in ERA and ratio. In other words, the average hitter has three "good things" to contribute to your stats; the average pitcher, but two. The hitter contributes 50 percent more and should be paid 50 percent more.

For standard leagues that means the average hitter earns $13, the average pitcher $8.67.

Fine by me. Next, you figure the stats of the average hitter, presumably by adding up the league stats and dividing by the number of players?

More or less. The trouble is, a lot of the players who figure in your league's final stats weren't available, and thus weren't paid for, in April. Rookies like Roberto Alomar and Bob Milacki, transfers like Tom Brunansky. No matter what your rules for acquiring these players are—no matter how much they cost—they don't figure into the $260 salary cap. Therefore, I total what I call the draft populations; I base my average players on just those stats that were available at the time of the draft.

Whose draft? Your draft?

My draft and about twenty other drafts, in both leagues. Jerry Heath of Heath Research, a stat service for more than a hundred leagues, compiles as a customer service "hypothetical final standings" that show how teams would have finished if no moves—no trades, waivers, etc.— had been made all season. It's fascinating stuff that you'll be hearing a lot about here.

Maybe I should just grab a moment to say Heath Research's address is: 3841 Croonenbergh Way, Dept. 9P, Virginia Beach, VA 23452. The phone number if (804) 498-8197.

He's error-free, he's fast, and he's even got a fax.

My partner—he's so weird he does our league stats for nothing. But how different are these various draft populations?

Not different at all. There wasn't a league in the country that I saw spend more than $10 for Doug Jones, but we all managed to squeeze him in somewhere. (In my league, the supposedly superalert American Dreams League, he just made it, the last player picked.) The only serious absence on some of the rosters was Bedrosian, who was injured, which I've made allowances for.

I'm willing to bet your league doesn't vary from the profile in the Masochist Notes by more than 1 percent.

I'll try to get my partner to take you up on that. How about the average players in the American and National Leagues—was there a big difference there?

A big, big difference. Darryl Strawberry actually hit more home runs than Canseco, in the Patton $ world.

You mean his 39 were worth more than Jose's 42?

Exactly. And Rickey Henderson, who's worth as much as Canseco in the American League, wouldn't be worth as much as Darryl in the National.

You're not telling me Strawberry outearned Canseco?

No, it wasn't that extreme. But before we get into this business, which can become something like a hall of mirrors, let's go back to why 39 was worth more than 42, which is the key to the pricing system.

I have to put out a few numbers here, I'm afraid.

	AB	H	HR	RBI	SB	BA
NL AVERAGE PLAYER	354	92	8	41	11	.259
AL AVERAGE PLAYER	379	100	10	47	8	.263

	IP	W	S	ERA	Ratio
NL AVERAGE PITCHER	86	8	4	3.31	11.02
AL AVERAGE PITCHER	84	8	4	3.85	11.87

To focus on the major differences, the NL hitter gets more steals than home runs, while in the AL it's the reverse. The NL pitcher is more than half a run better in ERA. Since they have different statistics, does that mean they earn different salaries?

No, because the two leagues have the same budgets and the same rules. Both pitchers are worth $8.67, both hitters are worth $13.

The question is, How do we get the four categories to add up to these figures? How do we express four numbers as one?

Let's see . . . for starters, things that are harder to get should cost more. A save, for instance, should be worth more than a win.

Ah, yes, the scarcity concept. In a pure scarcity model you could spin all the quantitative categories off each other. Each save should be worth twice as much as each win. In the National League, each home run should be five times more valuable than each RBI, each stolen base less than four times, and so forth. In fact, you could say that each save in the American League was almost twelve times as valuable as each RBI.

Now what about the qualitative categories? How does Wade Boggs fit in?

The way we fit Boggs in is we keep spending until we get him.

Uh-huh. Well, thanks to Heath, I've got prices from all around the country, and in some leagues last year he went in the low twenties and in others the high forties. That's a pretty big range. I try to narrow it down a little bit.

Pitchers, of course, have two qualitative categories. What do you do about Joe Magrane, who couldn't buy a win but led the league in ERA?

Curse, mainly.

Teddy Higuera, too. Compare his stats with Allan Anderson's: They look identical until you work out their ratios. Anderson's is good, Higuera's is unbelievable. There's no question who does more for your team.

Then there's the ratio king, Dennis Eckersley. How does he compare to Anderson? Seventy innings versus two hundred. Who helps your ratio more?

All these questions have mathematical answers. Take your team's stats and add Eckersley's; do it again with Anderson's. You will find that Eckersley lowers your ratio more.

No kidding? Well, I'll tell you one guy I bet he wishes he walked: Kirk Gibson.

On the other hand, Anderson lowers your ERA more. So, discounting wins and saves, which would you rather have?

I guess whichever one lowers it lower.

But they're not the same. Suppose my ratio drops from 11.50 to 11.40 with Eckersley and my ERA from 3.80 to 3.75 with Anderson. Which is likely to help my team more?

Depends on the standings.

Exactly. So, in fact, the qualitative (or calculated) categories *can* be weighed with the quantitative (or totaled). In each case you ask the question, how much does Player X help me in the standings? Add Wade Boggs to your team, and see how many points you gain. If you gain more with Boggs than you do with Molitor, then Boggs is more valuable.

Is that right? Do your prices put Boggs ahead of Molly?

No, they don't. But in the exact context of your league and your team, Boggs *could* be more valuable. Suppose you won steals anyway; Molitor's 41 won't gain you a single point. Boggs might jump you around five or six teams in batting average, and Molitor only two.

What we need to know is the spread in the standings of various leagues. How many wins make a difference, and how many saves? How many RBIs separate teams? How many decimal points in batting average? With the Heath figures, I do this for dozens of leagues. For the most part, our assumptions about scarcity are confirmed, but not all.

Hello?

Sorry. Didn't get much sleep last night. Our assumptions about scarcity are—?

I'll try to wind this up. In most cases, the standings are more spread out when there is more of something. It takes fifteen or twenty RBIs to gain a point, while it might take only four or five home runs to gain. The big exceptions are wins and saves: Over and over you find that the wins category bunches more tightly together than the saves category. Each win, therefore, is more likely to help you in the standings. By this reckoning, each win is more valuable, while according to scarcity, each save is twice as valuable. I've got myself a dilemma.

How do you solve it?

Compromise. The steadiest thing going in Rotisserie baseball (in baseball, too—in each game played there's always one) is the wins category. Year after year, in league after league, approximately three wins separate teams up and down the standings. I make three my wins denominator: To determine what Pitcher X's wins were worth, I divide his total by three.

5

Instead of making the saves denominator 1.5, as scarcity would dictate, I make it 2.5. It's still true that each day when you look in the paper, you're happier to see a save than a win, because they're so hard to come by. But you're not twice as happy. You're 20 percent more happy.

The Masochist Notes give all the denominators. The most important point to understand here is that they're not the same for each league. Viola's ERA and ratio are measured against the average American League pitcher, with the result that Viola overall is worth the same as Hershiser, even though Hershiser had the same number of wins and saves with a supposedly better ERA and Ratio.

I think I know what you're saying. If Hershiser faced the DH instead of some wimp like himself, his ERA would be the same as Viola's.

Not would be, is. Take a second to look in the appendix. There's Hershiser, third-best pitcher in the National League last year. There's Viola, fifth-best AL pitcher. Both are worth $34. The next column to the left is the points each pitcher contributes to a typical Rotisserie team. Almost seventeen points each. How do they get the points? Mainly from wins, ERA, and ratio (Hershiser had one regular-season save, too). The four next columns to the left break this down. In both cases under Rto+ you see 4.0: The amount the pitchers' ratios helped was exactly the same. Under ERA+ for Hershiser you see 4.3, for Viola 4.7.

For actual standings, of course it's a quibbling difference. The fact remains, Viola's ERA *was* better.

As you get used to the charts, you're going to see differences that are significant. Eckersley's ratio is clearly more helpful than Stewart's, for instance. Look at the way Higuera separates from Anderson on ratio alone. Even with eight fewer wins, Higuera helped the typical Rotisserie team just as much as Viola.

A team that ended with 50 points without them would end with somewhere around 67 points with them. The average pitcher contributes a little more than four points and is worth $8.67. On that basis Higuera and Viola get their salaries of $34.

Pretty neat.

Darn right. Everything is worked out in exact relationship to everything else. A hitter who gains 9.3 points earns the same as a pitcher who gains 9.3 points. Those 9.3 points are worth the same in each league. What can be confusing, though, is the way the different denominators for each league create different points out of the same raw stats.

It's not a problem with wins and saves—last year the two leagues had the same number of saves, and they always have the same number of wins per team—but it is a problem with home runs, RBIs, and stolen bases. You see that Strawberry's HR+ is 9.8 compared with Canseco's 8.4.

I see it, but I'm beginning to lose it again.

The National League was so power-deficient that Strawberry's 39 homers were likely to help a Rotisserie team more than Canseco's 42.

Similarly, the American League was so much less a running league that Willie Wilson's 35 steals were good for 7.8 points, whereas Brett Butler's 43 only got 7.2 in the NL. McReynolds's 99 RBI were more valuable than Winfield's 107, and so on.

I know what you're saying, but let's get down to the nitty-gritty. You've got Henderson and Canseco each worth $56, but I'm here to tell you there's not one owner in the country who would think twice about who they'd rather have.

Who?

Canseco.

Absolutely not so. I'm an owner, and if I had Henderson for $56 I'd probably keep him. If I had Canseco for $56, I'd throw him back in the pool—or, more likely, try to trade him to you.

Listen, I'm talking about what they did, not necessarily what they're going to do this year.

So am I. (Although that is a good point. All my prices are measurements, not predictions.) Henderson last year was every bit as much of a player—*in Rotisserie terms*—as Canseco. He lapped the field in stolen bases. The next best total was 44. A hitter getting the same percentage of the home run total would have to hit *116!*

Take it easy. But here's a question for you. In the appendix you've got Henderson's SB+ as 20.7. Correct me if I'm wrong: You're saying Rickey raises you between twenty and twenty-one places in the stolen-bases category? That's a pretty big league you're in.

Um. . . . Let me explain it like this: True, the most points you can gain in a category are eleven or nine, depending on the league (you get one free), but what is the base? It's the last-place team, obviously, but that can vary tremendously. (My team, Moose Factory, had 27 steals last year, which I imagine trailed the next worst in the country by more than that.) What happens is that teams as well as players start out from zero. From then on we're climbing an escalator that's going down. We never do get to the top. The object is to be farther up than anyone else when the escalator stops at the end of the season.

So you're saying it takes a real long escalator to hold Rickey?

Precisely. (Nice image. Thanks.) For the normal immortals, like the star relievers, it takes a long escalator, but at least they have company. There's John Franco on the sixteenth step, and there's Todd Worrell, only three behind.

What would Rickey be worth in the NL?

Forty-eight dollars. Not shabby, but appreciably less. Canseco, if he had had his season in the NL, would have earned $59. Suddenly he's way ahead of Henderson.

As for what Canseco did, I think the numbers give him sufficient respect. For a hitter or pitcher to earn more than $40 takes a great season; $56 is mind-boggling. Last year in my price guide I spent a lot of time arguing hitters' prices down. Neither George Bell ($36) nor Andre Dawson ($37) made the top ten. Here's that list:

1987 MVPs

TOM HENKE $51	STEVE BEDROSIAN $40
VINCE COLEMAN $45	JEFF REARDON $40
ERIC DAVIS $43	JIMMY KEY $40
TONY GWYNN $42	DAVE RIGHETTI $39
PAUL MOLITOR $42	ALAN TRAMMELL $39

And here's this year's:
(Before you read it, there are two repeaters. Who are they?)

1988 MVPs

RICKEY HENDERSON $56	JEFF REARDON $42
JOSE CANSECO $56	KIRBY PUCKETT $42
DENNIS ECKERSLEY $50	ANDY VAN SLYKE $41
DARRYL STRAWBERRY $45	ERIC DAVIS $39
DOUG JONES $42	MIKE GREENWELL $39

I'll be damned. Eric Davis took a lot of guff for dropping $4.

He sure did.

And meanwhile you've got Jimmy Key sneaking in there two years ago, but Hershiser and Viola don't come close.

No starting pitcher, and, for the first time, a hitter with almost no running game in Kirby Puckett. (Only six steals. Somehow Greenwell got 16.)

In the player profile section, this is going to be the cause of the biggest confusion. Over and over, people are going to look at numbers that don't seem to add up. Kevin McReynolds, 1987, $26; Kevin McReynolds, 1988, $38. Mark McGwire, 1987, $30; Mark McGwire, 1988, $24. Chet Lemon. Hershiser. Viola . . .

When it's a pitchers' year, the few people who manage to hit the ball go way up in price?

Just as when there's a rabbit ball, the few pitchers who survive are extremely valuable.

I'm sure glad Ubie's gone, because he was messing with our game badly. Wait until you see the strange stuff going on in the minors last year. In the Eastern League, I was really scratching my head over the home runs denominator: To keep the proportions right, it looked as though it should be less than three. Well, three is the magic wins denominator, the rock to which everything else is moored. So I checked the league totals again, and by God, there *were* fewer homers than wins—less than one home run by both teams in each game! And the batting average of the American Association dropped twenty-five points.

These radical changes are no good; we literally don't know what it is we're looking at. But they do make numbers crunching valuable, as seen by the following:

Suppose you took a player, named him Mr. Consistency, and gave him 600 AB, 30 SB, 100 RBI, and a .333 BA. What would he be worth according to the 1988 formulas for each league? Answer: Fifty dollars in the NL, $48 in the AL.

Next, suppose you changed the denominators by the exact amount that the hitting was different in 1987. For example, if there were 38% more home runs in the AL in '87, as there were, you make the home run denominator 38% larger; specifically, change it from 5 to 6.9.

If you did this across the board for 1987 and 1986 and then fed those denominators to Mr. Consistency, how consistent would his price be? In the NL, he'd earn $46 in '86, $41 in '87. For the AL, it's $45 in '86 and $40 in '87.

It looks as though his wages are fairly erratic, but they're not. He's being paid exactly what he should be in relation to the league he's in. He's consistent, but the context isn't.

It gets even more extreme if we take an actual player instead of rounded Mr. Consistency with his power/speed blend. Had Andre Dawson exactly repeated his 1987 MVP season last year (49 HR, 137 RBI, 11 SB, .287)—without changing the 1988 NL totals, of course—the value of this performance would have jumped from $39 to $51.

Whoa.

The point is, the overall context lately has fluctuated as much as the players do individually. In the player profile section, I measure players over the last three years according to the method I've just described; the dollar values tell how a player has progressed or declined, in each year's context, working back from 1988.

You still look puzzled.

Let me just check out these profiles, then we'll talk about it some more. Okay?

Fine.

Let's see . . . alphabetical by position. I like that. Sort of like Who's Who . . . Ashby—oh, man, what a stiff. Who are you kidding? He didn't earn nearly that much. No one in his right mind would pay that much for Ashby now.

I never said I'd pay that much for him, and I'm not making a prediction—I'm telling you what he earned last year.

And I'm telling you you're full of it. Hey, don't get touchy. I'm just giving you my gut reaction to these prices. Give me a second to flip through them. I'll get back to you.

Take your time.

For the benefit of those who skipped right to this, let me repeat myself briefly. The profiles of the hitters begin with a three-year scan of their past earnings. Each year requires a different formula, since each year had a different hitting context. The following chart will give you a quick example of the way salaries change even if the statistics don't. Think of it as scanning Mr. Consistency in both leagues over the last three years:

NL	AB	HR	RBI	SB	BA	HR+	RBI+	SB+	BA+	POINTS	$
1986	600	30	100	30	.333	6.3	6.1	4.8	5.3	22.4	46
1987	600	30	100	30	.333	5.3	5.6	4.8	4.5	20.2	41
1988	600	30	100	30	.333	7.5	6.5	5.0	5.6	24.6	50

AL	AB	HR	RBI	SB	BA	HR+	RBI+	SB+	BA+	POINTS	$
1986	600	30	100	30	.333	5.0	5.3	6.8	4.9	22.0	45
1987	600	30	100	30	.333	4.3	5.0	5.8	4.7	19.7	40
1988	600	30	100	30	.333	6.0	5.6	6.7	5.2	23.5	48

If the plus columns bother you, ignore them; they show how the leagues themselves differ, and people in only one league usually don't care. The important business is the big salary fluctuation in both leagues, especially between last year and the year before. When you're looking at individual players, keep in mind that the discrepancy will appear even greater if the player is a nonrunning power hitter, since the biggest change has been in home runs.

If a player has been traded during the off-season from one league to the other, naturally the formulas switch, too. If, however, the trade occurs in midseason, I have a problem.

I solve it by taking the player's combined statistics and placing them in the context of the league in which he got more at bats. The team that is not in parentheses is the team he played more for. Normally it's straightforward, but it can look peculiar when you first see something like Brunansky 1988 (MIN+)/STL. People who had Brunansky in the American League know what I mean.

You look for your player alphabetically by position, starting with catchers, ending with outfielders; if your player is not listed at his obvious position, he's a nobody or I've goofed or I think his obvious position is somewhere else, in which case I try to leave a note. I strongly recommend keeping a thumb in the appendix while you browse; it shows where these players stood last year at each position.

Many players have been uprooted; Keith Moreland is a good example. He was probably bought as a third basemen at most drafts but only played two games there for the Padres. I could have listed him in the appendix at first base or the outfield (or even at third, since one of the aims of the appendix is to be an exhaustive record of who did what where in the 1988 Rotisserie Leagues). I list him in the outfield where, from the standpoint of depth, he was needed more; owners probably found themselves shifting him there, once he qualified, to put a waiver claim on, say, Ricky Jordan for the 1B/3B slot.

By contrast, the profiles are more focused on who might do what where. For Moreland, it's irrelevant what Sparky Anderson decides, and my opinion isn't the issue either. Where are readers likely to look for a certain player? Moreland played the majority of his games at first last year, and regardless of whether he's needed more in the outfield, he'll probably fill one of the corner bases at the draft. Anyway, first is where he's been put.

A small band of fanatics—last year's customers—is going to find discrepancies between the prices in the player scans and the prices in last year's guide. They will notice, for instance, that Henke has dropped from $51 to $49. The technical explanation will be found in the Masochist Notes; I tried to give the rationale in the preceding Q & A. I'm going to try to explain it further, but if you agree there's very little difference between $51 and $49, by all means skip the next paragraph.

I had the choice, for these player profiles, of listing prices quoted in Golenbock's book for 1986 and in my guide for 1987, or of showing prices for those years in exact relationship to 1988 prices. I chose the latter course. If you reinvent the wheel for each year, it will always be round and the wagon will roll just as smoothly, but the wheel might have slightly different diameters. By concentrating on the 1988 wheel and using it to determine the diameters of the 1986 and 1987 wheels, I feel we get the best possible picture of what we're really looking for, and that's what the wheel in 1989 might look like.

If these discrepancies are a minor problem, the next one could be major. As I conclude my writing in early December, it's already obvious that two propositions—fashions, more accurately—have returned to baseball.

You *can* trade your way to a pennant.

You *can* buy your way to a pennant.

I'm not sure Ubie knows when Rocky Colavito has been traded for Harvey Kuenn, but he's all too aware of the latter fashion. Is there little wonder that his farewell speech was "tepid," as sports writers reported from Atlanta? First of all, he never really gave a hootenanny about real baseball (if he was introduced to Rotisserie baseball, he would immediately have been turned off by the zero-sum aspect). Secondly, even as he was still commissioner, he was surveying the spectacle of owners intoxicated with the effects of the collusion rulings, and shooting through the roof of Ubie's salary cap.

The result is that we are already well into a winter of unusual discontent, both from the standpoint of players and teams: for me it means that I've already had to trash dozens of player comments. Inter-league trades require more than simply changing the comments, and more than simply relocating the names, too—they alter, often profoundly, the overall assessment of what's available at the position.

Finally, after all this sorting of formulas and shuffling of players, I'm supposed to say something. The question is, what? I *hate* making predictions; the whole point is *you* stick *your* neck out. Besides, so much of what I say, even if it sounds good in November, is going to be obsolete by March. I've tried to solve this problem by asking myself questions that might at least help start the engines revving as you do the real work when the time comes. Sometimes I stray and ask utterly useless questions. Sometimes I can't think of any or am simply giving us both a rest. I hope that the comments are on the whole more helpful than otherwise, and that if I sometimes say next to nothing, the numbers above should tell the tale.

NL CATCHERS

ALAN ASHBY	AB	HR	RBI	SB	BA	$
1986 HOU	315	7	38	1	.257	7
1987 HOU	386	14	63	0	.288	14
1988 HOU	227	7	33	0	.238	7

When a 36-year-old catcher takes the kind of jump Ashby did in '87, do two things: (1) Put a stethescope to the baseball, and (2) *stay out of the bidding*. Craig Biggio is a better bet this year.

DAMON BERRYHILL	AB	HR	RBI	SB	BA	$
1988 CHI N	309	7	38	1	.259	9

Switch-hitter who will obviously play a lot; 18 home runs in Triple A in '87.

BOB BRENLY	AB	HR	RBI	SB	BA	$
1986 SF	472	16	62	10	.246	16
1987 SF	375	18	51	10	.267	15
1988 SF	206	5	22	1	.189	2

This kind of drop is hard to fathom; despite his age, he's probably worth a (very small) risk in the end-of-draft crapshoot.

GARY CARTER	AB	HR	RBI	SB	BA	$
1986 NY N	490	24	105	1	.255	22
1987 NY N	523	20	83	0	.235	11
1988 NY N	455	11	46	0	.242	10

Patton $ to the rescue! The real decline came in '87 but was masked by that deceptive HR total. And while his dollar decline doesn't look so bad for '88, for the last two-thirds of the season he looked just awful.

In any event, here are some market prices for the Kid last year: Marshmellows (CHL), $31; Dad's Devils (ATF), $16; Flushing Meadows (PTL), $18; Bagel Boys (OOTL), $25; McNameePackers (HPL), $15; Sacred Vessels (BAL), $29; Dick's Detective's (VIC), $18; Bobby Sox (BEA), $30; Vicious Fishes (MNO), $24. I make of this that five leagues do and four leagues don't believe in "position scarcity."

JODY DAVIS	AB	HR	RBI	SB	BA	$
1986 CHI N	528	21	74	0	.250	16
1987 CHI N	428	19	51	1	.248	10
1988 CHI N/ATL	257	7	36	0	.230	6

Pushed out of Chicago by Berryhill, he's another battered veteran heading home, like Buddy Bell to Cincy a few years back, and Tommy Herr this year to Lancaster. The clock seems to speed up when that happens.

BO DIAZ	AB	HR	RBI	SB	BA	$
1986 CIN	474	10	56	1	.272	13
1987 CIN	496	15	82	1	.270	15
1988 CIN	315	10	35	0	.219	6

Speaking of clocks, hasn't Bo's been thirty-five for about the last ten years?

MIKE LAVALLIERE	AB	HR	RBI	SB	BA	$
1986 STL	303	3	30	0	.234	3
1987 PIT	340	1	36	0	.300	7
1988 PIT	352	2	47	3	.261	9

In his fine '87, when he first started hitting to the opposite field, he explained that he used to be a pull hitter with no power.

BOB MELVIN	AB	HR	RBI	SB	BA	$
1986 SF	268	5	25	3	.224	3
1987 SF	246	11	31	0	.199	2
1988 SF	273	8	27	0	.234	6

Figures to get 350–400 AB, though you may not want them.

TONY PEÑA	AB	HR	RBI	SB	BA	$
1986 PIT	510	10	52	9	.288	17
1987 STL	384	5	44	6	.214	3
1988 STL	505	10	51	6	.263	15

Finished like the old Tony Peña. If it really was the glasses that finally remedied the trouble, how come Herzog and the Cardinals weren't watching a key investment more carefully?

BENITO SANTIAGO	AB	HR	RBI	SB	BA	$
1986 SD	62	3	6	0	.290	3
1987 SD	546	18	79	21	.300	26
1988 SD	492	10	46	15	.248	15

Sandy Alomar supposedly makes him trade bait. That's amazing. The Mets are probably the only team that can afford to give up what he's worth, and that's scary.

NELSON SANTOVENIA	AB	HR	RBI	SB	BA	$
1988 MON	309	8	41	2	.236	8

Hit 19 home runs in the Southern League in 1987, but no mention of him in *Baseball America* or the Mazeroski annual. Kind of makes you lose faith in the old-fashioned Rotisserie work ethic.

MACKEY SASSER	AB	HR	RBI	SB	BA	$
1988 NY N	123	1	17	0	.284	4

Good bat, combined with Carter's terrible arm, makes him worth considering.

MIKE SCIOSCIA	AB	HR	RBI	SB	BA	$
1986 LA	374	5	26	3	.251	5
1987 LA	461	5	38	7	.265	7
1988 LA	408	3	35	0	.257	6

If you buy him, don't forget to buy Rick Dempsey. Just kidding.

OZZIE VIRGIL	AB	HR	RBI	SB	BA	$
1986 ATL	359	15	48	1	.223	9
1987 ATL	429	27	72	0	.247	15
1988 ATL	320	9	31	2	.256	9

His knees were so shot it's surprising he did this well. The ultimate test of Dale Murphy's virtue would be if they asked him to put the mask back on.

Player Z

He's named this to ensure he's last on the list. (The only one who can slip in behind him is Paul Zuvella, and he'd fit perfectly here if he had caught enough.) Player Z, among the catchers, wears uniform numbers fifteen through twenty; Ashby through Virgil have numbers one through fourteen.

You need six Player Zs, that is to say, and the most comfort I can offer is to remind you that real baseball teams are looking around for even more.

I can name the obvious ones: Sandy Alomar, Craig Biggio. I can hunt through my stacks of *Baseball Americas* and come up with the fact that Todd Zeile, a Cardinals prospect, was the all-star catcher in Double A ball last year. You'll find him in the minor-league section but won't see that he had 33 doubles and walked more than he struck out. Later on in the summer, he very well might be one of the twenty catchers on rotisserie rosters. (By next year, he could cause more trouble than Zuvella, forcing Player Z to become Player Zzzz—not a bad name, since they're all sleepers.)

I'm going to do what I can to be thorough as I proceed through the player profiles. It would be a tremendous stroke of luck if—by dint of sheer volume of name-dropping—no one makes a big splash in the pool next year that I haven't mentioned somewhere. But that's all it would be: luck.

It's absolutely essential for you to have a list of catchers that goes at least twenty deep, for just when you're about to gleefully pounce on Biggio for $1, as the only owner left with a catching opening, the guy across from you is going to switch Tom Pagnozzi to first, point a $2 finger at you, and say, "Suck air."

Some people don't like this part of the game. They think we're warped, not letting Von Hayes qualify in the outfield, even though throughout March he's been shagging flies in Clearwater. Some leagues take verisimilitude so seriously they make special dispensations. My league *is* warped. We became excited out of all proportion last year when we discovered that Jim Morrison, who had been brought over to the American League by Sparky to be a DH against left-handers when Ray Knight didn't feel up to it, had played 17 games at shortstop for Pittsburgh in '87, and hence didn't qualify; he was three games short. But Sparky, when he got the wobbly veteran, inserted him into real baseball games *three times* at short; based on his play in both leagues, he qualified there.

The few owners who picked through the leaf pile this carefully and found this out become unreasonably attached to Jim Morrison. They let real shortstops like Bobby Meacham and Manny Lee go by in the draft for $1. Oh, in their heads they convince themselves that Morrison has a little more pop left in his bat than these younger guys, even if the move over to the AL did cause his batting average to plummet to .205. Yet the real reason they pass is to be there at the end, needing a shortstop, nominating Jim Morrison for $1, and hearing some pompous ignoramus whine: "Only 17 games at shortstop for Pittsburgh!"

And then, of course, all the teams that had been waiting, that had had their hearts set on Jim Morrison, shortstop, began a bidding war. These small skirmishes are really much more exciting, if you're sufficiently warped, than the big battles. The BB Guns wrestled him from the rest of us for $4. After the draft, the BB Gun owner, Bruce Buschel, asked me, who had shot my bolt at $2, "Do you think he can hit still?" "Not a chance," I said, positive I was wrong.

A roundabout way of saying, I'm the last person who's going to find Player Z for you. But if you think the pursuit of him to begin with is trivial, you're quite mistaken. In the Heath leagues last year, the fourth-most important hitter—judged by the number of winning teams that bought him in the draft, compared with the number of last-place teams that did—was Andy Allanson, the Cleveland catcher. If you think Andy Allanson is still boring, I can't argue with that, but you shouldn't be playing this game.

NL FIRST BASEMEN

SID BREAM	AB	HR	RBI	SB	BA	$
1986 PIT	522	16	77	13	.268	21
1987 PIT	516	13	65	9	.275	15
1988 PIT	462	10	65	9	.264	17

He looks very good against lefties, but Elias (not to mention what you see here) doesn't bear that out. I still wouldn't completely discount Orestes Destrade.

JACK CLARK	AB	HR	RBI	SB	BA	$
1986 STL	232	9	23	1	.237	5
1987 STL	419	35	106	1	.286	26
1988 NY A	490	27	91	2	.245	20

The lawyers' leagues are going to have fun with this one. Clark played 10 games at first, 19 in the outfield last year—so what is he? He's placed at first here because the Padres act as though they've acquired Steve Garvey. (Are they in for a surprise.) Personalities aside, he sure hits better than Garvey did and sure gets hurt more easily. George Steinbrenner scared him into playing 150 games for only the third time in his career.

I wonder about someone who's thirty-three, who's played in one World Series (and looked bad), and who's satisfied to go to the Padres at this point. Is he content to leave the stage remembered for nothing more than what he did to poor Tom Niedenfuer? (I could understand when it looked as if Dave Henderson was toe-dancing out of sight after his lucky swing against Donnie Moore—though now I'd take him over Clark.)

I realize they're excited in San Diego; I realize there are people excited all over the country. If you're one of those owners who couldn't get 27 homers from your entire infield last year, of course you're glad to see Jack back—a free agent for whom no one's even got a topper—but I wouldn't go nuts.

WILL CLARK	AB	HR	RBI	SB	BA	$
1986 SF	408	11	41	4	.287	14
1987 SF	529	35	91	5	.308	29
1988 SF	575	29	109	9	.282	36

If by some weird chance or combination he really does get traded to the Yankees for Don Mattingly, I think we'd find from the market prices what Rotisserie leaguers thought of the deal. He'd fetch more than Mattingly.

GLENN DAVIS	AB	HR	RBI	SB	BA	$
1986 HOU	574	31	101	3	.265	27
1987 HOU	578	27	93	4	.251	18
1988 HOU	561	30	99	4	.271	32

Great year, not just in the National League context but in the Houston context (Doran hurt, Young fading, Bass under fire, Hatcher still not quite getting the hang of his all-wood bats).

LEON DURHAM	AB	HR	RBI	SB	BA	$
1986 CHI N	484	20	65	8	.262	19
1987 CHI N	439	27	63	2	.273	18
1988 CHI N/CIN	124	4	8	0	.218	2

Reminds me of Willie Aikens, the way they're so quick to get rid of him.

NICK ESASKY	AB	HR	RBI	SB	BA	$
1986 CIN	330	12	41	0	.230	7
1987 CIN	346	22	59	0	.272	14
1988 CIN	391	15	62	7	.243	17

Nick didn't exactly seize the opportunity caused by Leon's problem, did he?

ANDRES GALARRAGA	AB	HR	RBI	SB	BA	$
1986 MON	321	10	42	6	.271	12
1987 MON	551	13	90	7	.305	22
1988 MON	609	29	92	13	.302	38

Amazing that he got virtually no consideration for MVP. Andy Van Slyke. Will Clark. Orel. Was it racism? Or state-ism: an unwillingness to vote for players in Canada who don't lead the league in homers and RBIs. Galarraga played a great first base, led the league in total bases, was second in slugging percentage. Market prices for last year indicate how little prejudice and provincialism exist in Rotisserie leagues.

MARK GRACE	AB	HR	RBI	SB	BA	$
1988 CHI N	486	7	57	3	.296	17

Good, and yet, like Roberto Alomar—probably because we've become so spoiled by rookies—maybe not as good as people expected. Made a lot of errors: relevant if it's an indication he's being pushed too fast. The bright side is, if you were a semidisappointment the first year, you're less likely to have a sophomore jinx.

PEDRO GUERRERO	AB	HR	RBI	SB	BA	$
1986 LA	61	5	10	0	.246	3
1987 LA	545	27	89	9	.338	32
1988 LA/STL	364	10	65	4	.286	18

A classic fire-sale trade: Tudor, perhaps worth nothing now, for a hitter who should really suit the Cardinals better than Jack Clark. I always thought Clark's patience as a hitter was a drawback for their kind of offense; by the time the first three hitters have done their thing, a single or somewhat possible home run is better than a walk or strikeout or somewhat more possible home run. Everything points to the kind of comeback the Cardinals seem to produce every other year. That's the one thing I don't like about this forecast: Going back through Clark, Joe Torre, and Orlando Cepeda, it's almost too déja vu.

MICKEY HATCHER	AB	HR	RBI	SB	BA	$
1986 MIN	317	3	32	2	.278	6
1987 LA	287	7	42	2	.282	9
1988 LA	191	1	25	0	.293	6

Of all the improbable postseason heroes over the years—Dusty Rhodes, Gene Tenace, Brian Doyle—this just might be the most unlikely. But in addition to not being prejudiced, we Rotisserie folk are icily unsentimental. Cash in quick, Mick—real life's coming.

VON HAYES	AB	HR	RBI	SB	BA	$
1986 PHI	610	19	98	24	.305	35
1987 PHI	556	21	84	16	.277	23
1988 PHI	367	6	45	20	.272	17

Hayes played a total of 16 games in the outfield last year, but every time I saw him at first, I was reminded why the Phillies were where they were. Hopelessly out of position, he was, for a Phillie, a good sport about it. Now he's back in the outfield. For all his talent, Hayes is far from a natural, and it will be interesting to see whether he can remember how to play there.

KEITH HERNANDEZ	AB	HR	RBI	SB	BA	$
1986 NY N	551	13	83	2	.310	23
1987 NY N	587	18	89	0	.290	19
1988 NY N	348	11	55	2	.276	15

By losing him to an injury, the Mets learned how important he was.

BOB HORNER	AB	HR	RBI	SB	BA	$
1986 ATL	517	27	87	1	.273	24
1987 YAK (Japan)	303	31	73	0	.327	24
1988 STL	206	3	33	0	.257	6

His 1987 salary is set in the NL context of that year. His 1989 salary, for what it will be worth, will most likely be set in an AL context. I wouldn't be surprised if he says *sayonara*. A shame. His start in baseball, without benefit of a day in the minors, was better than his protégé Inky's, better than Winfield's, better than Kaline's, better than Banks's, better than anybody's.

RICKY JORDAN	AB	HR	RBI	SB	BA	$
1988 PHI	273	11	43	1	.308	15

Eighth in the Rookie of the Year voting? Probably because nobody had advance warning of this guy. Sportswriters don't read *Baseball America* for nothing. (I'm giving them too much credit, I know.) I would certainly not go overboard bidding on him—Tony Oliva, he ain't. But if I were in a league that allowed you to freeze your waiver pickups for $15, I wouldn't hesitate.

JOHN KRUK	AB	HR	RBI	SB	BA	$
1986 SD	278	4	38	2	.309	11
1987 SD	447	20	91	18	.313	28
1988 SD	378	9	44	5	.241	10

Most people are going to bet on his coming back strong; I'm not sure why, but I don't think so. I'd pencil in a price better than last year for him, but keep it conservative. With Clark in town, he moves to the outfield, where he already qualifies.

DAVE MAGADAN	AB	HR	RBI	SB	BA	$
1986 NY N	18	0	3	0	.444	1
1987 NY N	192	3	24	0	.318	6
1988 NY N	314	1	35	0	.277	7

If he really were the next Wade Boggs, Keith Hernandez would be Wally Pipp.

MIKE MARSHALL   *(see outfield)*

CARMELO MARTINEZ   *(see outfield)*

EDDIE MURRAY	AB	HR	RBI	SB	BA	$
1986 BAL	495	17	84	3	.305	21
1987 BAL	618	30	91	1	.277	20
1988 BAL	603	28	84	5	.284	27

This trade, when it took place, struck me as the most interesting illustration of two observations I had been making in other comments: the trend of sending natural DH-types over to the NL from the AL; and the trend of sending old or oldish soldiers home again before they fade away.

Murray is more interesting, I think, than Jack Clark or Kirk Gibson (and, I still predict, George Bell) as an example of the first trend, because he really has deteriorated as a fielder; the others may have never been any good to begin with. In any case, Eddie has become practically a stationary object; it's very hard to know whether his mobility just isn't there anymore or he's been in a perpetual zombie-like state.

If the latter, then the move to LA may snap him out of it. My dire predictions concerning the second trend (see Tommy Herr and Jody Davis) may not hold here. Obviously, I'm not sure (obviously, I'm waffling). One thing that was said in the newspapers when the trade was made—that Murray clearly hasn't been the same hitter in the last two years—is shown in Patton $ to be incorrect: Murray's bat was extremely effective last year. Preceded by somebody other than Billy Ripken, it would have been even better.

National League Rotisseries have to be very excited now. The appendix shows how egregiously thin the corner bases were last year, and the picture has suddenly changed radically. I'm pretty sure I'd chase Murray further than Clark in a draft, simply because of his durability, but Clark has seen—and thoroughly enjoyed—National League pitchers before; for Murray, there are the examples of Von Hayes, Lance Parrish, and Phil Bradley (I'm having trouble thinking of non-Phillies, but there must be a few) to give one pause.

In the end, I worry about that mood of Eddie's. Not that you could tell when he was in a good mood in his great years for the Orioles, but I do wonder if he's simply lost all appetite for baseball. If it's the unhappiness in his family that's at the root of it, will being closer to his family cheer him up or simply make him sadder?

Pee Wee Reese is supposed to have said, "A player who is in a hurry to leave the lockerroom after the game is in a hurry to leave the game." Eddie has struck me as being so depressed the last few years he couldn't even hurry.

GERALD PERRY	AB	HR	RBI	SB	BA	$
1986 ATL	70	2	11	0	.271	2
1987 ATL	533	12	74	42	.270	26
1988 ATL	547	8	74	29	.300	30

In our game, his very weaknesses—getting caught stealing a lot and not drawing many walks—are strengths. But even though he's a great Rotisserie first baseman, he doesn't give a major-league team what it wants from the position. Good thing he doesn't play for one.

FRANKLIN STUBBS	AB	HR	RBI	SB	BA	$
1986 LA	420	23	58	7	.226	15
1987 LA	386	16	52	8	.233	10
1988 LA	242	8	34	11	.223	10

Without a trade, he doesn't have much to cheer about. Apparently the World Series didn't save his career, but I'll bet it got a few scouts fired.

Player Z

It's hard to tell how many uniform numbers to assign him, because—as seen by the flurry of trades with the American League already—National League GMs are themselves disgusted with the production at this position.

One thing I've been able to glean from rosters is that few Rotisserie teams are able to get their utility men from either this position or third base. There's so little depth at the corner bases, as well as in the outfield, that the utility slot actually gets filled with utility ballplayers.

NL SECOND BASEMEN

ROBERTO ALOMAR	AB	HR	RBI	SB	BA	$
1988 SD	545	9	41	24	.266	19

Unlike Mark Grace, he began shaky but was really cooking by the end.

BILL DORAN	AB	HR	RBI	SB	BA	$
1986 HOU	550	6	37	42	.276	23
1987 HOU	625	16	79	31	.283	27
1988 HOU	480	7	53	17	.248	15

Supposedly he will be as good as new physically. Even so, I wouldn't fall for the illusion that he was getting stronger in '87.

RON GANT	AB	HR	RBI	SB	BA	$
1988 ATL	563	19	60	19	.259	24

As with Alomar, many Rotisserie owners were waiting for him, and he really delivered. Hit so well—and fielded so poorly—that the Braves moved him to third; the position flexibility could be very useful.

TOMMY HERR	AB	HR	RBI	SB	BA	$
1986 STL	559	2	61	22	.252	14
1987 STL	510	2	83	19	.263	15
1988 (+STL)/MIN	354	2	32	13	.262	10

In my Jody Davis comment, I make Herr seem as close to the end of the line; actually, I think he's closer. He's the same age and might have older knees; he didn't get beat out last year, he sat out. He couldn't get excited about Minnesota—a nice state and by far the most excited baseball region in the country. If he is depressed, it's nice he'll be working nearer his home, but the Phillies might not be the right employer.

REX HUDLER	AB	HR	RBI	SB	BA	$
1988 MON	216	4	14	29	.273	15

Wasn't on one reserve list that I saw. I don't really know whether he's beaten out Tom Foley, but he takes up less space.

MARK LEMKE	AB	HR	RBI	SB	BA	$
1988 ATL	58	0	2	0	.224	0

If Hudler gets a line, so should this guy. Small, but has shown some power. Check him out carefully in the spring.

JOSE LIND	AB	HR	RBI	SB	BA	$
1987 PIT	143	0	11	2	.322	4
1988 PIT	611	2	49	15	.262	13

A great glove who ended last year at the plate the way he ended 1987.

Time out for an editorial. At one Pirates-Mets game this year, I heard some guy yell at Lind from the third row, ''Hey, Jose, you gotta start stealing more bases!'' Now, you know as well as I do what that was all about, and we should all cut it out right now. It's not the fault of any major-league ballplayer that we play this silly game, or rather, this serious game with its silly rules.

RON OESTER   *see Jeff Treadway*

JOSE OQUENDO   *see shortstops, etc.*

WILLIE RANDOLPH	AB	HR	RBI	SB	BA	$
1986 NY A	492	5	50	15	.276	15
1987 NY A	449	7	67	11	.305	17
1988 NY A	404	2	34	8	.230	5

Willie took the pinstripes more seriously than any other Yankee—he may have been the only Yankee left who took them seriously. He'll get over it, in the sense that he's got plenty of baseball left. But he won't really ever get over it.

RANDY READY	AB	HR	RBI	SB	BA	$
1987 SD	350	12	54	7	.309	16
1988 SD	331	7	39	6	.266	11

He's placed here because this will probably be his Rotisserie position; however, all other pretenders to third base appear to have been cleared away on the Padres. It's the classic opportunity that good-hitting scrubs so often botch.

JUAN SAMUEL	AB	HR	RBI	SB	BA	$
1986 PHI	591	16	78	42	.266	31
1987 PHI	655	28	100	35	.272	33
1988 PHI	629	12	67	33	.243	24

He must be as bad as they say he is at second base, or they wouldn't say it (would they?), but the stats give a clear edge only to Lind and Sandberg. A great offensive player, anyway, who probably reached his nadir last year. The play of his team upset him greatly. (If it's a comfort, Juan, you were on many first-place teams in the Heath leagues.) I think he's going to come roaring back, wherever he plays.

RYNE SANDBERG	AB	HR	RBI	SB	BA	$
1986 CHI N	627	14	76	34	.284	30
1987 CHI N	523	16	59	21	.294	22
1988 CHI N	618	19	69	25	.264	28

Mr. Perfect who would be Mr. Dumped-On in New York. So he hasn't repeated 1984; have you repeated the best year of *your* life?

TIM TEUFEL	AB	HR	RBI	SB	BA	$
1986 NY N	279	4	31	1	.247	5
1987 NY N	299	14	61	3	.308	16
1988 NY N	273	4	31	0	.234	4

So many of his shots landed on the warning track this year that he decided he had a wrist problem.

ROBBIE THOMPSON	AB	HR	RBI	SB	BA	$
1986 SF	549	7	47	12	.271	14
1987 SF	420	10	44	16	.262	13
1988 SF	477	7	48	14	.264	15

When you've got a little, scrappy guy like this batting .304 in June, trade him.

JEFF TREADWAY	AB	HR	RBI	SB	BA	$
1987 CIN	84	2	4	1	.333	3
1988 CIN	301	2	23	2	.252	4

Glancing through the market prices for Treadway last year: $9, $6, $8, $12, $9. Reds management felt the same way, but by season's end had dug up Ron Oester again.

CURTIS WILKERSON	AB	HR	RBI	SB	BA	$
1986 TEX	236	0	15	9	.237	4
1987 TEX	138	2	14	6	.268	4
1988 TEX	338	0	28	9	.293	10

Of all the trades at the winter meetings in Atlanta, this one intrigues me the most.

When the Rangers made this deal, they presumably had the next one—which brought Franco from Cleveland—in place. They were picturing DPs of Fletcher-to-Franco-to-Palmeiro instead of Fletcher-to-Whoever-to-O'Brien. They were satisfied that Cecil Espy—incredible as it may seem—really is better than Oddibe McDowell. They were willing to gamble (or perhaps realized it was the Cubs who were gambling?) that Drew Hall could replace Mitch Williams.

The reason for these reflections here? It's my first chance to talk about it, and besides, Curtis never has gotten any ink of his own.

Or . . . ? Are the Cubs—every bit as methodically as the Rangers—getting set to ship both Dunston and Sandberg?

Dave Winfield, Dale Murphy—just to name two who probably wouldn't mind playing more than two in Wrigley.

Player Z

I've managed to list quite a few second basemen, if we count cheating ("Oester—see Treadway," "Oquendo—see shortstops"); the strict count and the appendix show many teams without clearly established regulars.

While not a deep position, it's got a fair amount of strength in it. It will probably get a little stronger: the loss of Sax counteracted by the addition of Randolph, the return to form of Doran, the development of Roberto Alomar, and so forth.

I'm not aware of many promising rookies, outside of Lemke, whom I've mentioned, and, of course, Ty Griffin.

NL SHORTSTOPS

SHAWON DUNSTON	AB	HR	RBI	SB	BA	$
1986 CHI N	581	17	68	13	.250	18
1987 CHI N	346	5	22	12	.246	6
1988 CHI N	575	9	56	30	.249	21

For all the criticism he takes—from me, at least; I think it's clear he's never going to learn to lay off the curve, which is the least he can do since he can't hit it—he still ranks fourth among NL shortstops.

KEVIN ELSTER	AB	HR	RBI	SB	BA	$
1988 NY N	406	9	37	2	.214	5

And I know this guy may be useless to us, but I can't help feeling he's the kind of shortstop major-league teams win pennants with. I think he's heading for a long career, though not with the Mets—Davey Johnson has a block about shortstops who can field. You'd think those years playing next to Belanger would have taught him better.

ALFREDO GRIFFIN	AB	HR	RBI	SB	BA	$
1986 OAK	594	4	51	33	.285	25
1987 OAK	494	3	60	26	.263	16
1988 LA	316	1	27	7	.199	1

I think the Dodgers are going to miss Juan Bell.

HOWARD JOHNSON	AB	HR	RBI	SB	BA	$
1986 NY N	220	10	39	8	.245	11
1987 NY N	554	36	99	32	.265	34
1988 NY N	495	24	68	23	.230	25

Despite his troubles, the third best you could have at this position last year.

BARRY LARKIN	AB	HR	RBI	SB	BA	$
1986 CIN	159	3	19	8	.283	7
1987 CIN	439	12	43	21	.244	13
1988 CIN	588	12	56	40	.296	33

The first best, as a lot of people predicted. Heath shows him as ranking third among all National League players, behind Daniels and Galarraga, for appearing on winning rosters. Now you know none of these players were secrets last year; what the three have in common is that they were highly promising but somewhat obscure rookies in 1986. My guess is that people were bringing them along at cheap prices all the way since then: the value of scouting. Of the three, Larkin was by far the most disappointing in 1987, hence by far the most gratifying to these patient owners last year.

JOSE OQUENDO	AB	HR	RBI	SB	BA	$
1986 STL	138	0	13	2	.297	4
1987 STL	248	1	24	4	.286	5
1988 STL	451	7	46	4	.277	13

With four more games at first, five more in the outfield, and 19 more at catcher, he would have qualified everywhere.

SPIKE OWEN	AB	HR	RBI	SB	BA	$
1986 SEA/BOS	528	1	45	4	.231	2
1987 BOS	437	2	48	11	.259	9
1988 BOS	257	5	18	0	.249	3

Spike can hit a little bit from the right side; if the Expos had planned to use him that way, he might have been a good $1 infielder. But if he can't earn more than these dollars in Seattle and Boston, what's he going to do in Montreal?

RAFAEL RAMIREZ	AB	HR	RBI	SB	BA	$
1986 ATL	496	8	33	19	.240	11
1987 ATL	179	1	21	6	.263	4
1988 HOU	566	6	59	3	.276	14

Strong effort, in the Astrodome no less. And if you still don't believe in him, there's always Craig Reynolds at the end of the draft for $1.

ERNEST RILES	AB	HR	RBI	SB	BA	$
1986 MIL	524	9	47	1	.252	7
1987 MIL	276	4	38	3	.261	6
1988 (MIL+)/SF	314	4	37	3	.277	10

The funny thing is that Jeff Leonard had to make a salary drive in September to outearn Ernie. He mostly played third base, but between the Giants and the Brewers he did play enough to qualify here—something to keep quiet, of course.

OZZIE SMITH	AB	HR	RBI	SB	BA	$
1986 STL	514	0	54	31	.280	19
1987 STL	600	0	75	43	.303	27
1988 STL	575	3	51	57	.270	29

Just like Ozzie to start hitting homers with the dead ball.

GARRY TEMPLETON	AB	HR	RBI	SB	BA	$
1986 SD	510	2	44	10	.247	7
1987 SD	510	5	48	14	.222	5
1988 SD	362	3	36	8	.249	8

Since he comes right after him alphabetically, the temptation is yet
again to comment on The Trade, but if I were Garry, I would be looking
down, not up. And if not at Thon, who in December seems to have
bolted, then at least Mike Brumley.

DICKIE THON	AB	HR	RBI	SB	BA	$
1986 HOU	278	3	6	1	.248	1
1987 HOU	66	1	3	3	.212	1
1988 SD	258	1	18	19	.264	10

In real life, someone would still be paying him for the long-term contract given him in the spring of '84.

ANDRES THOMAS	AB	HR	RBI	SB	BA	$
1986 ATL	323	6	32	4	.251	7
1987 ATL	324	5	39	6	.231	5
1988 ATL	606	13	68	7	.252	17

I wonder if, on December 8, 1987, they were dancing in the streets of
San Pedro de Macoris. (Also Boca Chica, which must be next door.)
That's the day Rafael Ramirez was shipped off to Houston, and look
at what it did for both players. In the box scores, you started to see
the name Thomas behind the name Murphy. Sure, the names Mc-
Reynolds or McGwire would have been preferable, but Andres held
his own. The NL shortstops, in fact, were a feisty bunch in general
last year: While people like Doran, Sveum, and Boggs were watching
their fly balls once again settle on the warning track, Thomas, Ramirez,
Oquendo, and, yes, even Ozzie were pounding them over the fence. If
I were Andres, however, I wouldn't party too hard this winter; in the
box scores in September, fairly often, you started to see the name
Blauser at shortstop.

JOSE URIBE	AB	HR	RBI	SB	BA	$
1986 SF	453	3	43	22	.223	9
1987 SF	309	5	30	12	.291	11
1988 SF	493	3	35	14	.252	10

Somehow he managed to play as well after he started playing again as
he'd been playing before.

Player Z

As I noted in the individual comments, this position had some surprising pop in it last year. However, it's almost impossible to assess the overall picture while we're waiting for the noticeably dissatisfied teams—the Cubs and the Pirates among them—to decide what they're going to do about it.

NL THIRD BASEMEN

BUDDY BELL	AB	HR	RBI	SB	BA	$
1986 CIN	568	20	75	2	.278	21
1987 CIN	522	17	70	4	.284	17
1988 CIN/HOU	323	7	40	1	.241	8

He says he's not retiring, but has he quit?

BOBBY BONILLA	AB	HR	RBI	SB	BA	$
1986 CHI/(+PIT)	426	3	43	8	.256	8
1987 PIT	466	15	77	3	.300	19
1988 PIT	584	24	100	3	.274	29

At a game in Sarasota in 1986, I watched him three times take three called strikes, and nine times shake his head with a huge smile. Is it possible this strange behavior revisited him over the second half last year?

JEFF HAMILTON/TRACY WOODSON

I've done an exhaustive study of these two, and I even watched the World Series, and I still can't figure out which is which.

CHRIS JAMES	AB	HR	RBI	SB	BA	$
1986 PHI	46	1	5	0	.283	1
1987 PHI	358	17	54	3	.293	15
1988 PHI	566	19	66	7	.242	18

Fielded .921 in 31 games here, but with Hayes and Samuel going to the outfield, he better keep picking those grounders.

GREGG JEFFERIES	AB	HR	RBI	SB	BA	$
1987 NY N	6	0	2	0	.500	1
1988 NY N	109	6	17	5	.321	9

I suspect there won't be many bidding wars on him because whoever got hold of him last year isn't about to turn him loose. (For that reason, I doubt many leagues will allow him to qualify at second base.)

VANCE LAW	AB	HR	RBI	SB	BA	$
1986 MON	360	5	44	3	.225	5
1987 MON	436	12	56	8	.273	13
1988 CHI N	556	11	78	1	.293	21

In his own modest way, he'll be as scarce as Jefferies.

KEVIN MITCHELL	AB	HR	RBI	SB	BA	$
1986 NY N	328	12	43	3	.277	13
1987 SD/SF	464	22	70	9	.280	20
1988 SF	505	19	80	5	.251	21

The Padres ripped themselves off in the McReynolds trade by not keeping this guy.

KEN OBERKFELL	AB	HR	RBI	SB	BA	$
1986 ATL	503	5	48	7	.270	11
1987 ATL	508	3	48	3	.280	8
1988 ATL/PIT	476	3	42	4	.271	10

Wherever Syd Thrift ends up, he'll end up. Of course, that could be in real estate.

TERRY PENDLETON	AB	HR	RBI	SB	BA	$
1986 STL	578	1	59	24	.239	12
1987 STL	583	12	96	19	.286	24
1988 STL	391	6	53	3	.253	11

Had knee surgery, but the real trouble is that those big thighs have too many muscles that go pop.

CHRIS SABO	AB	HR	RBI	SB	BA	$
1988 CIN	538	11	44	46	.271	29

The NL equivalent to Doug Jones: didn't cost a nickel, earned a fortune, and isn't available unless you want to trade your five best keepers for him.

MIKE SCHMIDT	AB	HR	RBI	SB	BA	$
1986 PHI	552	37	119	1	.290	35
1987 PHI	522	35	113	2	.293	29
1988 PHI	390	12	62	3	.249	14

Some market prices last year for Schmidt: Southwesterly Winds (WGL), $37; Cortlandt Cougars (WOR), $33; Lips (MNO), $35; Bums (CHL), $32; Conn Dements (HPL), $37; Mom-Mom's Boys (ATF), $28; Merry Larrys (BAL), $31; Kieran Beers (BEA), $37; Tommy's T-Bones (OOTL), $39; L.E. Dodgers (VIC), $35.

Plenty of respect shown for the greatest third baseman ever; even a little restraint, inasmuch as he came close to these prices the two previous years, and there is something to be said for sewing up a chunk of money in the bottom of your mattress where it won't collect interest but it won't go away either. Supposedly.

It was a question of when he would break down—a question that's still being asked of Nolan Ryan. But I can't quite tell whether he broke down as a result of his injury, or whether the injury occurred as he fought too hard to stave off the breakdown of his skills.

There's certainly going to be a larger spread of prices this year than those above (much cheaper overall, of course), depending on how Rotisserie owners make up their minds about which came first: irreparable old age or his piddling little rotator tear that's been taken care of. Supposedly.

TIM WALLACH	AB	HR	RBI	SB	BA	$
1986 MON	480	18	71	8	.233	15
1987 MON	593	26	123	9	.298	30
1988 MON	592	12	69	2	.257	16

In 200 more at bats, he had as bad a season as Schmidt (and therefore worse, for our purposes). He wasn't hurt, he's eight years younger, he's supposed to be even more dedicated. Some of the explanation was the new baseball, some was Tim Raines, but his season essentially was one of those quiet little mysteries that happen every year.

Pendleton, Schmidt, Wallach—it's not hard to see why the value of the average NL 3B took such a plunge.

DENNY WALLING	AB	HR	RBI	SB	BA	$
1986 HOU	382	13	58	1	.312	18
1987 HOU	325	5	33	5	.283	8
1988 HOU/STL	234	1	21	2	.239	3

Worth listing because of Terry Pendleton's thighs.

MATT WILLIAMS	AB	HR	RBI	SB	BA	$
1987 SF	245	8	21	4	.188	1
1988 SF	156	8	19	0	.205	4

Worth listing because, but for the small detail of last year, his career so far is a clone of Mike Schmidt's. And because of the small detail, it's worth mentioning Ernest Riles.

Player Z

Here, even counting the Hamilton/Woodson entry as one, I've managed to list more players than there are NL teams. The appendix tells the true story of dire weakness at this position. If Gant switches to third, Chris James doesn't get killed at third, and Schmidt rallies, wherever he is, the picture might improve a little.

Too many ifs, face it. Unlike over at first base, this position is going to be weaker. It's a situation that won't change, as far as I'm concerned, if Mike Pagliarulo and/or Jim Presley show up in the league. And there's nothing in the minors that makes much of a blip on my radar screen.

NL OUTFIELDERS

MIKE ALDRETE	AB	HR	RBI	SB	BA	$
1986 SF	216	2	25	1	.250	3
1987 SF	357	9	51	6	.325	16
1988 SF	389	3	50	6	.267	11

They moved Jeff Leonard to make room for him, and now they've moved him. Not a ringing endorsement.

KEVIN BASS	AB	HR	RBI	SB	BA	$
1986 HOU	591	20	79	22	.311	33
1987 HOU	592	19	85	21	.284	25
1988 HOU	541	14	72	31	.255	27

You'd have a hard time persuading them in Houston that he earned more money last year. He'll probably be earning elsewhere this year.

BARRY BONDS	AB	HR	RBI	SB	BA	$
1986 PIT	413	16	48	36	.223	20
1987 PIT	551	25	59	32	.261	25
1988 PIT	538	24	58	17	.283	29

Has caught up to and maybe passed Pop as a hitter, but 11 CS suggest he inherited Mom's legs.

HUBIE BROOKS	AB	HR	RBI	SB	BA	$
1986 MON	306	14	58	4	.340	21
1987 MON	430	14	72	4	.263	13
1988 MON	588	20	90	7	.278	28

Hubie, like Robin Yount, is a real outfielder now, and hits like one.

TOM BRUNANSKY	AB	HR	RBI	SB	BA	$
1986 MIN	593	23	75	12	.256	20
1987 MIN	532	32	85	11	.259	21
1988 (MIN+)/STL	572	23	85	17	.240	26

Of all the hitters who look like they're getting phony raises between 1987 and 1988, Bruno may be the most glaring. That's because both the league context and the baseball were switched on him.

BRETT BUTLER	AB	HR	RBI	SB	BA	$
1986 CLE	587	4	51	32	.278	23
1987 CLE	522	9	41	33	.295	23
1988 SF	568	6	43	43	.287	28

In contrast to Brunansky, Butler would have been worth significantly more if he hadn't changed leagues. Judging from the market prices, more people thought he would have trouble adjusting than Bradley.

VINCE COLEMAN	AB	HR	RBI	SB	BA	$
1986 STL	600	0	29	107	.232	**34**
1987 STL	623	3	43	109	.289	**44**
1988 STL	616	3	38	81	.260	**34**

In Heath's leagues, nine owners who bought Coleman in the draft finished first, ten finished last. It would be interesting to pencil in twenty-five more steals for each team that Coleman was on and calculate the resulting standings.

KAL DANIELS	AB	HR	RBI	SB	BA	$
1986 CIN	181	6	23	15	.320	**13**
1987 CIN	368	26	64	26	.334	**31**
1988 CIN	495	18	64	27	.291	**31**

One of the many players kept in the minors by Pete Rose's pursuit of the hit record.

ERIC DAVIS	AB	HR	RBI	SB	BA	$
1986 CIN	415	27	71	80	.277	**48**
1987 CIN	474	37	100	50	.293	**44**
1988 CIN	472	26	93	35	.273	**39**

I used to wait for Bob Horner to get 500 at bats. Well, consider what Davis earns without them. Imagine how he would look in a uniform projection, as I've done with the minor leagues. As it is, his $131 total in the last three years is exceeded only by Rickey.

There's definitely something peculiar about the Reds—they all, Sabo included, look as if they should be in jungle fatigues, which doesn't mean they're tough. I'd like to see Kal Daniels and Eric Davis stay together for at least one more year.

MIKE DAVIS	AB	HR	RBI	SB	BA	$
1986 OAK	489	19	55	27	.268	**25**
1987 OAK	494	22	72	19	.265	**21**
1988 LA	281	2	17	7	.196	**1**

Talk about not adjusting! Last year I questioned the credentials of the Twins as a Rotisserie team; these Dodgers, though, were something else. Imagine buying Mike Davis, Alfredo Griffin, and Fernando; trading away Welch, trading away Guerrero; making a waiver claim for Rickey Horton . . .

ANDRE DAWSON	AB	HR	RBI	SB	BA	$
1986 MON	496	20	78	18	.284	27
1987 CHI N	621	49	137	11	.287	39
1988 CHI N	591	24	79	12	.303	34

A few more ducks on second, and he would have earned the same as his MVP year. Wait a minute? There weren't ducks? What about Sandberg, Grace, and Palmeiro? We'll have to wait for Elias to figure this one out.

LENNY DYKSTRA	AB	HR	RBI	SB	BA	$
1986 NY N	431	8	45	31	.295	23
1987 NY N	431	10	43	27	.285	19
1988 NY N	429	8	33	30	.270	20

I just can't see Lenny Dykstra platooning with Dale Murphy.

KIRK GIBSON	AB	HR	RBI	SB	BA	$
1986 DET	441	28	86	34	.268	35
1987 DET	487	24	79	26	.277	26
1988 LA	542	25	76	31	.290	38

A legend, at last, in his own time. Even so, I can't help wondering whether Frank Robinson would have been the AL MVP in 1966 with Gibson's stats.

TONY GWYNN	AB	HR	RBI	SB	BA	$
1986 SD	642	14	59	37	.329	36
1987 SD	589	7	54	56	.370	42
1988 SD	521	7	70	26	.313	29

One thing about Rotisserie baseball, you can be totally schizoid; no reason to be consistent at all. Having earlier ridiculed Jack Clark for going to the Padres, I here find myself wondering if and if and if: If Clark stays healthy, if Roberto Alomar keeps progressing, if his brother or Benito is Johnny Bench, if the pitchers, etc.; and, of course, if Gwynn's thumb is all right, I see the Padres winning the pennant and Gwynn being the MVP.

BILLY HATCHER	AB	HR	RBI	SB	BA	$
1986 HOU	419	6	36	38	.258	19
1987 HOU	564	11	63	53	.296	32
1988 HOU	530	7	52	32	.268	23

Is it possible that the first time he corked his bat was in the playoffs against the Mets in 1986? That ball he hit in the greatest game I've ever seen . . . good Lord.

MICKEY HATCHER   *see first base*

VON HAYES   *see first base*

DION JAMES	AB	HR	RBI	SB	BA	$
1987 ATL	494	10	61	10	.312	19
1988 ATL	386	3	30	9	.256	8

Players like James are a problem. As a left fielder, he's clearly a stopgap move on a team this bad; if the Braves are ever going to go anywhere, they'll need more power out of the position. If they go the complete rebuilding route, James could see his at bats dwindle into the low two hundreds.

RON JONES	AB	HR	RBI	SB	BA	$
1988 PHI	124	8	26	0	.290	9

Great to have something nice to say about Philadelphia. A 550 AB season would project to $40. You can surely get him for less, and in what shapes up as the Year of the Rookie Backlash, he could be a nice gamble.

TRACY JONES	AB	HR	RBI	SB	BA	$
1986 CIN	86	2	10	7	.349	7
1987 CIN	359	10	44	31	.290	30
1988 CIN/MON	224	3	24	18	.295	13

This is the kind of player the Dion Jameses should be losing their playing time to. He'll be tough teaming with Butler at the top of the lineup.

CANDY MALDONADO	AB	HR	RBI	SB	BA	$
1986 SF	405	18	85	4	.252	18
1987 SF	442	20	85	8	.292	22
1988 SF	499	12	68	6	.255	17

As with Kevin Bass, the gnashing of teeth from his hometown fans masks some surprisingly consistent dollar values. Like Wallach, it's not clear what happened, but it should drive his price down.

MIKE MARSHALL	AB	HR	RBI	SB	BA	$
1986 LA	330	19	53	4	.233	13
1987 LA	402	16	72	0	.294	16
1988 LA	542	20	82	4	.277	25

Bob Costas got a lot of ink for calling the Dodgers' lineup in Game 4 the weakest in World Series history. Sabermetricians this spring are going to list 29 lineups that were worse; still, Costas was right. The statement that offended me—and it might have been by Costas, or it might have been by Al Michaels in the playoffs, they have the same ring—occurred earlier when Mike Marshall was called ''probably the worst cleanup hitter in baseball.'' Whoever said it (a) overrates Andres Thomas, and (b) knows as much about baseball as the crib cards in front of him, and should stick to what they say.

CARMELO MARTINEZ	AB	HR	RBI	SB	BA	$
1986 SD	244	9	25	1	.238	6
1987 SD	447	15	70	5	.273	15
1988 SD	365	18	65	1	.236	16

Hey, Bob or Al—this guy batted cleanup, too.

DAVE MARTINEZ	AB	HR	RBI	SB	BA	$
1987 CHI N	459	8	36	16	.292	15
1988 CHI N/MON	447	6	46	23	.255	17

Not shown here is his .139 average in 108 AB in 1986. If you stuck with him through that, congratulations, but he sure looked better running into ivy.

WILLIE MCGEE	AB	HR	RBI	SB	BA	$
1986 STL	497	7	48	19	.256	14
1987 STL	620	11	105	16	.285	23
1988 STL	562	3	50	41	.292	27

Here is why I keep taking shots at sabermetricians. They don't like McGee; he doesn't walk enough, he doesn't run enough (or he gets caught too often), he doesn't hit the ball far enough; who wouldn't—they ask—knock in a lot of runs with his number of chances? Whitey Herzog just laughs. Since Willie doesn't walk, Herzog has the runner ahead of him steal, and that gives him tons of chances. Elias will tell us how many Willie muffed last year, but if the lineup in spring training reads Coleman, O.Smith, McGee, Guerrero, Brunansky—as it ought to—Rotisserie owners should spend their biggest bucks on the guy in the middle.

KEVIN McREYNOLDS	AB	HR	RBI	SB	BA	$
1986 SD	560	26	96	8	.288	29
1987 NY N	590	29	95	14	.276	26
1988 NY N	552	27	99	21	.288	38

My favorite three-year scan. Look at those consistent stats; look at the way his salary jumps around. What people are going to be pondering, however, is his 1989 stolen-base total. It's well known he hasn't been caught in a very long time; he's obviously crafty. Does he care about his string? Will he be more cautious? Or will he let fly and see what he can do? My answer: There's no one in baseball who's a little like Jose Canseco but less like Canseco. Big Mac doesn't give a damn about joining any clubs. I suspect he also doesn't give a damn about his string. I figure about 25 stolen bases.

DALE MURPHY	AB	HR	RBI	SB	BA	$
1986 ATL	614	29	83	7	.265	25
1987 ATL	566	44	105	16	.295	36
1988 ATL	592	24	77	3	.226	19

This will be no comfort to you, Dale, and no surprise, but it wasn't just the Braves that finished last. Fourteen Heath teams that paid for you finished in the cellar; out of 171 players ranked by this method, you're number 171.

PAUL O'NEILL	AB	HR	RBI	SB	BA	$
1988 CIN	485	16	73	8	.252	20

He wasn't chopped liver, coming on strong at the end, yet I'll bet his owners were secretly expecting more. However, since no one paid close to $20 for him—the highest I've found is $13—he won't come up in many auctions. If he was mine, I'd make Van Snider a reserve pick.

TIM RAINES	AB	HR	RBI	SB	BA	$
1986 MON	580	9	62	70	.334	45
1987 MON	530	18	68	50	.330	39
1988 MON	429	12	48	33	.270	25

Unlike so many other people who suddenly hit some long balls in 1987, Raines was continuing to hit them at roughly the same pace before he was hurt last year. (Otis Nixon might be mentioned here for his valiant effort, but I doubt he'll make the team.)

GARY REDUS	AB	HR	RBI	SB	BA	$
1986 PHI	340	11	33	25	.247	16
1987 CHI A	475	12	48	52	.236	25
1988 CHI A/(+PIT)	333	8	38	31	.249	21

For some reason, Gary's real-life salary is comparable to his Rotisserie one, and it's guaranteed; meanwhile, he batted .197 and stole five bases for the Pirates. Rotisserie owners weren't surprised when Syd Thrift was fired, and they've already fired Gary.

R.J. REYNOLDS	AB	HR	RBI	SB	BA	$
1986 PIT	402	9	48	16	.269	16
1987 PIT	335	7	51	14	.260	12
1988 PIT	323	6	51	15	.248	14

Surprised? I am; he can do a little of everything, and the Pirates keep letting him do it. He'll never break out big, but he'll never be bid big either. The perfect fifth outfielder.

JOHN SHELBY	AB	HR	RBI	SB	BA	$
1986 BAL	404	11	49	18	.228	13
1987 (BAL+)/LA	508	22	72	16	.272	21
1988 LA	494	10	64	16	.263	20

Handled the game-winning run that McReynolds scored on him while he double clutched in the playoffs quite well, I thought. Mental toughness is what he was thought to lack. Given where the ball happened to go so often, he might have been the one Dodger besides Hershiser whom they could least afford to lose in the postseason.

DARRYL STRAWBERRY	AB	HR	RBI	SB	BA	$
1986 NY N	475	27	93	28	.259	32
1987 NY N	532	39	104	36	.284	39
1988 NY N	543	39	101	29	.269	45

The numbers here don't lie; the raise in his salary might even understate how much better Straw's 1988 season was than his 1987. In my guide last year, by the way, I advised spending a few bucks extra for him, perhaps $42, to put your money safely somewhere; I recommend not chasing him to $45, a surefire substantial loss.

MILT THOMPSON	AB	HR	RBI	SB	BA	$
1986 PHI	299	6	23	19	.251	11
1987 PHI	527	7	43	46	.302	27
1988 PHI	378	2	33	17	.288	14

See second basemen, Juan Samuel, and first basemen, Von Hayes.

ANDY VAN SLYKE	AB	HR	RBI	SB	BA	$
1986 STL	418	13	61	21	.270	21
1987 PIT	564	21	82	34	.293	31
1988 PIT	587	25	100	30	.288	41

In *USA Today,* I still look this guy up under St. Louis; wonder whether Whitey does. Yes, he had a career year, but he's so mad about not getting enough recognition (although it seemed to me he got plenty) that he might even have a better year.

MITCH WEBSTER	AB	HR	RBI	SB	BA	$
1986 MON	576	8	49	36	.290	25
1987 MON	588	15	63	33	.281	25
1988 MON/CHI N	523	6	39	22	.260	16

This wasn't just a drop in stats; when you see a big drop in dollars like this, watch out. He was terrible.

GLENN WILSON	AB	HR	RBI	SB	BA	$
1986 PHI	584	15	84	5	.271	19
1987 PHI	569	14	54	3	.264	11
1988 SEA/(+PIT)	410	5	32	0	.256	5

He was adequate with the Pirates, and they'll keep him around. It would be cruel to call Glenn a sleeper, in view of the medication he has to take, but he might surprise at a cheap price.

MOOKIE WILSON	AB	HR	RBI	SB	BA	$
1986 NY N	381	9	45	25	.289	20
1987 NY N	385	9	34	21	.299	17
1988 NY N	378	8	41	15	.296	18

In a sea of uncertainty—yearly hitting context, status on team—Mookie's a rock.

MARVELL WYNNE	AB	HR	RBI	SB	BA	$
1986 SD	288	7	37	11	.264	11
1987 SD	188	2	24	11	.250	6
1988 SD	333	11	42	3	.264	13

If he keeps playing, it will be because Abner and Mack still can't.

GERALD YOUNG	AB	HR	RBI	SB	BA	$
1987 HOU	274	1	15	26	.321	14
1988 HOU	576	0	37	65	.257	27

Wore himself out trying to run with Coleman. Also, apparently he didn't know that you can steal first: not one bunt base hit all season. Don't be surprised if that average comes up while the steals hold steady; he's exactly the kind of player that the market prices undervalue.

Player Z

There are so many outfielders already in the NL that can play halfway decent but don't really have a regular position—Dion James, Milt Thompson, Tracy Jones, etc.—and there are so few minor-league outfielders who had good numbers last year (but may be better than we think, judging by Ron Jones) that it's hard to guess whether there will be much turnover. But two contrasting situations are worth at least thinking about.

When the Dodgers refused to include Mike Devereaux with Juan Bell to get Murray, it surprised me. He looks to me like one more in the long line of good PCL hitters, especially Albuquerque hitters, who can't hit at the next level. I thought the Orioles did better in picking up Brian Holton for the bullpen instead. Mike disagrees and would love to have gone to Baltimore; he's fed up with the Dodgers. The Dodgers disagree and aren't fed up with Mike. The fact that I'm still not convinced is almost irrelevant; it would seem they now *have* to give him a decent shot.

Of course, the question is, where? If you're part of the legion of Shelby nay-sayers, you know your answer. Even if you're not, you can figure on Gibson and Marshall spending enough time hurt to give Devereaux his chance.

The other outfielder is Van Snider. Playing in a tougher hitting context, I think he showed he's a better hitter than Devereaux. As I indicated in the O'Neill comment, I see him forcing his way into the Reds' outfield, either in spring training or in the course of the season.

NOTES ON THE PITCHER PROFILES

All the quantitative fluctuations that batters have—home runs, RBIs, steals—really only affect pitchers in their qualitative categories, ERA and ratio. As we try to understand how a pitcher is doing each year in his context, all we basically want to know is: What were the league ERA and ratio that year? To be more exact—since they're different—what were the Rotisserie League ERA and ratio? This is the three-year picture:

NL	ERA	RATIO
1986	3.60	11.50
1987	4.00	12.22
1988	3.31	11.03

AL	ERA	RATIO
1986	4.12	12.21
1987	4.31	12.36
1988	3.85	11.87

This is what counts. Slight variations from year to year in how many wins and saves are bought in drafts in April don't matter (with one big exception). Consequently, in the pitcher profiles, these items are precisely uniform. The number of points that the average pitcher gets, since it's based on these items, is precisely the same each year. Finally, since the number of wins and saves don't change, the denominators—the key to determining the dollar value of the wins and saves—don't change.

Now, about that exception. The American League in 1987 had such slugfests, with relievers often getting battered even worse than starters, that saves became an endangered species. Normally there's about one save for every two wins; in the AL that year almost 100 of these saves simply vanished. In my price guide last year, to show exactly how much scarcer American League saves were than National League saves, I made the denominators 2 in the AL, 2.66 in the NL.

It was valid. It showed Henke to be a more powerful performer in his league than Bedrosian in the other, and he was. But this year, as I've explained earlier, the saves denominators for both leagues are a nice, simple 2.5. For the three-year scan for both leagues, to concentrate on ERA and ratio fluctuations, they remain 2.5, *except* for the American League in 1987, where it will be 2.

Having suffered through all that, we now can behold, with some degree of demystification, a friend of the Mr. Consistency from the hitters' profile introduction. This is what Mr. Unbelievably Reliable Pitcher looks like in both leagues over the past three years.

NL	IP	W	S	ERA	RATIO	W+	S+	ERA+	RATIO+	PTS	$
1986	200	10	10	2.50	9.50	3.3	4.0	2.7	2.5	12.6	26
1987	200	10	10	2.50	9.50	3.3	4.0	4.8	5.4	17.5	36
1988	200	10	10	2.50	9.50	3.3	4.0	2.6	3.1	13.1	27

AL	IP	W	S	ERA	RATIO	W+	S+	ERA+	RATIO+	PTS	$
1986	200	10	10	2.50	9.50	3.3	4.0	4.0	3.4	14.7	30
1987	200	10	10	2.50	9.50	3.3	5.0	5.8	5.7	19.8	41
1988	200	10	10	2.50	9.50	3.3	4.0	4.3	4.7	16.4	34

It's apparent that pitchers as a group, not just individually, fly up and down in their salaries even more than the hitters do. (How come? Well, I'm not sure I even know, but I can figure out that 4.31 is to 3.85 as X is to .269; that is, what would the pitchers' improvement last year in earned-run average translate into in batting average?

Granted, there's some distortion because of the different bases, but X = .301.)

Now, couple Mr. Unbelievably Reliable's salary flying up and down with the fact that individual pitchers' performances fly up and down with a vengeance, and you have an unstable situation. The charts reflect it.

Surveying such confusion, time and again shaking my head over how little we value even decent starting pitchers, I find myself turning the mike down more often. There's just not that much to say.

As many pitchers as there are, it's a more select group than the hitter sections. I don't get my fun from zapping Al Nipper—in real baseball he's more valuable than Nick Esasky—but someone's got to go. If I zapped one of your favorites, don't be irritated; buy him for $1.

NL PITCHERS

STEVE BEDROSIAN	IP	W	S	ERA	RATIO	$
1986 PHI	90	8	29	3.39	11.30	**30**
1987 PHI	89	5	40	2.83	10.82	**43**
1988 PHI	74	6	28	3.75	12.35	**24**

He got a win or a save in more than half the Phillies' wins, so he had a pretty good year on a bad team. On the other hand, those rises in ERA and ratio are pretty ominous in such a weak offensive season. He dropped almost $20; owners all over the country want to lynch Jesse Barfield for dropping $2.

TIM BELCHER	IP	W	S	ERA	RATIO	$
1987 LA	34	4	0	2.38	9.79	**7**
1988 LA	180	12	4	2.91	9.72	**19**

The chart doesn't show that Belcher did some other pitching in in 1987: Tacoma, Triple A, the Oakland chain. He walked 133 batters in 163 innings. He came over to LA on September 2, and the Dodgers—no doubt thinking, what the hell?—brought him right up. Did any Rotisserie owner in his right mind claim this guy immediately on waivers and pick up all seven of those lovely dollars? Yet somehow Tim Belcher has the chance of finishing his career without a ratio over 10. What happened?

TOM BROWNING	IP	W	S	ERA	RATIO	$
1986 CIN	243	14	0	3.81	10.93	10
1987 CIN	183	10	0	5.02	12.89	−2
1988 CIN	251	18	0	3.41	9.66	18

It could be that Ubie not only saved Tom Browning's career but his life. With the old baseball he would have given up, what, fifty-one home runs? And yet people had great faith in Browning. One team paid $21 for him.

TIM BURKE	IP	W	S	ERA	RATIO	$
1986 MON	101	9	4	2.93	13.54	8
1987 MON	91	7	18	1.19	8.01	37
1988 MON	82	3	18	3.40	11.96	15

I suppose there's no reason to feel that sorry for pitchers when a Belcher comes along to get bathed in glory and a Tim Burke can so radically deteriorate while barely drawing attention. His ERA doesn't look awful at all, and yet imagine if a hitter batted .340 one year and .119 the next. If that's unfair, and it is, look at it this way: The enemy hit around .270 against him last year; the year before, .196. The only batters who are that unpredictable are Tim Laudner and Dave Winfield.

DON CARMAN	IP	W	S	ERA	RATIO	$
1986 PHI	134	10	1	3.22	11.08	10
1987 PHI	211	13	0	4.22	11.22	11
1988 PHI	201	10	0	4.29	12.56	−6

Worst Patton $ pitcher with as many as 10 wins in the NL. That means he's for sure a bad Rotisserie pitcher, not necessarily a bad pitcher. However, the $17 drop, when on the face of it his stats look very similar, ought to give even a real general manager a moment of concern.

DAVID CONE	IP	W	S	ERA	RATIO	$
1987 NY N	99	5	0	3.71	11.91	5
1988 NY N	231	20	0	2.22	10.04	26

Let's talk a bit more about real general managers. In 1987 in one of the winter leagues, Cone's name was at the top—way at the top—of everything. As the Rotisserie owners came out of their groundhog holes and started talking, he was one name nobody mentioned. Because they didn't follow winter ball? No, because they did! Nobody owned him, everybody prayed no one else had noticed him. Then the trade, for a schlep. Humble Rotisserie owners said, ''Gee, he must have been getting Manny Mota out.'' He went cheap in the NL drafts, and he's the pitcher as responsible as anyone, according to the Heath rosters, for finishing first this year. No sympathy for the Royals! None!

DANNY COX	IP	W	S	ERA	RATIO	$
1986 STL	220	12	0	2.90	10.19	16
1987 STL	199	11	0	3.88	13.34	4
1988 STL	86	3	0	3.98	11.93	−2

Well over the league average in ERA and ratio; if you think he'll give you some wins, you risk a buck on him. In certain leagues, he'll go right through the draft and be an early reserve pick.

RON DARLING	IP	W	S	ERA	RATIO	$
1986 NY N	237	15	0	2.81	10.78	17
1987 NY N	208	12	0	4.29	12.07	7
1988 NY N	241	17	0	3.25	10.40	15

It was fascinating to hear him described as a crafty guy without much stuff in the playoffs. Do the announcers have better eyes than we do? Does some prankster like Roger McDowell sneak in to substitute Bobby Ojeda's crib cards? Darling's got stuff. He's even learned to control his stuff. Whether he's got the right stuff remains to be seen.

MARK DAVIS	IP	W	S	ERA	RATIO	$
1986 SF	84	5	4	2.99	10.39	9
1987 SF/SD	133	9	2	3.99	12.32	7
1988 SD	98	5	28	2.01	10.25	33

The difference a manager makes: The people who owned him then will tell you Mark was even nastier in 1986.

KEN DAYLEY	IP	W	S	ERA	RATIO	$
1986 STL	39	0	5	3.26	12.23	4
1987 STL	61	9	4	2.66	12.54	12
1988 STL	55	2	5	2.51	10.90	7

For a while, he had a 1:1 walk/strikeout ratio last year, but finished looking very sharp.

JOSE DELEON	IP	W	S	ERA	RATIO	$
1986 (PIT+)/CHI A	95	5	1	3.87	11.80	5
1987 CHI A	206	11	0	4.02	11.97	8
1988 STL	225	13	0	4.02	11.34	5

The pitcher who brought the American League drafts Lance Johnson.

JIM DESHAIES	IP	W	S	ERA	RATIO	$
1986 HOU	144	12	0	3.25	11.44	10
1987 HOU	152	11	0	4.62	12.20	4
1988 HOU	207	11	0	3.00	10.26	13

For the same amount of wins, he won three times more dollars. Does he hang around with Bob Knepper? Do different gods have jurisdiction over Houston lefties in even-numbered years?

ROB DIBBLE	IP	W	S	ERA	RATIO	$
1988 CIN	59	1	0	1.82	9.71	6

As you scan down the list of pitchers in the appendix, keep going until you find someone with almost no wins and no saves. His name is Rob Dibble. Then check the second player below and above him: Who do you see? Jose DeLeon and Nolan Ryan. That, I hope, demonstrates the Rotisserie power of a nonentity reliever, one who's never there when it counts, seldom there at all, but throws like hell when he is.

Dibble may *not* be a nonentity this year; he was very tough in the minors, and for Cincinnati he struck out 12 of the last 24 batters he faced and got 11 of the other 12 out.

DOUG DRABEK	IP	W	S	ERA	RATIO	$
1986 NY A	132	7	0	4.10	12.00	5
1987 PIT	176	11	0	3.88	10.79	13
1988 PIT	220	15	0	3.07	10.00	17

IP going up, ERA going down, has never given up more hits than innings; perfect guy to buy in a hitter's market.

DAVE DRAVECKY	IP	W	S	ERA	RATIO	$
1986 SD	161	9	0	3.07	11.35	9
1987 SD/SF	191	10	0	3.43	11.78	12
1988 SF	37	2	0	3.16	9.97	3

Hope he's all right. In the words of W.C. Fields, I'd rather have a rotator cuff.

MIKE DUNNE	IP	W	S	ERA	RATIO	$
1987 PIT	163	13	0	3.03	11.63	16
1988 PIT	170	7	0	3.92	13.29	−7

Nothing says there won't be a $23 swing the other way this year.

SID FERNANDEZ	IP	W	S	ERA	RATIO	$
1986 NY N	204	16	1	3.52	11.12	13
1987 NY N	156	12	0	3.81	11.37	12
1988 NY N	187	12	0	3.03	9.48	16

No one is harder to hit, and he even hits pretty well—even though El Sid gets a little too hefty for los knees. Yet I'll bet his owners aren't showing much profit on him. Everyone keeps waiting for "that one big year," and he probably just had it. He throws a lot of pitches, walks guys when that's the one thing you can't afford, and is an abysmal fielder—the kind of pitcher who makes his own hard luck.

JOHN FRANCO	IP	W	S	ERA	RATIO	$
1986 CIN	101	6	29	2.94	11.94	29
1987 CIN	82	8	32	2.52	11.30	38
1988 CIN	86	6	39	1.57	9.10	45

It disturbs me when I see Franco going for $17 or $18 last year. Was it that he didn't strike people out? Buy Dibble this year, if that's your thing, but jeepers creepers—Franco was no secret, look at the prices he was earning before last year. In fact, he ties with Todd Worrell and Dave Righetti as the biggest pitching earner in the three-year scan. Heath rosters rank him first, tied with Cone, as the pitcher most frequently found on a winner.

SCOTT GARRELTS	IP	W	S	ERA	RATIO	$
1986 SF	174	13	10	3.11	11.28	**20**
1987 SF	106	11	12	3.22	10.61	**24**
1988 SF	98	5	13	3.58	11.57	**12**

Solid ratios in view of how many he walks.

DWIGHT GOODEN	IP	W	S	ERA	RATIO	$
1986 NY N	250	17	0	2.84	9.97	**21**
1987 NY N	180	15	0	3.21	10.75	**20**
1988 NY N	248	18	0	3.19	10.84	**14**

The person thought of by most people first as The Pitcher hasn't approached $30 in quite a while. You can hardly blame the average baseball fan; the more moderate market prices for Gooden last year indicate that Rotisserie owners, like Doc himself, are coping with reality. But I'm not sure about Davey Johnson. Clemens was set aside for Hurst in the playoffs; it didn't work, but it made sense. There was even talk in Dodgerland in September of pitching Tudor ahead of Hershiser; at the time that made sense—Orel himself said it did, but he then pitched as though it was a lunatic idea. So there was Davey Johnson, and there was David Cone, the hottest pitcher in baseball since he'd started starting. Yet Davey starts Gooden in Game 1, and what happens? Johnson's right; Doc Gooden looked like and was The Pitcher; victory went to somebody else, but it was Doc's.

Switch to the fourth game. Because of rain, he's now matched against Tudor, and it's no contest, although the Mets bother to build only a two-run lead. Doc walks John Shelby in the ninth; this is entirely, 100 percent Doc's fault. But precisely because it is, shouldn't Johnson do something? Gooden finally gets his first postseason W if Myers comes in and snuffs Scioscia, so it's not sentiment, it's unblinking belief in The Pitcher. People in the bar I was sitting in were nervous. I was sitting in a New York bar; I'm sure the rest of the country, sitting there rather glumly, was as startled by what followed as Davey Johnson.

The more Gooden struggles, the more he grows. He was a changed person this season: honest, perceptive, amusing. The burden of having pitched his greatest season early in his career is shared by many; he's beginning to carry it better than any of them. The highest praise I can think of—and it will not seem like much if you don't know me—is that I'd bid him to $15.

RICH GOSSAGE	IP	W	S	ERA	RATIO	$
1986 SD	65	5	21	4.45	12.32	**18**
1987 SD	52	5	11	3.12	11.42	**15**
1988 CHI N	44	4	13	4.33	13.40	**10**

Can't call him Goose anymore; the Goose was a guy who threw heat and breathed fire. This one's just Rich, a so-so reliever who's got no business being in there in save situations. The only thing he's got left is his fearlessness, which has become a liability.

JIM GOTT	IP	W	S	ERA	RATIO	$
1986 SF	13	0	0	4.45	20.08	**−2**
1987 SF/PIT	87	1	13	3.12	12.52	**13**
1988 PIT	77	6	34	3.49	10.47	**33**

Thanks are due Tom Fulghum of Atlanta for calling me up and trying to bribe me to send him the prices early, because in the process of feeding him crumbs I discovered somehow Gott got forgotten and wasn't even in the appendix.

The obvious and spectacular change is in the ratio, but it's also clear that San Francisco wasn't quite sure what to do with him, while Pittsburgh saw him as the closer right away. By all reports, what turned it around for Gott was the confidence shown in him; in tossing bouquets at Syd Thrift, let's not forget the day-to-day contributions of Jim Leyland in cases like this.

KEVIN GROSS	IP	W	S	ERA	RATIO	$
1986 PHI	242	12	0	4.02	12.42	**3**
1987 PHI	201	9	0	4.35	13.07	**0**
1988 PHI	232	12	0	3.69	11.58	**3**

Gross is said to be a whiner; imagine the ruckus if he learned what being a pretty solid starting pitcher for three years netted him. The Expos clearly decided they'd rather have his reliable 200+ innings than a solid middle reliever and an unpredictable number of innings from the more talented Mr. Youmans.

Since we don't count innings, for the same price I'd bet on the talent.

ATLEE HAMMAKER	IP	W	S	ERA	RATIO	$
1986 SF			did not play			
1987 SF	168	10	0	3.58	11.57	11
1988 SF	145	9	5	3.73	11.01	8

The main effect of his injury seems to be that he gives up more walks.

OREL HERSHISER	IP	W	S	ERA	RATIO	$
1986 LA	231	14	0	3.85	11.63	8
1987 LA	265	16	1	3.06	10.92	26
1988 LA	267	23	1	2.26	9.47	34

Orel commanded the biggest market prices of any pitcher in the National League, so his hard-luck '87—near the end of which he was heard daring to propose he was a Cy Young candidate anyway—was fully respected by Rotisserie owners. As for this year, does the public at large even remember Danny Jackson?

JAY HOWELL	IP	W	S	ERA	RATIO	$
1986 OAK	53	3	16	3.38	12.83	16
1987 OAK	44	3	16	5.89	14.01	14
1988 LA	65	5	21	2.08	9.00	27

I'm no Dodgers fan. Before you get mad on the West Coast, I should tell you I'm just the right age to still be incensed by O'Malley. So it was funny as hell to see Howell surrounded and kicked off the field, his glove handed over the railing to one of the spectators. But I certainly found Giamatti's punishment to be absurd—even he did, finally—and the remarks by Don Baylor were beyond the pale. Therefore, I hurt for him when McGwire smoked him; watching Jay Howell walk off the field (even though he was able to hide it a lot better than Eckersley had earlier) made me for a moment stop wishing I was a professional athlete. I gave him a long, quiet clap after the next game.

BRUCE HURST	IP	W	S	ERA	RATIO	$
1986 BOS	174	13	0	2.99	11.33	16
1987 BOS	239	15	0	4.41	11.86	12
1988 BOS	217	18	0	3.66	11.92	13

Those prices are for real; he hasn't earned more. Obviously, people will be overspending massively for him this year; I'll be tracking the results next spring for the morbidly curious.

DANNY JACKSON	IP	W	S	ERA	RATIO	$
1986 KC	186	11	1	3.20	12.41	12
1987 KC	224	9	0	4.02	13.18	4
1988 CIN	261	23	0	2.73	9.56	28

John Schuerholz supposedly tape-records his rationale for making a trade after it's made; Rotisserie owners understand. Heaven knows what he said about David Cone, but it made sense to move Jackson along, and if he had just gotten Larkin in exchange, it would have been even.

PAUL KILGUS	IP	W	S	ERA	RATIO	$
1988 TEX	203	12	0	4.16	11.55	7

I had written, before he was traded. "The hitters seemed to be learning about him as the season continued, but I have a feeling he's one of those lefties who then learns what to do next."

I'll stand by that—with the added advantage for Kilgus, of course, that hitters are starting from scratch with him. The worry is—need it be said?—Wrigley Field. You can certainly look for a good April from Kilgus, at which point you might start talking to people who already are in dire need of a starting pitcher.

BOB KNEPPER	IP	W	S	ERA	RATIO	$
1986 HOU	258	17	0	3.14	10.26	18
1987 HOU	178	8	0	5.27	14.18	−9
1988 HOU	175	14	0	3.14	11.47	9

A typical yo-yo.

MIKE KRUKOW	IP	W	S	ERA	RATIO	$
1986 SF	245	20	0	3.05	9.51	23
1987 SF	163	5	0	4.80	12.59	−2
1988 SF	125	7	0	3.54	10.25	6

The string might have run out on Krukow.

MIKE LACOSS	IP	W	S	ERA	RATIO	$
1986 SF	204	10	0	3.57	10.97	8
1987 SF	171	13	0	3.68	13.00	8
1988 SF	114	7	0	3.62	11.49	3

A Rotisserie hot potato—crams the bulk of his value into one hot month each year, but Elias gives us no clue which.

TIM LEARY	IP	W	S	ERA	RATIO	$
1986 MIL	188	12	0	4.21	12.88	2
1987 LA	108	3	1	4.76	13.08	−2
1988 LA	229	17	0	2.91	10.12	19

The people who bought him for $1 swear they noticed his dominance in winter ball, but they'll be extremely upset if he tries it again. By September, he had nothing.

CRAIG LEFFERTS	IP	W	S	ERA	RATIO	$
1986 SD	108	9	4	3.09	11.83	10
1987 SD/SF	99	5	2	3.83	11.36	7
1988 SF	92	3	11	2.92	9.46	16

Because of our position restrictions and the fact that we're not actually trying to win games, it's rare that major-league teams make an in-season trade we can relate to. But here was one: Lefferts, Dravecky, and Kevin Mitchell—two pitchers and a third baseman—for Mark Davis, Mark Grant, Chris Brown, and a minor-leaguer. Despite what Davis has become, Al Rosen must be pretty happy with his end of it. I would be, too. Rosen got a divisional title out of it; I'd have shown a $25 profit on it in '87, with another $7 coming from '88.

GREG MADDUX	IP	W	S	ERA	RATIO	$
1986 CHI N	31	2	0	5.52	15.97	−3
1987 CHI N	156	6	0	5.61	14.71	−13
1988 CHI N	249	18	0	3.18	11.24	12

In the Heath leagues, he only ranks thirty-sixth as a pitcher on winning teams (five firsts, four lasts). How come? First, we can infer that a lot of people didn't pick him at all, with good reason. The total of nine is well below average. Second, I would propose that the four people who still finished last with him didn't have any idea what they were doing when they were selecting pitchers. As for the five who won, they *must* have been in leagues that allow you to dump pitchers at will.

JOE MAGRANE	IP	W	S	ERA	RATIO	$
1987 STL	170	9	0	3.54	11.49	11
1988 STL	165	5	0	2.18	10.02	13

Has to be the lowest victory total of any ERA champion ever.

RICK MAHLER	IP	W	S	ERA	RATIO	$
1986 ATL	237	14	0	4.88	14.35	−7
1987 ATL	197	8	0	4.98	13.57	−6
1988 ATL	249	9	0	3.69	11.60	1

Solid plugger. Avoid.

DENNIS MARTINEZ	IP	W	S	ERA	RATIO	$
1986 (BAL+)/MON	105	3	0	4.71	12.26	−2
1987 MON	145	11	0	3.30	10.74	15
1988 MON	235	15	0	2.72	10.33	18

No, it wasn't a fluke; he really is back. Another marvelously cheering example of Yogi's maxim.

ROGER MCDOWELL	IP	W	S	ERA	RATIO	$
1986 NY N	128	14	22	3.02	10.48	31
1987 NY N	89	7	25	4.16	12.44	24
1988 NY N	89	5	16	2.63	11.22	19

Rumored to be available, he's one of the many things my editor and I don't agree on. He'd trade him, I wouldn't, if we were Cashen. We both would gladly keep him on our Rotisserie teams.

ANDY MCGAFFIGAN	IP	W	S	ERA	RATIO	$
1986 MON	143	10	2	2.65	10.66	14
1987 MON	120	5	12	2.39	10.99	23
1988 MON	91	6	4	2.76	11.63	8

I'll bet even the people who owned him in '87 didn't realize he was worth that much.

ROB MURPHY	IP	W	S	ERA	RATIO	$
1986 CIN	50	6	1	0.72	8.46	11
1987 CIN	101	8	3	3.04	10.96	14
1988 CIN	85	0	3	3.08	11.37	3

Like Tom Henke in '87, couldn't find a win last year. There the similarity ends.

RANDY MYERS	IP	W	S	ERA	RATIO	$
1987 NY N	75	3	6	3.96	10.92	9
1988 NY N	68	7	26	1.72	8.21	35

He wanted more responsibility and more work, and only got one. The innings-pitched column will be interesting to see next year.

BOB OJEDA	IP	W	S	ERA	RATIO	$
1986 NY N	217	18	0	2.57	9.83	22
1987 NY N	46	3	0	3.88	10.76	4
1988 NY N	190	10	0	2.88	9.03	18

It worked for Mordecai Brown.

ALEJANDRO PENA	IP	W	S	ERA	RATIO	$
1986 LA	70	1	1	4.89	13.37	−3
1987 LA	87	2	11	3.50	12.31	12
1988 LA	94	6	12	1.91	9.73	22

An interesting question in projecting stats, given the fickle nature of Lasorda's use of relievers. Nominate Howell first, if you can, then decide; you may very well end up with the real closer.

PASCUAL PEREZ	IP	W	S	ERA	RATIO	$
1986			out of baseball			
1987 MON	70	7	0	2.30	8.74	15
1988 MON	188	12	0	2.44	8.47	24

Those are possibly the best ERAs and ratios for any starting pitcher, or anyone with that much more than two hundred innings, in the last two years.

DENNIS RASMUSSEN	IP	W	S	ERA	RATIO	$
1986 NY A	202	18	0	3.88	10.43	18
1987 NY A/(+CIN)	191	13	0	4.57	11.83	9
1988 CIN/SD	205	16	0	3.43	11.30	9

Wouldn't he look good in pinstripes now, George? And how did Bill Gullickson do in Japan last year?

RICK REUSCHEL	IP	W	S	ERA	RATIO	$
1986 PIT	216	9	0	3.96	12.04	3
1987 PIT/SF	227	13	0	3.09	9.87	26
1988 SF	245	19	0	3.12	10.43	17

His walks went down, but his ratio went up, a warning sign. His ERAs look the same and truly aren't; the ERA+ in the appendix reads 0.7, signifying that he gained the typical Rotisserie team under a point in the ERA standings last year. His ERA+ for 1987 was 3.4.

JOSE RIJO	IP	W	S	ERA	RATIO	$
1986 OAK	194	9	0	4.65	12.99	−3
1987 OAK	82	2	0	5.90	16.13	−12
1988 CIN	162	13	0	2.39	10.17	17

The biggest leap from the red to the black, by far. How could the Reds gain Rijo and Danny Jackson, giving up nothing they needed, and still not make a race of it?

DON ROBINSON	IP	W	S	ERA	RATIO	$
1986 PIT	69	3	14	3.38	11.48	14
1987 PIT/SF	108	11	19	3.42	12.08	25
1988 SF	177	10	6	2.45	10.24	20

Ended strong as a starter, but these dollars won't stand up if he's going to be in the rotation all year.

JEFF ROBINSON	IP	W	S	ERA	RATIO	$
1986 SF	104	6	8	3.36	10.73	12
1987 SF/PIT	123	8	14	2.85	10.46	26
1988 PIT	125	11	9	3.03	10.97	16

It was bad enough when the Giants and Pirates swapped Robinsons; then along came the guy in Detroit. The Robinsons are threatening to overtake the Davises; they already lead in Hall of Famers, 4–0.

RON ROBINSON   *omitted, to lessen the confusion*

BRUCE RUFFIN	IP	W	S	ERA	RATIO	$
1986 PHI	146	9	0	2.46	11.19	11
1987 PHI	205	11	0	4.35	13.59	−1
1988 PHI	144	6	3	4.43	14.40	−9

The dollar figure is one with which Lee Elia would, no doubt, heartily concur.

CALVIN SCHIRALDI	IP	W	S	ERA	RATIO	$
1986 BOS	51	4	9	1.41	9.00	16
1987 BOS	84	8	6	4.41	12.37	11
1988 CHI N	166	9	1	4.38	12.39	−4

My editor is a Red Sox fan. He went to a Mets-Cubs game in June without knowing who was going to pitch. When he saw it was Schiraldi, he remembered the last time he had been at Shea Stadium with Schiraldi on the mound, and he wept piteously. He would like it known that anyone who bought this guy last year deserved it. (I would like to note that my editor probably knew who was pitching for both teams for the next two weeks, perhaps even before Zimmer and Johnson did.)

MIKE SCOTT	IP	W	S	ERA	RATIO	$
1986 HOU	275	18	0	2.22	8.31	32
1987 HOU	245	16	0	3.23	10.21	26
1988 HOU	219	14	0	2.92	8.85	22

Here's why I refuse to spend $20 for my starters: Suppose I had paid $20 for Scott. I get a very respectable year—and a $2 profit. For the risk I'm taking (all pitchers should be looked at as venture capital) that's not enough. And I doubt there are five leagues in the country in which $20 would have gotten Scott.

ERIC SHOW	IP	W	S	ERA	RATIO	$
1986 SD	136	9	0	2.97	11.78	8
1987 SD	206	8	0	3.84	11.93	8
1988 SD	235	16	0	3.26	9.74	18

Another test in projection. Where's the upside if you buy him based on his '88 season? Will Jack Clark really mean more than 16 wins for Show? Will the Padres' improvement help those ERAs or ratios? Not likely. Expect him to earn something like $10 to $13 in '89, and underbid accordingly.

JOHN SMILEY	IP	W	S	ERA	RATIO	$
1987 PIT	75	5	4	5.76	14.28	−2
1988 PIT	205	13	0	3.25	10.14	13

Much more canny bet on a pitcher who was in the red last year than Greg Maddux, and the Heath rosters agree with me: eight firsts, one last. (And a lot of people still not taking.)

BRYN SMITH	IP	W	S	ERA	RATIO	$
1986 MON	187	10	0	3.94	11.79	4
1987 MON	150	10	0	4.37	11.70	6
1988 MON	198	12	0	3.00	9.59	16

See Eric Show, add in the possibility of injury again, and be even more careful.

DAVE SMITH	IP	W	S	ERA	RATIO	$
1986 HOU	56	4	33	2.73	9.80	32
1987 HOU	60	2	24	1.65	9.00	30
1988 HOU	57	4	27	2.67	12.40	25

When I see that kind of jump in ratio (the ERA rise for a reliever in this few innings could be random) I get very, very nervous, just as the manager must have.

ZANE SMITH	IP	W	S	ERA	RATIO	$
1986 ATL	205	8	1	4.05	13.79	−2
1987 ATL	242	15	0	4.09	12.50	8
1988 ATL	140	5	0	4.30	13.02	−7

Bobby Cox would just get his pants stolen in a Rotisserie League. He waits and waits and waits when the market is hot for one of his players. Then it gets cold. Okay, he's still got his pants, but overcoats cost almost as much as Damaco Garcia.

RICK SUTCLIFFE	IP	W	S	ERA	RATIO	$
1986 CHI N	177	5	0	4.64	13.32	−6
1987 CHI N	237	18	0	3.68	12.49	13
1988 CHI N	226	13	0	3.86	12.03	1

I have no quarrel with sabermetricians who will explain his ERA and ratio as the result of the park, but we Rotisserie types just have to accept it.

BRUCE SUTTER	IP	W	S	ERA	RATIO	$
1986 ATL	19	2	3	4.34	12.32	3
1987 ATL			did not play			
1988 ATL	45	1	14	4.77	11.91	9

For a while it did look like he was back.

WALT TERRELL	IP	W	S	ERA	RATIO	$
1986 DET	217	15	0	4.56	12.32	7
1987 DET	245	17	0	4.05	12.78	12
1988 DET	206	7	0	3.97	12.08	3

A third-starter addition to a pitching staff of third starters.

JOHN TUDOR	IP	W	S	ERA	RATIO	$
1986 STL	219	13	0	2.92	10.27	16
1987 STL	96	10	0	3.84	12.38	7
1988 STL/LA	198	10	0	2.32	10.47	16

Except for '85, he was never that great a Rotisserie pitcher, a fact he would no doubt greet with the enthusiasm he usually reserves for reporters, dugout fans, and life in general.

FERNANDO VALENZUELA	IP	W	S	ERA	RATIO	$
1986 LA	269	21	0	3.14	10.41	21
1987 LA	251	14	0	3.98	13.55	3
1988 LA	142	5	1	4.24	13.78	−8

If you bought him in '88 you only have yourself—and Tommy Lasorda, for making him throw so many innings so often so young—to blame.

BOB WALK	IP	W	S	ERA	RATIO	$
1986 PIT	142	7	2	3.75	12.23	4
1987 PIT	117	8	0	3.31	12.15	8
1988 PIT	213	12	0	2.71	10.50	15

I don't think he'll be available much—a lot of people should have carried him cheap after '87—but if you buy now, you could well be paying peak price in a market about to crash.

ED WHITSON	IP	W	S	ERA	RATIO	$
1986 (NY A+)/SD	113	6	0	6.21	15.85	−11
1987 SD	206	10	0	4.73	11.40	5
1988 SD	205	13	0	3.77	10.83	7

Now that he's out of the Zoo, he shouldn't kill you, but save him for the crapshoot; '88 is about as good as it's going to get for Ed.

MITCH WILLIAMS	IP	W	S	ERA	RATIO	$
1986 TEX	98	8	8	3.58	13.59	11
1987 TEX	109	8	6	3.23	12.96	14
1988 TEX	68	2	18	4.63	12.57	13

It's possible that the Rangers shipped the Cubbies a bill of goods. The IP column above doesn't bode well. Mitch was given the closer job by Valentine and he did reasonably well for half the season. Late in the season, he had certainly thrown his hellendish arm out temporarily, and it was put on ice.

If all Mitch needs is a winter's rest, there's going to be some real excitement in Wrigley Field. You can see that his ratio has been steadily descending, and that's the key. It's still a mystery why the Cubs dumped Lee Smith, and they're taking a big chance in exchanging proven—but more prosaic—talent in the form of Palmeiro, but they may have brought the bleacher bums the kind of folk hero the Goose would have been ten years ago.

TODD WORRELL	IP	W	S	ERA	RATIO	$
1986 STL	104	9	36	2.08	10.99	41
1987 STL	95	8	33	2.66	11.37	39
1988 STL	90	5	32	3.00	10.30	32

Some market prices for Worrell: Bert's Sognatores (WOR), $20; Hill Street Blues (WGL), $30; Sherr Shots (MNO), $29; A-200's (CHL), $19; Dad's Devils (ATF), $27; Vodka Forevers (BAL), $41; Foxtrots (HPL), $25; Kerr's Cocktail Club (VIC), $36; Jomammas (BEA), $39; Robin's Hoods (OOTL), $25; Flushing Meadows (PTL), $19.

Nice profits, overall, on an "off year."

FLOYD YOUMANS	IP	W	S	ERA	RATIO	$
1986 MON	219	13	0	3.53	10.81	11
1987 MON	116	9	0	4.64	12.34	3
1988 MON	84	3	0	3.21	11.25	2

How could the Phillies *not* make this trade? Such a huge upside, still, on this guy, and Jeff Parrett isn't chopped liver. The Expos probably had to make this trade, too, just to avoid the same old press releases, but getting a pitcher with this kind of talent is the right move for a team with no downside to make, whatever his problems.

Curiously, the Heath rosters show Youmans ranked number 15 (appearing on eight first-place teams and four last-place teams) out of 120 pitchers: a game of luck? Hey, damn right. Just keep your bets under $10 on Youmans and close your eyes.

Pitcher Z

Some of the pitchers who were tough calls on whether they should be given a three-year scan were: Kent Tekulve, Jeff Parrett, Danny Darwin, Terry Leach, Juan Agosto, and Brian Fisher. Obviously, much more compelling Pitcher Zs will be American Leaguers who follow the lead of Bruce Hurst.

As far as rookies go, the spring-training camps are going to be loaded with pitchers bearing great-looking 1988 minor league stats. I'd look at the two-year minor-league scans of Randy Milligan, Mark Carreon, Alonzo Powell, and a host of other hitting prospects, and be just as skeptical that all these pitchers became phenoms overnight.

AL CATCHERS

ANDY ALLANSON	AB	HR	RBI	SB	BA	$
1986 CLE	293	1	29	10	.225	4
1987 CLE	154	3	16	1	.266	3
1988 CLE	434	5	50	5	.263	10

Turned out to be a solid regular, but nine CS would indicate his running days are behind him.

BOB BOONE	AB	HR	RBI	SB	BA	$
1986 CAL	442	7	49	0	.222	3
1987 CAL	389	3	33	0	.242	1
1988 CAL	352	5	39	2	.295	11

According to the newspapers, the rebirth of the free-agent bidding wars occurred the day the Royals signed Boone for $1 more than the Angels were offering him. Gene Autry is said to have gone into a rage; is it possible he didn't know his team had already picked up Lance Parrish?

The shock waves from that one dollar are still going out. In the Rotisserie combat zone, Boone's conscription by the Royals is going to raise the price of Royals starting pitchers an average of $5. While the AL West shapes up as an epic battle between Oakland and Minnesota, Kansas City—so conspicuously but indefinably out of it last year—might have leapt back into the fray.

And Bob Boone, who last year earned a good part of his $11 while he was a free agent unclaimed by any Rotisserie team, will go for $2, if he's lucky, in the April auctions.

SCOTT BRADLEY	AB	HR	RBI	SB	BA	$
1986 CHI A/SEA	220	5	28	1	.300	8
1987 SEA	342	5	43	0	.278	7
1988 SEA	335	4	33	1	.257	5

Study the Mariners carefully in spring training, because you get the idea they don't like either him or Valle.

CARLTON FISK	AB	HR	RBI	SB	BA	$
1986 CHI A	457	14	63	2	.221	7
1987 CHI A	454	23	71	1	.256	13
1988 CHI A	253	19	50	0	.277	15

He's riding his exercise bike right now, going for the Hall.

RICH GEDMAN	AB	HR	RBI	SB	BA	$
1986 BOS	462	16	65	1	.258	12
1987 BOS	151	1	13	0	.205	−1
1988 BOS	299	9	39	0	.231	6

Looked good, especially against Cadaret, in the playoffs. Still, it's hard to take seriously anyone who loses part of his job to Rick Cerone. Rich, why didn't you just sign in '87? Are money and principle worth the last two years?

RON HASSEY	AB	HR	RBI	SB	BA	$
1986 NY A/CHI A	341	9	49	1	.323	14
1987 CHI	145	3	12	0	.214	0
1988 OAK	323	7	45	2	.257	9

Will be thirty-five, knees will be forty-five, swing will be twenty-five.

MIKE HEATH	AB	HR	RBI	SB	BA	$
1986 STL/(+DET)	288	8	36	6	.226	7
1987 DET	270	8	33	1	.281	7
1988 DET	219	5	18	1	.247	4

Since "full time" for a catcher these days seems to mean about 100 games, Heath's a decent backup for a buck; Sparky seems unsure about Nokes behind the plate, even though (admittedly misleading) fielding stats compare Nokes favorably with Heath.

TERRY KENNEDY	AB	HR	RBI	SB	BA	$
1986 SD	432	12	57	0	.264	12
1987 BAL	512	18	62	1	.250	10
1988 BAL	265	3	16	0	.226	1

Sixteen RBIs?

TIM LAUDNER	AB	HR	RBI	SB	BA	$
1986 MIN	193	10	29	1	.244	6
1987 MIN	288	16	43	1	.191	4
1988 MIN	375	13	54	0	.251	10

His batting average last year was the equivalent of Tony Gwynn batting .486. He was an All-Star last year, folks—a sad commentary on the state of modern catching.

MATT NOKES	AB	HR	RBI	SB	BA	$
1987 DET	461	32	87	2	.289	21
1988 DET	382	16	53	0	.251	12

My guess is that the new baseball hurt him more than the sophomore jinx. Patton $, of course, allow for the new baseball; the people whose salaries suffer aren't so much the Mark McGwires as the guys who in '87 just did lift 'em over the fence. McGwire's pay cut was 20 percent; Nokes' is 43 percent. Many sophomores do collapse—sometimes, like Joe Charboneau, forever—but I thought these two kept their cool awfully well.

LANCE PARRISH	AB	HR	RBI	SB	BA	$
1986 DET	327	22	62	0	.257	13
1987 PHI	466	17	67	0	.245	10
1988 PHI	424	15	60	0	.215	11

Of course he'd rather be in California, if not an Angel, but I'm betting we're going to discover that his declining skills predated his poor morale.

GENO PETRALLI	AB	HR	RBI	SB	BA	$
1986 TEX	137	2	18	3	.255	4
1987 TEX	202	7	31	0	.302	7
1988 TEX	351	7	36	0	.282	9

Big jump in RBIs due. Good hitter.

DON SLAUGHT	AB	HR	RBI	SB	BA	$
1986 TEX	314	13	46	3	.264	11
1987 TEX	237	8	16	0	.224	1
1988 NY A	322	9	43	1	.283	11

Batting .346 at the All-Star break. The Yankees surprised me, though, by signing him to a two-year contract. Perhaps Slaught inserted a must-trade clause.

MIKE STANLEY	AB	HR	RBI	SB	BA	$
1987 TEX	216	6	37	3	.273	7
1988 TEX	249	3	27	0	.229	2

Puzzling. You sort of feel he heard Chad Kreuter coming when no one else did. He was many people's most expensive mistake—a fatal meeting of "sleeper expectations" and "position scarcity."

TERRY STEINBACH	AB	HR	RBI	SB	BA	$
1987 OAK	391	16	56	1	.284	12
1988 OAK	351	9	51	3	.265	11

Surhoff may outearn him, but there will be no better catcher this year in the three hitting categories.

B.J. SURHOFF	AB	HR	RBI	SB	BA	$
1987 MIL	395	7	68	11	.299	16
1988 MIL	493	5	38	21	.245	14

It will be interesting to see in the Elias book how B.J. batted against lefties (.318 in '87). Provides an extra dollar's worth of flexibility by qualifying at third base.

MICKEY TETTLETON	AB	HR	RBI	SB	BA	$
1986 OAK	211	10	35	2	.204	5
1987 OAK	211	8	26	7	.194	4
1988 BAL	283	11	37	0	.261	9

Between Terry Kennedy and Carl Nichols, he might finally have some job security.

DAVE VALLE	AB	HR	RBI	SB	BA	$
1986 SEA	53	5	15	0	.340	4
1987 SEA	324	12	53	2	.256	9
1988 SEA	290	10	50	0	.231	8

Strat-O-Matic says he can throw, so why doesn't he play more? RBI/AB ratio is excellent.

ERNIE WHITT	AB	HR	RBI	SB	BA	$
1986 TOR	395	16	56	0	.268	12
1987 TOR	446	19	75	0	.269	13
1988 TOR	398	16	70	4	.251	15

By stealing second when no one was looking, and otherwise standing still, old Ernie finally rose to the top last year. But Pat Borders will be crowding him this year. (And I have a hunch Francisco Cabrera might sneak past Borders.)

Player Z

Unlike in the National League, where this position is truly in tatters, the American League has plenty of catching talent; the trouble was that it was too young last year—there were too many sophomores—and I expect a big rise in the "average, top 20" earnings in next year's appendix.

In fact, I'll predict that the appendix will show average earnings of over $10 next year—not bad at all for the position. Depth of position will, inevitably, remain a problem.

AL FIRST BASEMEN

STEVE BALBONI	AB	HR	RBI	SB	BA	$
1986 KC	512	29	88	0	.229	15
1987 KC	386	24	60	0	.207	7
1988 KC/SEA	413	23	66	0	.235	14

It was great for the people who had him that Phelps was traded and Davis was hurt, allowing Bye-Bye to seriously lose baseballs indoors and also qualify at first. Considering what Kingman was able to do, they should give him a good, long shot at DH. Should doesn't mean they will.

TODD BENZINGER	AB	HR	RBI	SB	BA	$
1987 BOS	223	8	43	5	.278	9
1988 BOS	405	13	70	2	.254	13

I'd be interested in what he could do with 600 at bats.

GEORGE BRETT	AB	HR	RBI	SB	BA	$
1986 KC	441	16	73	0	.290	16
1987 KC	427	22	78	0	.290	17
1988 KC	589	24	103	14	.306	34

He's much funnier about his great rivals, Boggs and Mattingly, than they are—about anything. In August he looked at his .340 batting average while he was shaving and yelled, ''Look out, Boggsey!'' In September, he was telling about it. And, of course, his ''there'll be a woman president before Wade Boggs gets called out on strikes'' may yet come true.

GREG BROCK	AB	HR	RBI	SB	BA	$
1986 LA	325	16	52	2	.234	11
1987 MIL	532	13	.85	5	.299	18
1988 MIL	364	6	50	6	.212	6

For all the upset about his not being the next Steve Garvey—hell of a thing to call anybody—'88 was his first really bad year. But it was really bad.

ALVIN DAVIS	AB	HR	RBI	SB	BA	$
1986 SEA	479	18	72	0	.271	15
1987 SEA	580	29	100	0	.295	22
1988 SEA	478	18	69	1	.295	20

Tino Martinez is coming soon.

DARRELL EVANS	AB	HR	RBI	SB	BA	$
1986 DET	507	29	85	3	.241	17
1987 DET	499	34	99	6	.257	21
1988 DET	437	22	64	1	.208	11

In Darrell's case, Keith Moreland has come already.

KENT HRBEK	AB	HR	RBI	SB	BA	$
1986 MIN	550	29	91	2	.267	21
1987 MIN	477	34	90	5	.285	23
1988 MIN	510	25	76	0	.312	25

If I had an endless winter, I'd add up the Patton $ earnings of all the World Series teams that have failed to repeat over the last decade and compare those figures with their real-life salary increases. The lesson would be obvious; it would also have absolutely nothing to do with the 1988 performance of the Minnesota Twins.

The Twins were both a better baseball team and a better Rotisserie team despite failing to repeat. This actually reversed their trend from 1986–87; sure, they won, but in Rotisserie terms, even with Viola's $21 gain, the regulars dropped $16 overall (discounting the newcomers Reardon and Berenguer). I made the blanket statement that I doubted the World Champion Twins brought many pennants to Rotisserie teams in 1987. Whereas last year, thanks to the efforts of Puckett, Viola, and even Hrbie, they probably did.

WALLY JOYNER	AB	HR	RBI	SB	BA	$
1986 CAL	593	22	100	5	.290	24
1987 CAL	564	34	117	8	.285	27
1988 CAL	597	13	85	8	.295	24

Wally kept telling the world he wasn't having that bad a year, and he was right.

GENE LARKIN	AB	HR	RBI	SB	BA	$
1987 MIN	233	4	28	1	.266	4
1988 MIN	505	8	70	3	.267	13

Larkin and Bush (and Moses and a few others) did an adequate job replacing Brunansky. That leaves the swap of dubious assets—Tommy Herr and Shane Rawley.

DON MATTINGLY	AB	HR	RBI	SB	BA	$
1986 NY A	677	31	113	0	.352	37
1987 NY A	569	30	115	1	.327	29
1988 NY A	599	18	88	1	.311	25

A related malady to the Defending Champions Syndrome, which the Twins survived through player fortitude and management luck, is the more widely recognized Home Team Love Affair; naturally, the majority of veterans reading this will scoff and say they're not susceptible. But just about everybody reading this is a veteran (if you're a rookie, I hope you read some other books first), and we *know* that players from the home teams cost more.

The proof of this would be quite simple: Add Mattingly's prices on the East Coast, then add them up on the West. I'll bet there's a $10 difference.

Now the real question: Is Mattingly finished?

All right, he's not, but is he still Stan Musial? My prices do show that he wasn't all that bad last year—and that the serious slip occurred in 1987. The man called the best player in baseball hasn't been the best hitter in baseball in years. Ignore steals; I'm using the prices as a very simple and valid way of saying who hits best. In the last two years, it's Kirby Puckett, no contest. But you'd be surprised how much company Mattingly has in his sector: George Bell. Greenwell. Tartabull. Winfield—yes, Winfield's right with him. McGwire and Boggs are a fascinating pair of contenders. Some of these guys, it's true, steal a little bit, and that's not fair. So erase the SB column totally and recalculate; with the appendix, you can almost do that with the eye.

Look at Canseco. Subtract his SB+, and he still has 18.6 points. That puts him between Carter and Greenwell, so give him $37 without any steals, which means he's also hit better than Mattingly in the last two years.

As for being the best all-around player? He is indeed a very good first baseman, but he's no better at first than Puckett is in center field. Not that versatility is necessarily one of the criteria, but I'd like to see them switch positions.

FRED MCGRIFF	AB	HR	RBI	SB	BA	$
1987 TOR	295	20	43	3	.247	10
1988 TOR	536	34	82	6	.282	29

A lot of leagues, I see, permitted him at first base in their drafts last year. Based on the previous season, he didn't qualify, but it was clear he'd be playing there, so it was a sensible ruling. My league wastes a lot of energy trying to make sensible rulings—always balanced with everyone's self-interest—so he was thrown to the auction as a DH only and went for a mere $10.

MARK MCGWIRE	AB	HR	RBI	SB	BA	$
1987 OAK	557	49	118	1	.289	30
1988 OAK	550	32	99	0	.260	24

He says he and Jose next year are going to be "salty veterans."

JOEY MEYER	AB	HR	RBI	SB	BA	$
1988 MIL	327	11	45	0	.263	10

Played much, much better after I got rid of him.

KEITH MORELAND	AB	HR	RBI	SB	BA	$
1986 CHI N	586	12	79	3	.271	17
1987 CHI N	563	27	88	3	.266	20
1988 SD	511	5	64	2	.256	11

While Jack Clark keeps saying how excited he is to be back in the National League, Moreland, leaving the Padres, says he's excited ''to be going back to the major leagues.'' Alas, the only place he's been a major-league hitter, Wrigley Field, isn't on the itinerary.

PETE O'BRIEN	AB	HR	RBI	SB	BA	$
1986 TEX	551	23	90	4	.290	23
1987 TEX	569	23	88	0	.286	18
1988 TEX	547	16	71	1	.272	17

The unsettling aspect of O'Brien's gradual decline, both in stats and in Patton $, is that it occurred while Arlington Stadium was becoming a much better hitter's ballpark. Perhaps, in some odd way, this indicates the spacious confines of Cleveland won't bother him.

I hope not, because otherwise the Indians have made an excellent Rotisserie trade—quantity over quality—and an awful real baseball trade. Franco is topnotch at a difficult position; O'Brien and McDowell are both good fielders but are not even average offensively at positions that are meant to supply offense. Jerry Browne—well, I *could* be wrong . . .

Joe Carter, meantime, is once again footloose. If he ends up on the Mets instead of in left field, and the Indians end up with Cone and McDowell and Mark Carreon and a few others, then I'll eat all these words. Right now it looks like the Indians are very confused.

JIM TRABER	AB	HR	RBI	SB	BA	$
1986 BAL	212	13	44	0	.255	9
1987 BAL	did not play in majors					
1988 BAL	352	10	45	1	.222	6

Finally got the chance to show the Orioles they were right about him.

GREG WALKER	AB	HR	RBI	SB	BA	$
1986 CHI A	282	13	51	1	.277	11
1987 CHI A	566	27	94	2	.256	16
1988 CHI A	377	8	42	0	.247	7

For years people have paid more for Greg Walker's swing than his statistics; this year, with any luck, his statistics will exceed what you'll have to pay to take a chance on him.

Player Z

Player Z wears uniform number eighteen; he gets it because there have been seventeen first basemen listed so far, and unless we're going to nip nineteen third basemen—which is no easy feat, either—we still need one. Should we borrow him from the outfield, where Dewey Evans lurks? Should we ask for a recount on Pat Tabler and his 17 games? Should I not have zapped the law firm of Bergman, Buckner, Knight, and Parrish? Should I have taken Mike Diaz more seriously?

Everything in its time and place. I suggest March as the time and Arizona and Florida as the places for resuming the hunt for Player Z.

AL SECOND BASEMEN

WALLY BACKMAN	AB	HR	RBI	SB	BA	$
1986 NY N	387	1	27	13	.320	14
1987 NY N	300	1	23	11	.250	5
1988 NY N	294	0	17	9	.303	9

His last thirty-stolen-base year doesn't even make this chart. If the Twins thought they were getting some speed, they've made a mistake you should avoid in your bidding. His batting averages on artificial turf: 1986, .346; 1987, .158 (in only 57 at-bats); 1988, ? Something to look for in Elias.

The most important factor is, of course, the difficulty of facing new pitchers. I'd be tempted, if I were the Twins, to call the Dodgers up and discuss a straight-up trade for Willie Randolph.

MARTY BARRETT	AB	HR	RBI	SB	BA	$
1986 BOS	625	4	60	15	.286	18
1987 BOS	559	3	43	15	.293	15
1988 BOS	612	1	65	7	.283	14

Wins pennants in real and Rotisserie life.

The $14 that I assign to him asserts he's a little better than the average hitter, who earns $13. Is he?

The average hitter in a typical league, multiplied by 14, is going to produce an average offense, which will get 6.5 points in each category, adding up to 26 hitting points (which, combined with 26 pitching points, produces 52 total points the perfect tied-for-sixth team). In the American Dreams League last year, a team of fourteen Marty Barretts would have finished last in home runs, first in RBI, eleventh in steals, first in batting average: twenty-seven hitting points, so he is, indeed, a little better than the average player.

The thing is, though, that Marty is almost never paid what he's worth in market prices. His American Dreams salary was $10. A $4 profit may not seem like much—until you realize that if you could get away with that twenty-three times, you'd have just turned $260 into $352, and whatever 50 percent of the year-end pot is worth.

JULIO FRANCO	AB	HR	RBI	SB	BA	$
1986 CLE	599	10	74	10	.306	22
1987 CLE	495	8	52	32	.319	26
1988 CLE	613	10	54	25	.303	28

He's sort of Barrett at another level for a different reason. Just as reliable, much more productive, as often underpaid—the latter probably stemming from his failure to punch in once when the Indians were visiting the Bronx. Now that he's in Texas, he seems to have a slightly better chance of winning a real life pennant before he retires. Slightly.

JIM GANTNER	AB	HR	RBI	SB	BA	$
1986 MIL	497	7	38	13	.274	13
1987 MIL	265	4	30	6	.272	7
1988 MIL	539	0	47	20	.276	16

Another solid little profit-maker.

GLENN HUBBARD	AB	HR	RBI	SB	BA	$
1986 ATL	408	4	36	3	.230	4
1987 ATL	443	5	38	1	.264	5
1988 OAK	294	3	33	1	.255	5

On the market at this writing. His strengths—doubles, walks, turning the DP—are exactly the things our game ignores.

MANNY LEE	AB	HR	RBI	SB	BA	$
1986 TOR	78	1	7	0	.205	0
1987 TOR	121	1	11	2	.256	2
1988 TOR	381	2	38	3	.291	9

Toronto loved his talent, was not happy with his hustle. Nelson Liriano will be scuffling with him in the spring.

STEVE LOMBARDOZZI	AB	HR	RBI	SB	BA	$
1986 MIN	453	8	33	3	.227	3
1987 MIN	432	8	38	5	.238	5
1988 MIN	287	3	27	2	.209	1

The invasion from the National League must be thoroughly discouraging him by now.

MARK MCLEMORE	AB	HR	RBI	SB	BA	$
1987 CAL	433	3	41	25	.236	11
1988 CAL	233	2	16	13	.240	7

See the next comment.

JOHNNY RAY	AB	HR	RBI	SB	BA	$
1986 PIT	579	7	78	6	.301	20
1987 PIT/(+CAL)	599	5	69	4	.289	13
1988 CAL	602	6	83	4	.306	20

If McLemore has any chance at all of pushing Ray back into the outfield, it's because fielding statistics lie. Ray had more assists in fewer games than both Randolph and Whitaker, for instance. He had more DPs than Whitaker. In fact, he had more DPs per game than Hubbard. Finally, he seemed to hit better as a second baseman. No, not finally: He was the world's worst outfielder, so I don't see how McLemore has a prayer.

HAROLD REYNOLDS	AB	HR	RBI	SB	BA	$
1986 SEA	445	1	24	30	.222	12
1987 SEA	530	1	35	60	.275	28
1988 SEA	598	4	41	35	.283	25

If we subtracted times caught stealing, as purists propose, Harold's salary would be $12. If you subtracted 2 × CS, as sabermetricians propose, Harold would be Jim Walewander.

BILLY RIPKEN	AB	HR	RBI	SB	BA	$
1987 BAL	234	2	20	4	.308	7
1988 BAL	512	2	34	8	.207	1

When you see his fielding statistics, you learn it wasn't just his name that kept him in the lineup. I'd give him another shot for a few bucks.

STEVE SAX	AB	HR	RBI	SB	BA	$
1986 LA	633	6	56	40	.332	34
1987 LA	610	6	46	37	.280	21
1988 LA	632	5	57	42	.277	27

This is what Dallas Green is all about—taking over, kicking ass, kicking the least deserving ass there was on the Yankees. It's not pretty, but it's based on a very simple proposition: The Yankees weren't going to win with Randolph, and with Sax they might.

LOU WHITAKER	AB	HR	RBI	SB	BA	$
1986 DET	584	20	73	13	.269	21
1987 DET	604	16	59	13	.265	15
1988 DET	403	12	55	2	.275	14

Did Lou have his little dancing mishap earlier and just not tell anyone? His fielding stats look as though he were picking 'em from a wheelchair. Good hands, though: only eight errors, and the only second baseman in the league with more than ten home runs.

FRANK WHITE	AB	HR	RBI	SB	BA	$
1986 KC	566	22	84	4	.272	19
1987 KC	563	17	78	1	.245	10
1988 KC	537	8	58	7	.235	9

Frank White has always been honest, has always told us how he's playing (particularly in relation to how other people are playing). Last year, he says, he fielded better than his stats and hit worse than his stats.

Player Z

Jerry Browne will certainly get another shot in Cleveland; I don't think they dealt for him to back up Tommy Hinso. There is so much riffraff to mention here: Jimmy Walewander, Mike Gallego, Donnie Hill or Fred Manrique, Brad Wellman, Mike Woodard. . . . It's all in the appendix. This is where the game gets really tough, and I bow out.

AL SHORTSTOPS

JAY BELL	AB	HR	RBI	SB	BA	$
1987 CLE	125	2	13	2	.216	1
1988 CLE	211	2	21	4	.218	3

Fielding, not hitting, was meant to be his problem, which, to the chagrin of Rotisserie owners, turned out to be all wrong. Since the Indians have to, he's worth giving another shot.

TONY FERNANDEZ	AB	HR	RBI	SB	BA	$
1986 TOR	687	10	65	25	.310	29
1987 TOR	578	5	67	32	.322	28
1988 TOR	648	5	70	15	.287	21

The Heath leader among American League rosters: the hitter found on the most first-place teams, the fewest last. I find that puzzling. Yes, on a team that might have had one of the foulest atmospheres ever seen in the major leagues, working with a body that was creaking in all the shortstop's most critical parts, Tony Fernandez put in an absolutely heroic year. But he's been around; unless leagues give out Quisenberry contracts, he reached his fair market price long ago. Because of his problems, he was tossed into the pool in many instances last year, but he didn't stay down very long. In my league he was let go at $33 and then chased back to $32. I dropped out at $24 and remember being pleased; two of the teams that were continuing on had good, solid low-priced keepers, and Tony F seemed to me precisely the way to self-destruct.

SCOTT FLETCHER	AB	HR	RBI	SB	BA	$
1986 TEX	530	3	50	12	.300	17
1987 TEX	588	5	63	13	.287	16
1988 TEX	515	0	47	8	.276	11

People talk about the lack of loyalty these mercenaries show their teams. It's partly the fans who say this, understandably; a fan is by definition loyal to his players, much as he puts up all sorts of Freudian defenses in certain towns. The owners, who give no loyalty whatsoever back, say it, also understandably. What I don't understand is why any players are, in fact, loyal.

Scott, if you ever get a better offer from another team again, if you even get an equal offer from a better team, take off, my friend—git. Go someplace that knows how to put together a winner. It's not right that more Americans—maybe even more Texans—know Walt Weiss's name than yours.

GREG GAGNE	AB	HR	RBI	SB	BA	$
1986 MIN	472	12	54	12	.250	14
1987 MIN	437	10	40	6	.265	9
1988 MIN	461	14	48	15	.236	15

Let's see . . . this Twin improved his earnings 66 percent; I seriously doubt he got that big a raise from them.

OZZIE GUILLEN	AB	HR	RBI	SB	BA	$
1986 CHI A	547	2	47	8	.250	7
1987 CHI A	560	2	51	25	.279	17
1988 CHI A	566	0	39	25	.261	16

It's hard to figure out how the White Sox can make so many great trades and be so bad. They got Guillen for LaMarr Hoyt. Ivan Calderon was dumped on them as the player-to-be-named later for Scott Bradley. Melido Perez for Floyd Bannister was a next-year and this-year trade. Dan Pasqua may have been a slight dud, but they gave the Yankees a bomb in Rich Dotson. Shawn Hillegas looks good; Ricky Horton was awful.

I guess one of the problems is that Reinhorn and Einsdorf have the gall to play baseball in the country's third-largest market with the $260 salary cap.

Ozzie Guillen (sorry, I almost forgot you, and you're a good player), in roughly the same number of games, had more putouts, more assists, more double plays, and fewer errors than Ozzie Smith. No other short-stop comes close to them.

REY QUINONES	AB	HR	RBI	SB	BA	$
1986 BOS/SEA	312	2	22	4	.218	1
1987 SEA	478	12	56	1	.276	10
1988 SEA	499	12	52	0	.248	9

I've been to Seattle, and it's a nice place; but when Rey gets the urge to dash home in the middle of the season, although it's not very professional, I can sort of understand how he must feel.

JODY REED	AB	HR	RBI	SB	BA	$
1987 BOS	30	0	8	1	.300	1
1988 BOS	338	1	28	1	.293	7

As it happens, I was sitting in Fenway Park on a rainy day in April when, to the horror of screaming teeny-bops, Spike Owen was given a "rest." Jody Reed charged out onto the field and paid no attention to the high-pitched abuse. He hit a rope to the third baseman's shoe-tops, rammed one up the middle that Trammell was cheating over for, and knocked one toward the Wall that in any other month wouldn't have suddenly stopped dead and dropped. He took the collar.

Question: What was Spike doing resting in April? Answer: Sitting it out because McNamara was already trying to replace him. Question: What did Jody do wrong? Answer: Nothing, he was sensational. Question: Why was *he* being rested the next day? Answer?

CAL RIPKEN JR.	AB	HR	RBI	SB	BA	$
1986 BAL	627	25	81	4	.282	22
1987 BAL	624	27	98	3	.252	16
1988 BAL	575	23	81	2	.264	20

He comes out four-against-four in the Heath leagues; as many teams lost with him as won. Unlike the Tony Fernandez situation, I can easily guess the reason. Cal did fine last year, and in leagues that know what they're doing he can be bought for around $25. That's an acceptable loss to take if you have enough profits elsewhere. On four occasions, however, I imagine teams continued to bid until they had the one AL shortstop they were certain would give them twenty home runs. And they were right; he was the only one. And they finished last.

LUIS SALAZAR	AB	HR	RBI	SB	BA	$
1986 CHI A	7	0	0	0	.143	0
1987 SD	189	3	17	3	.254	3
1988 DET	452	12	62	6	.270	16

He qualifies here (there, and everywhere), but his battle is going to be over at third. As far as I know, he and Brookens are nice guys, but they're gutsy survivors for sure. I'll save the rest for the Chris Brown comment.

RAFAEL SANTANA	AB	HR	RBI	SB	BA	$
1986 NY N	394	1	28	0	.218	−1
1987 NY N	439	5	44	1	.255	5
1988 NY A	480	4	38	1	.240	4

Raffie smokes cigarettes. Other than that, I think he's got it just about totally together.

DICK SCHOFIELD	AB	HR	RBI	SB	BA	$
1986 CAL	458	13	57	23	.249	19
1987 CAL	479	9	46	19	.251	13
1988 CAL	527	6	34	20	.239	12

You watch him hit, you watch him run, you wonder why he can't bat .275.

GARY SHEFFIELD	AB	HR	RBI	SB	BA	$
1988 MIL	80	4	12	3	.238	4

He gets admired in the minor-league section and is simply placed here as a name that will command higher market prices than all but three of these other shortstops.

KURT STILLWELL	AB	HR	RBI	SB	BA	$
1986 CIN	279	0	26	6	.229	3
1987 CIN	395	4	33	4	.258	5
1988 KC	459	10	53	6	.251	12

After the draft, I asked the BB Guns—definitely one of the more informed teams in the American Dreams—what the heck they paid $9 for Stillwell for. His speed, said the Guns. *Speed?* said I. Stillwell has stolen 12 bases in his career! His minor-league career, said the Guns. I'm *including,* said I, his minor-league career! It looked as if I had made the Guns very sad.

Undoubtedly they cheered up as Stillwell stole a few bases and hit nine more homers than the Guns' other two middle infielders together.

DALE SVEUM	AB	HR	RBI	SB	BA	$
1986 MIL	317	7	35	4	.246	6
1987 MIL	535	25	95	2	.252	16
1988 MIL	467	9	51	1	.242	8

This one is a conflict of interest.

I got my share of derision when I bought this guy two years ago for $2. Chortles started up again last year when he came back out of the phone booth dressed as Clark Kent, a.k.a., Warning Track Power. Other aliases are Stone Hands, Rag Arm, and Lead Legs. None of these unkind epithets have ever been flung at Gary Sheffield.

Now for the conflict of interest: I've got the topper on him, and Dale Sveum ain't through. He's got a great wristy swing from both sides of the plate, Trebelhorn likes him, and he's going to play. Shortstop, third base, maybe even first base, where the Brewers don't exactly have Cecil Cooper.

Assuming my jaundiced comrades read this book, they now have an important bit of information: Patton actually wants this turkey, let's run the price up!

This leaves me with no alternative other than to plant a seed of doubt. Is Patton such a desperate customer that he would *lie* to his readers? He *knows* Sveum is a turkey, *wants* to run the price up, then plans to stick someone else with him!

I'm trusting you don't think I would do that, and they're not sure.

ALAN TRAMMELL	AB	HR	RBI	SB	BA	$
1986 DET	574	21	75	25	.277	28
1987 DET	597	28	105	21	.343	38
1988 DET	466	15	69	7	.311	23

You'll still hear arguments for Ripken, and he may not be comparable to Fernandez, but at least Trammell's reached the point in his career where he's no longer tracked alongside Lou Whitaker.

WALT WEISS	AB	HR	RBI	SB	BA	$
1987 OAK	26	0	1	1	.462	2
1988 OAK	452	3	39	4	.250	6

In a kind of reverse Stillwell, Weiss did a fair amount of running in the minors and seemed to be stopped at the next level (he was caught stealing four times). For that reason, it could well be that the Rookie of the Year gets dropped in droves in Rotisserie Leagues.

Let's say you bought him, though, at Stillwell's market price in my league ($9). The chart says you lost $3. Before I dropped him, I'd weigh two factors. What will he earn this year? What will the market bid him back to? If I was quite sure he'd earn $15, but equally sure no one else thought so, I'd drop him.

The only reason to think he's worth $15 is if he's going to be a base stealer after all, and he might. As of August 25, he was just 0-for-3; LaRussa might have seen Weiss dusting his pants off after he was nailed the first two times and said, Let him just field the ball. But the little guy didn't wear out, he didn't get discouraged, and he finished up like a $15 ballplayer.

Player Z

I don't even care to count the number of uniforms needed after totaling the players profiled for the middle-infield positions. One of the problems is that these positions are fairly settled in the AL; the scrubs just don't play that much.

In November, there are only two that even bother to wave at me through the mist:

Randy Velarde. He started out in Billy Martin's penthouse but didn't stay there long. Nevertheless, it's harder to start there than, say, in Sparky Anderson's. Martin thought he saw something, and the few times I've seen Velarde play, I think I did too.

Monty Farriss. Why did Greg Olson take so much heat for skipping the Olympics while we never heard a word about this guy? Maybe you did, but I didn't. In any event, he was great at his first minor-league stop last season, lousy at his second. Facing the same pitchers as Robin Ventura at Oklahoma State, he outhit him.

AL THIRD BASEMEN

WADE BOGGS	AB	HR	RBI	SB	BA	$
1986 BOS	580	8	71	0	.357	23
1987 BOS	551	24	89	1	.363	29
1988 BOS	584	5	58	2	.366	25

Wade Boggs, a married man, had sex often with another woman while he was on the road.

One day she said, Wade, you're such a compulsive guy, you've even

83

got to have the same groupie every night. Some of your teammates can turn all groupies down, and some can't turn down any. But you've built up such a record of fidelity to me that I think you owe me some money.

He said, I don't think so. She said, Well, I'm going to tell on you. He said, Go ahead.

Headlines were made. For some reason, his wife wouldn't throw Boggs out of the house, but he was the laughingstock of Boston. Such fierce morality and unflinching principles existed in some quarters that it was suggested, both during and after the season, that he be banished from the club.

It went to the courts. The first judge sided with Boggs on the grounds that selling sex is against the law; one of our sillier laws, I think. The second is going to side with him because blackmail is against the law, one of our better laws.

Is Boggs a terrible person? It could be. Not only is he a cheater who must have hurt his wife terribly, but he may just have been too cheap to buy this woman off, which could have been accomplished easily. Nevertheless, when he told her to stuff it, he knew what he was getting into.

If his wife didn't, she did soon. As she walked into Fenway Park to watch her husband play, loyal fans chanted, "Margo, Margo." I don't really know very much at all about the morality and principles of either Boggs or his wife, but based on her coming to watch him play and on the level of his performance, I conclude they are both fiercer and more unflinching than I could ever be.

I was tested, however. Just after Boggs was reported fighting with some of his teammates on a flight—teammates who preferred not to be subpoenaed—I got a call from someone gently suggesting I trade Boggs before he was banished to, God forbid, the National League. It was a very gentle trade offer.

Perfectly fair. I didn't mind; it's the way the game is played. And I told him to stuff it.

CHRIS BROWN	AB	HR	RBI	SB	BA	$
1986 SF	416	7	49	13	.317	19
1987 SF/SD	287	12	40	4	.237	7
1988 SD	247	2	19	0	.235	2

The question, in just a couple of years, has switched from: Is Sparky Anderson the worst manager who ever won it all? To: Is he one of the best managers ever? All this without winning it all again.

If he can make Chris Brown into a ballplayer, then he's both re-deemed himself for Chris Pittaro and earned my vote.

STEVE BUECHELE	AB	HR	RBI	SB	BA	$
1986 TEX	461	18	54	5	.243	12
1987 TEX	363	13	50	2	.237	7
1988 TEX	503	16	58	2	.250	13

The Rangers were talking about moving him to second before they made the Franco deal. The fact that it was easier for them to get Franco than a better 3B says a lot about how this position slipped last year.

GARY GAETTI	AB	HR	RBI	SB	BA	$
1986 MIN	596	34	108	14	.287	33
1987 MIN	584	31	109	10	.257	22
1988 MIN	468	28	88	7	.301	29

His slugging average was the best on the team. Kirby Puckett is the center fielder.

KELLY GRUBER	AB	HR	RBI	SB	BA	$
1986 TOR	143	5	15	2	.196	2
1987 TOR	341	12	36	12	.235	9
1988 TOR	569	16	81	23	.278	29

The Blue Jays had about as bad a year as you could have, and they still scored more runs than, say, the Twins. McGriff covered for a lot of the malingerers, and Gruber tried to cover for the rest.

JACK HOWELL	AB	HR	RBI	SB	BA	$
1986 CAL	151	4	21	2	.272	5
1987 CAL	449	23	64	4	.245	12
1988 CAL	500	16	63	2	.254	14

I traded for this guy, cussed him all season long, then—when I had worked out my formulas and pressed some buttons—learned he'd been doing better than he had the year before.

BROOK JACOBY	AB	HR	RBI	SB	BA	$
1986 CLE	583	17	80	2	.288	19
1987 CLE	540	32	69	2	.300	21
1988 CLE	552	9	49	2	.241	7

Would a Rotisserie owner try to trade this guy? Absolutely not. We might dump him, the greatest advantage we have over real general managers; we consider loyalty a sucker's problem and never honor a contract we don't like. But we realize that the time to trade a player is when his stock is high. Don't the Indians remember how they got Jacoby in the first place? For Len "I've-Got a Lifetime Stash" Barker? And now, supposedly, he's being shopped around as a throw-in. Well, Atlanta still needs a third baseman.

CARNEY LANSFORD	AB	HR	RBI	SB	BA	$
1986 OAK	591	19	72	16	.284	24
1987 OAK	554	19	76	27	.289	27
1988 OAK	556	7	57	29	.279	25

Did I say we know better than to trade someone when he's at the bottom of his value? Well, Lansford in May in my league fetched Mattingly.

PAUL MOLITOR	AB	HR	RBI	SB	BA	$
1986 MIL	437	9	55	20	.281	20
1987 MIL	465	16	75	45	.353	40
1988 MIL	609	13	60	41	.312	38

Even with over 600 at bats, you feel the injury factor is still there, lurking. It shaves a few dollars off his price, making him a good gamble if you're willing to crash and burn along with the Brewers.

MIKE PAGLIARULO	AB	HR	RBI	SB	BA	$
1986 NY A	504	28	71	4	.238	16
1987 NY A	522	32	87	1	.234	14
1988 NY A	444	15	67	1	.216	9

In a year of apparent decline, his was for real.

JIM PRESLEY	AB	HR	RBI	SB	BA	$
1986 SEA	616	27	107	0	.265	21
1987 SEA	575	24	88	2	.247	14
1988 SEA	544	14	62	3	.230	10

Ditto.

KEVIN SEITZER	AB	HR	RBI	SB	BA	$
1986 KC	96	2	11	0	.323	3
1987 KC	641	15	83	12	.323	26
1988 KC	559	5	60	10	.304	19

No, Seitzer is not like Pags and Presley. Like Nokes, Steinbach, even
Big Mark McGwire, he didn't hit it as far as his rookie year, and so it
appears as if he didn't hit it as often. But let's give him those ten home
runs that Ubie took from him; those ten times the outfielder stood at
the fence, tapping his glove: 170 hits become 180, and his batting
average becomes .322.

Player Z

There's a whole team of him to think about: Craig Worthington and
Edgar Martinez will get opportunities to take over for the Orioles and
the Mariners. Hensley Meulens would seem further away; but perhaps
if they loan him to the Pacific Coast League, he'll get his confidence
in a hurry. I noticed that when the Tigers released Ray Knight, Doug
Strange went on their forty-man roster. Yes, we heard about this Strange
fellow last year—God save him, another of Sparky's phenoms—and he
was awful at Triple A, so-so at Double A, but Sparky's determined to
be right *once*.

There's Tom Brookens, to be sure. Probably some people are ticked
off that he's been demoted unceremoniously to the Player Zs (others
don't like to see him anywhere, since they always get him for $1), but
Brookens has thoroughly established by now that he's one of those
excellent scrubs who should not play regularly. His offense and defense
last year were subpar; Sparky's jaw goes up and down about how the
whole of his Tigers is more than the sum the parts, but why start off
with subpar parts?

There's one last Player Z worth mentioning. Perhaps I shouldn't,
for he's in the appendix, and there really should be some special re-
wards for those who spend their time there. Nevertheless, it's something that occurred on the White Sox last year that I'm going to manage
to blame on Ken Harrelson. Everyone must recall him telling Carlton
Fisk, "You're a big, husky guy. You want to help the team, don't
you? See those skinny guys shagging flies in left field? I know you're
a catcher, but why don't you go out there and start shagging some?"

Last year there was this conversation in Sarasota. "You're a big guy.
You want to help the team, don't you? See those skinny guys fielding
grounders at third? I know you're an outfielder, but why don't you go
over there and start fielding some?"

And so Ken Williams did. If you see him at third this spring, head on to Winter Haven, because you don't want to have anything to do with the White Sox. But if he's playing in the outfield for them—and there aren't many reasons why he shouldn't—then Ken Williams could turn out to be a fine third baseman, after all, on *your* team.

AL OUTFIELDERS

JESSE BARFIELD	AB	HR	RBI	SB	BA	$
1986 TOR	589	40	108	8	.289	32
1987 TOR	590	28	84	3	.263	17
1988 TOR	468	18	56	7	.244	15

The disaster was really two years ago. Those of us who paid lots of money for him thought he had simply had an off year in '87, caused by a wrist problem; we thought he did well, considering. Well, he did not do well, considering people like Dale Sveum did just as well, and the wrist problem may have become chronic. All last summer he was rumored to be on his way to the Astrodome, where the most the Astros could have hoped for—they must have finally realized—was a slow Kevin Bass.

GEORGE BELL	AB	HR	RBI	SB	BA	$
1986 TOR	641	31	108	7	.309	32
1987 TOR	610	47	134	5	.308	35
1988 TOR	614	24	97	4	.269	24

Another guy who should, and probably will, be going to the National League, even though he should be a DH.

PHIL BRADLEY	AB	HR	RBI	SB	BA	$
1986 SEA	526	12	50	21	.310	25
1987 SEA	603	14	67	40	.297	31
1988 PHI	569	11	56	11	.264	18

One more player who went into shock his first year on the Phillies. (Come to think of it, does the law of competitive balance say this *won't* happen to Herr?) By season's end, Bradley was playing better and saying he liked where he was—perhaps recognizing that both would make him more tradable. But Baltimore can't have been what he had in mind.

GLENN BRAGGS	AB	HR	RBI	SB	BA	$
1986 MIL	215	4	18	1	.237	2
1987 MIL	505	13	77	12	.269	16
1988 MIL	272	10	42	6	.261	12

Was headed for a pretty good year before he was hurt.

MICKEY BRANTLEY	AB	HR	RBI	SB	BA	$
1986 SEA	102	3	7	1	.196	0
1987 SEA	351	14	54	13	.302	18
1988 SEA	577	15	56	18	.263	21

Will have a very big year if the Mariners will only let him. To me a sign that there's some hope in Seattle would be Brantley in left, Buhner in center, Coles in right—with no butting in by Henry Cotto, Bruce Fields, or even Nelson Simmons before each has had a good 200 at bats.

ELLIS BURKS	AB	HR	RBI	SB	BA	$
1987 BOS	558	20	59	27	.272	23
1988 BOS	540	18	92	25	.294	34

Blue chip: $40.

RANDY BUSH	AB	HR	RBI	SB	BA	$
1986 MIN	357	7	45	5	.269	10
1987 MIN	293	11	46	10	.253	11
1988 MIN	394	14	51	8	.261	15

Trading Brunansky gave him the at bats, and he responded.

IVAN CALDERON	AB	HR	RBI	SB	BA	$
1986 SEA/CHI A	164	2	15	3	.250	3
1987 CHI A	542	28	83	10	.293	24
1988 CHI A	264	14	35	4	.212	8

Hit the hell out of the ball for a guy with a torn shoulder. I assume that's been repaired. However, it may not be so easy to tell in spring training, with Walt Hriniak trying to preach his let-go method to him. I just can't see Ike being as willing a pupil as Dewey Evans.

JOSE CANSECO	AB	HR	RBI	SB	BA '	$
1986 OAK	600	33	117	15	.240	27
1987 OAK	630	31	113	15	.257	25
1988 OAK	610	42	124	40	.307	56

Well, this is easy. In the line above I switch 42 to 50 and 40 to 50 and I get . . . $64. Pay $64 for Jose this year.

No, no—forgot something. Ten more homers are ten more hits, .323 batting average—$67.

And then—you know what?—ten more homers are ten more ribbies, conservatively, so—$68. A buck's a buck.

I'm not all that impressed that this 40-40 feat was finally accomplished; many people could have done it before, if we were as numbers-conscious then, and many came close anyway. But accomplishing this 40-40 business *last year*—that's a whole other matter. There were 38 percent more home runs hit in 1987. Thirty-eight percent more than Canseco's 42 is 58. There were also 15 percent more stolen bases in 1987. The equivalent of Canseco's 40 is 46. Imagine if he had almost broken Maris's record, while stealing 40 with ease.

In my guide last year I speculated on what people like Mantle and Mays would be worth in their contexts; I said they clearly broke the $50 barrier, it was only a question of how often and by how much. I sent a letter out asking whether anybody cared to have this pursued; the answer was unanimous: *I wouldn't pay a dollar for either one of those codgers now.*

So, Jose, what are you going to do next year? Fifty homers? I know he's going to try for them. Fifty steals? Is it worth it? You can get beat up sliding. You can get bushed after 15 pickoff attempts. Suppose Tony LaRussa has anything to say in the matter?

Why run when it doesn't matter? Because baseball, oddly enough, isn't all numbers. Like any tough, physical game, it has a lot to do with sticking it in your face. With forearm bashing. With taking a long, slow trot. With glaring from the mound. With not shaving. With flexing your muscles to the fans.

And what will Jose earn next year? I have no idea. That's why I don't worry about this book spoiling anyone's fun.

JOE CARTER	AB	HR	RBI	SB	BA	$
1986 CLE	663	29	121	29	.302	42
1987 CLE	588	32	106	31	.264	32
1988 CLE	621	27	98	27	.271	36

If he goes to Boston for Boggs, I'm going to be extremely upset. And when I've recovered, I'm going to bid higher on him than I will on Canseco.

DARNELL COLES	AB	HR	RBI	SB	BA	$
1986 DET	521	20	86	6	.273	20
1987 DET/(+PIT)	268	10	39	1	.201	3
1988 PIT/(+SEA)	406	15	70	4	.261	16

Since he put up most of his stats after going back to Seattle, 1988 is computed in the AL context, even though he had slightly more than half his at bats in Pittsburgh. (The NL formula puts his combined season at $19.) Whatever way you figure the numbers, Darnell's salaries make him look like he's a starting pitcher.

HENRY COTTO	AB	HR	RBI	SB	BA	$
1987 NY A	149	5	20	4	.235	4
1988 SEA	386	8	33	27	.259	19

He had 139 at bats in the second half.

CHILI DAVIS	AB	HR	RBI	SB	BA	$
1986 SF	526	13	70	16	.278	21
1987 SF	500	24	76	16	.250	20
1988 CAL	600	21	93	9	.268	24

I didn't realize Chili had a sense of humor, but he laughed harder than anyone at his fielding.

ROB DEER	AB	HR	RBI	SB	BA	$
1986 MIL	466	33	86	5	.232	19
1987 MIL	474	28	80	12	.238	17
1988 MIL	492	23	85	9	.252	22

Consistently undervalued; when he's bad he's really bad but in the end he produces.

DWIGHT EVANS	AB	HR	RBI	SB	BA	$
1986 BOS	529	26	97	3	.259	20
1987 BOS	541	34	123	4	.305	29
1988 BOS	559	21	111	5	.293	28

How about Dewey to the White Sox—where he can keep working on letting that hand go with Walt Hriniak—for . . . Carlton Fisk!

DAVE GALLAGHER	AB	HR	RBI	SB	BA	$
1988 CHI A	347	5	31	5	.303	12

He's invented some weird gizmo like a horse's hobble that has certainly helped his hitting. I don't understand much about it, except you must not wear it in the games.

DAN GLADDEN	AB	HR	RBI	SB	BA	$
1986 SF	351	4	29	27	.276	15
1987 MIN	438	8	38	25	.249	14
1988 MIN	576	11	62	28	.269	25

Good year, good player, but he'll never live down batting .351 as a rookie. It's as if Willie McCovey turned out to be Pete O'Brien.

MIKE GREENWELL	AB	HR	RBI	SB	BA	$
1986 BOS	35	0	4	5	.314	3
1987 BOS	412	19	89	5	.328	23
1988 BOS	590	22	119	16	.325	39

You'd expect the stolen bases would come down a little; on the other hand, if Jose keeps insulting him . . .

DAVE HENDERSON	AB	HR	RBI	SB	BA	$
1986 SEA/BOS	388	15	47	2	.265	11
1987 BOS/(+SF)	205	8	26	3	.234	4
1988 OAK	507	24	94	2	.304	27

Who knows what he'll do, but since he won't be available in any league, it doesn't really matter. (He looked for real in the Series and—maybe it was playing on the same field with Mickey Hatcher—almost normal.) Oddly, though, he didn't figure that powerfully in the Heath leagues. Nobody paid more than a few dollars for him, and he's split right down the middle: six first-place teams, five cellar-dwellers.

RICKEY HENDERSON	AB	HR	RBI	SB	BA	$
1986 NY A	608	28	74	87	.263	58
1987 NY A	358	17	37	41	.291	27
1988 NY A	554	6	50	93	.305	56

If Boggs simply has to go, if the best psychiatrists and most powerful pills can't calm down Mrs. Jean Yawkey, then this is the trade to make, probably the only trade that would deliver sufficient value. I was surprised, because he really does have some muscles, but the combination of new baseball and Stadium dimensions was too much for him, obviously. For a player who's considered both a flake and a rockhead (he *is* a flake), he did a nice job adjusting. He'll bat .320 this year if he makes up his mind to go for singles.

PETE INCAVIGLIA	AB	HR	RBI	SB	BA	$
1986 TEX	540	30	88	3	.250	19
1987 TEX	509	27	80	9	.271	20
1988 TEX	418	22	54	6	.249	17

I was at Mardi Gras once and watched a car go by with the guy in the passenger seat, perfectly conscious, bouncing his head along the pavement. That's the way Inky seems to me; I mean, that tough. So why isn't he getting 600 at bats every year? People always pay $25 for him in the draft, and that's what he'd give them with a full season.

BO JACKSON	AB	HR	RBI	SB	BA	$
1986 KC	82	2	9	3	.207	2
1987 KC	396	22	53	10	.235	12
1988 KC	439	25	68	27	.246	29

Steve Stoneburn of the Bags in my league follows Bo so closely he knows what bike he rides in the Nike ads, and he tells me he's headed for a BIG running year in baseball.

STAN JAVIER	AB	HR	RBI	SB	BA	$
1987 OAK	151	2	9	3	.185	− 1
1988 OAK	397	2	35	20	.257	13

Well, he did improve.

CHET LEMON	AB	HR	RBI	SB	BA	$
1986 DET	403	12	53	2	.251	**9**
1987 DET	470	20	75	0	.277	**14**
1988 DET	512	17	64	1	.264	**15**

Is it a good or a bad sign when a veteran is seen belly-flopping into first base trying to beat out routine grounders in spring training? Just a question, but I don't know where Chet got the rep of not hustling.

JEFFREY LEONARD	AB	HR	RBI	SB	BA	$
1986 SF	341	6	42	16	.279	**14**
1987 SF	503	19	63	16	.280	**20**
1988 (SF+)/MIL	534	10	64	17	.242	**16**

One of the oddest careers in the history of baseball. And in Seattle, he'll be getting his final paychecks from one of the oddest franchises.

FRED LYNN	AB	HR	RBI	SB	BA	$
1986 BAL	397	23	67	2	.287	**18**
1987 BAL	396	23	60	3	.253	**12**
1988 BAL/DET	391	25	56	2	.246	**16**

The man who was once the least reliable of superstars now puts up numbers, albeit lunchpail numbers, you can assign to your team right after the draft. He's been this way so long—much longer than the chart shows, check him out in *Who's Who*—that people seldom even knock him anymore. When they bother to, it's usually to say he never was a superstar outside a few ballparks. Fenway, obviously, was his favorite; Tiger Stadium might have been his second. Elias will probably tell us. Even if he's hit .400 there (wasn't Don Baylor meant to hit .300 in Fenway?), I'm going to try hard to be unimpressed.

ODDIBE MCDOWELL	AB	HR	RBI	SB	BA	$
1986 TEX	572	18	49	33	.266	**27**
1987 TEX	407	14	52	24	.241	**16**
1988 TEX	437	6	37	33	.247	**20**

Oh, not to be Oddibe! This poor guy is having a rough time: The first '84 Olympian to arrive, maybe the first to leave. But the important message in his curriculum vitae lies just off the screen: 1985. After 31 games at Oklahoma City, batting an even .400, he was called up to the Rangers. New context chipped away at his batting average, off 161 points, but he got 18 home runs and stole 25 bases.

Robin Ventura, Ty Griffin, Tino Martinez, Jim Abbott—there's gold in one or two of those hills, maybe this year.

LLOYD MOSEBY	AB	HR	RBI	SB	BA	$
1986 TOR	589	21	86	32	.253	29
1987 TOR	592	26	96	39	.282	35
1988 TOR	472	10	42	31	.239	20

His $15 drop was the biggest of the Toronto Three, and he ended up deepest in the doghouse; barking the loudest, too.

JOE ORSULAK	AB	HR	RBI	SB	BA	$
1986 PIT	397	0	21	24	.300	15
1987 PIT		did not play in majors				
1988 BAL	379	8	27	9	.288	13

One of the better efforts on the Orioles last year.

RAFAEL PALMEIRO	AB	HR	RBI	SB	BA	$
1987 CHI N	221	14	30	2	.276	9
1988 CHI N	580	8	53	12	.307	22

He came within a dink here and a nubber there of leading the league in batting and gets traded to Texas! This is why the trade fascinates me. Normally you say, "Both teams are improving themselves," but it's pretty clear in this instance that each team thinks it has fleeced the other. The amusing possibility exists that both are wrong, that both *did* improve by the trade.

In any event, a line-up of Espy, Franco, Palmeiro, and Inky makes me tempted to spend a few bucks on this guy.

DAVE PARKER	AB	HR	RBI	SB	BA	$
1986 CIN	637	31	116	1	.273	29
1987 CIN	589	26	97	7	.253	20
1988 OAK	377	12	55	0	.257	11

Dave seemed to do for his Rotisserie owners exactly what he did for Oakland: just enough. Eight teams in Heath leagues won with him, four came in last.

That was then, which is also the way Parker seems to feel. Throughout the World Series debacle, he caught my attention by his choice of pronoun ("they" referred to his teammates) and his interesting tense changes: "They had a good year. They're just showing their inexperience. They will be back."

Okay, Dave. It was nice seeing you.

DAN PASQUA	AB	HR	RBI	SB	BA	$
1986 NY A	280	16	45	2	.293	13
1987 NY A	318	17	42	0	.233	6
1988 CHI A	422	20	50	1	.227	11

Here's an exception to the rule that you want to see your hitters hitting every day; if they'd only stop letting him hit against lefthanders, he'd be a lot more valuable.

GARY PETTIS	AB	HR	RBI	SB	BA	$
1986 CAL	539	5	58	50	.258	30
1987 CAL	394	1	17	24	.208	5
1988 DET	458	3	36	44	.210	19

He looks like a wiffle-ball player.

LUIS POLONIA	AB	HR	RBI	SB	BA	$
1987 OAK	435	4	49	29	.287	20
1988 OAK	288	2	27	24	.292	17

One of Bill James's most difficult and quixotic attempts was to compare a player's offensive and defensive contributions. I'm quite sure, if such a thing could be done, the negative weight of Polonia's defense would tip the scales against the positive contribution of his offense, mainly because the latter weighs so little. But that's completely irrelevant to us—this little ballplayer weighs a lot on our scales, unless LaRussa gets fed up with him.

KIRBY PUCKETT	AB	HR	RBI	SB	BA	$
1986 MIN	680	31	96	20	.328	40
1987 MIN	624	28	99	12	.332	33
1988 MIN	657	24	121	6	.356	42

In the three years that we're surveying, no one has played the real game of baseball as well. Even Rotisserie owners can't complain; the less he runs, the more he hits.

JIM RICE	AB	HR	RBI	SB	BA	$
1986 BOS	618	20	110	0	.324	27
1987 BOS	404	13	62	1	.277	11
1988 BOS	485	15	72	1	.264	15

Rice has always been in a hurry to leave after games, but at least he shows up early. Or used to; he may have said, "Screw it" last season. In the old days, though, he hit under the stands, went out and had a thousand balls fungoed to him, then went back to the indoor cage. Rice worked for his living. It's not his fault that the aging process hit him like a brick; we don't have any say in these things. The test comes in choosing how to react to them, and Rice got a *D* last year. This year, I fear big problems in Boston. I see an *F*.

LARRY SHEETS	AB	HR	RBI	SB	BA	$
1986 BAL	338	18	60	2	.272	14
1987 BAL	469	31	94	1	.316	25
1988 BAL	452	10	47	1	.230	6

Do the Orioles not like to play because they play badly, or is it possibly the other way?

Fortunately, Sheets was not available in my league. Like Pasqua in '88, he was given the chance to play full time in 1987, and he was superb: .303 batting average, .538 slugging average against lefthanders. I would have bet the bank on him.

It's so easy to say now, but I never believed in Larry Sheets. Big guy, tremendous hitting mechanics, but he doesn't like to play. How do I know? Because he quit baseball in 1981. Quit! Long time ago. But he quit!

Such people do exist. Some are intense head cases, like Mike Ivie. Some are clever, almost invisible head cases, like Wes Parker. Some are so opaque that you can't even tell whether they had any talent or not, like Joe Foy.

Well, we know Sheets has talent. On a scale of one for Ivie to ten for Parker, I'd give Sheets a six.

PAT SHERIDAN	AB	HR	RBI	SB	BA	$
1986 DET	236	6	19	9	.237	6
1987 DET	421	6	49	18	.259	13
1988 DET	347	11	47	8	.254	13

Hard to believe that the home run jump is real.

RUBEN SIERRA	AB	HR	RBI	SB	BA	$
1986 TEX	382	16	55	7	.264	14
1987 TEX	643	30	109	16	.263	25
1988 TEX	615	23	91	18	.254	27

Because in his by now rather extensive career he's always been a slow starter, it's time for change: fast out of the blocks, big numbers, lots of ink, pundits who have been beating his drums for years now beating their chests. So here's the plan: Buy him (up to $30), ride him; trade him. Ruben's good, but he's not José-good. He'll have a bad second half, and you'll have Canseco.

CORY SNYDER	AB	HR	RBI	SB	BA	$
1986 CLE	416	24	69	2	.272	17
1987 CLE	577	33	82	5	.236	15
1988 CLE	511	26	75	5	.272	23

It was nice to see him cut down his strikeouts so dramatically. It must have taken incredible force of will to stop flailing quite so hard, to take a few more pitches, to foul some off, and once in a while let that critical 3–2 pitch go by. You improved, Cory; don't be discouraged. And don't relapse.

The cruel fact remains that one more of those '84 Olympians is proving mortal; the only potential gods remaining are Will Clark and Mark McGwire.

PAT TABLER	AB	HR	RBI	SB	BA	$
1986 CLE	473	6	48	3	.326	16
1987 CLE	553	11	86	5	.307	19
1988 CLE/KC	444	2	66	3	.282	12

It must be quite a rush to own this guy and watch him come up with the bases loaded. No reason why he shouldn't return to batting .300.

DANNY TARTABULL	AB	HR	RBI	SB	BA	$
1986 SEA	511	25	96	4	.270	21
1987 KC	582	34	101	9	.309	30
1988 KC	507	26	102	8	.274	28

Wouldn't you like to hear what Scheurholz is saying into his tape recorder now, before he makes his trade? This guy must be more obnoxious than Doyle Alexander, the way he gets peddled around.

CLAUDELL WASHINGTON	AB	HR	RBI	SB	BA	$
1986 NY A	272	11	30	10	.254	11
1987 NY A	312	9	44	10	.279	12
1988 NY A	455	11	64	15	.308	24

Here's an interesting thing from Elias: In 1987, Claudell batted .361 against left-handers. Didn't play much against them, but he was ready when Roberto Kelly didn't cut it, and then I guess he just kept doing so well that he made Jay Buhner expendable.

DEVON WHITE	AB	HR	RBI	SB	BA	$
1986 CAL	51	1	3	6	.235	3
1987 CAL	639	24	87	32	.263	28
1988 CAL	455	11	51	17	.259	18

Because of the big prices paid for him last year, he'll be widely available; the big prices gambled on him this year will determine many fates.

KEN WILLIAMS	AB	HR	RBI	SB	BA	$
1986 CHI A	31	1	1	1	.129	0
1987 CHI A	391	11	50	21	.281	18
1988 CHI A	220	8	28	6 ·	.159	3

I'm only saying it once.

WILLIE WILSON	AB	HR	RBI	SB	BA	$
1986 KC	631	9	44	34	.269	24
1987 KC	610	4	30	59	.279	29
1988 KC	591	1	37	35	.262	21

It's amazing that he can no longer be counted on to help your team in batting average.

DAVE WINFIELD	AB	HR	RBI	SB	BA	$
1986 NY A	565	24	104	6	.262	22
1987 NY A	575	27	97	5	.275	21
1988 NY A	559	25	107	9	.322	35

Winfield is considered a solid citizen, good head on his shoulders, straight shooter; he's also thought of as a good, steady ballplayer.

But if you just lounge back in your chair and stare at *Who's Who*, you're looking at one of the *weirdest* hitting resumes of all time. The games played and at bats columns belong to the steady ballplayer and solid citizen, and that's why the rest is so peculiar. Al Kaline's offensive stats jumped around a little like Winfield's, but he always had half a dozen injuries to explain why he could hit for average this year but not power; or, in their absence, why he suddenly felt frisky enough to steal. Winfield must invent his own reasons, and as a result, Rotisserie owners don't really know what they're buying, just that they're going to get a lot of it.

ROBIN YOUNT	AB	HR	RBI	SB	BA	$
1986 MIL	522	9	46	14	.312	21
1987 MIL	635	21	103	19	.312	31
1988 MIL	621	13	91	22	.306	33

Trebelhorn, asked why he played Molitor and Yount so much: "I like to win."

Player Z
Well, you're going to need a lot of him, and my recommendations aren't any better than anyone else's here, so read everything you can get your hands on this spring. You'll need about fifteen of him, depending on how many outfielders end up in other position slots, and vice versa.

My personal favorite is Jay Buhner, though the statistical evidence is pretty grim. I think the Brewers are going to need Lavell Freeman's left-handed bat in their lineup, and if the Blue Jays clean house, this might finally be the year for Ducey and Campusano; they also have a curious talent in Geronimo Berroa. Having dealt Boddicker for him, the Orioles may have no choice but to give Brady Anderson another shot, and if he hits, he'll steal some bases. And every year some corpses like Tony Armas and Dwayne Murphy rise up just when you think you've finished the burial. It's very hard to evaluate the talent in the minors last year, but if the hitters were as bad as they appeared, these old fellows will be needed.

DESIGNATED HITTERS

HAROLD BAINES	AB	HR	RBI	SB	BA	$
1986 CHI	570	21	88	2	.296	22
1987 CHI	505	20	93	0	.293	18
1988 CHI	599	13	81	0	.277	17

Seems to have been fading for years, but he's only thirty. As a DH only, you could get him for a bargain price.

BRIAN DOWNING	AB	HR	RBI	SB	BA	$
1986 CAL	513	20	95	4	.267	19
1987 CAL	567	29	77	5	.272	19
1988 CAL	484	25	64	3	.242	16

I've got him for $17. If he'd played enough OF, as he did in '87, I might even keep him, although he's been getting older for years. As a DH, I let him go.

RON KITTLE	AB	HR	RBI	SB	BA	$
1986 CHI A/NY A	376	21	60	4	.218	11
1987 NY A	159	12	28	0	.277	7
1988 CLE	225	18	43	0	.258	12

Wouldn't it be awful, after all this time, if he and Greg Walker end up as a platoon?

RANCE MULLINIKS	AB	HR	RBI	SB	BA	$
1986 TOR	348	11	45	1	.259	8
1987 TOR	332	11	44	1	.310	12
1988 TOR	337	12	48	1	.300	14

The homework litmus test in drafts will be when he gets nominated at 3B.

KEN PHELPS	AB	HR	RBI	SB	BA	$
1986 SEA	344	24	64	2	.247	14
1987 SEA	332	27	68	1	.259	14
1988 SEA/NY A	297	24	54	1	.263	17

Jay Buhner couldn't have brought Mike Boddicker? (Not that Boddicker could have gotten the Yankees the pennant, but in real baseball you're supposed to keep trying.) Of course, now the Yankees have McCullers and a DH who is as good as Clark—two-thirds of the time.

Player Z—or, Sam, We Hardly Knew Ye

It's pretty obvious that Mickey Hatcher now needs to return to the American League to provide help at this position. Perhaps Cleveland will sign him and platoon him with Terry Francona.

What's the real explanation of this sudden mass extinction of the DH? Old age overtaking everyone from Hal McRae to Don Baylor can't account for it, since old age is overtaking everyone else, too. It seems to me that there is something about the DH that really grates on the soul.

Jack Clark was expected to have problems with his teammates and the New York press; he got along fine with both. He was expected to positively delight in being relieved of the leather; it made him miserable. He even ran back out into the outfield when anyone would let him; Herzog either couldn't or wouldn't order such a move.

For Rotisserie auctions, what this spells is the end to one of our more enjoyable gambits. In the old days, the trick was to run "DH-onlys" out in the draft, filling up the DH slot on everyone else's roster; then bring out some flukey DH-only like Greg Walker (based on his cup-of-coffee service in the majors as a rookie) and say $1. He was yours.

This end-game maneuvering proved so much fun in the Amercan Dreams that many of us ultimately became $1 DH addicts. See the Fred McGriff comment for a perfect illustration in his market price. Here was a guy who hit 20 home runs in half a season the year before and who at Dunedin was hitting balls every day over the palm trees. You could read this in *USA Today,* and if you had ever been to Dunedin, as the majority of Dreamers had, you knew the palm trees were in left field.

Anyway, some spoilsport threw McGriff's name into the draft early. The DH addicts were truly saddened. The Residuals had the topper on McGriff and the addicts fantasized that if we only waited long enough he would blow it by saying $2 for Don Baylor and get him. Now, however, we had to bid on McGriff.

Each dollar that the bidding rose above $1 was a terrible psychological hurdle. You could feel it in the room: even at the absurdly low price of $5, the addict who had made the bid showed a furrow in his brow as the auctioneer started to count—he didn't at all look forward to actually getting him.

I'm an addict, and I was as sorry as anyone to see McGriff go early, but I had no trouble bidding on him, simply because of the Residuals' topper. When someone grudgingly said $8, I quickly said $9.

The auctioneer started his count. Going once, going twice.

If I'd had my wits about me, I would have called time-out. The addicts weren't going to help me? There was never any question of my getting McGriff—they weren't that addicted—but were they really willing to let the ever-harmless Residuals have McGriff at $10, just to be good and certain they didn't fill their DH slot?

I could have blurted, "Fifteen dollars!" That would have saved me a time-out (each team gets a limit of two), since the legality of bidding against yourself had never come up before. I'm sure I would have been declared to have misspoken, but at least one other addict might have come to his senses in the interval.

In any event, Fred McGriff for $10, much more than Doug Jones for $1, was the biggest disgrace of our draft.

By the time Sam Horn came up—well, there were enough addicts left to bid him to $6. He, of course, was the hidden agenda. Screw Fred McGriff; Sam Horn—we called him Little Beeg Horn—was the man for this year! We all believed that we could get him for $1. We all believed he would hit 50 home runs.

We were not alone. Some market prices for Sam Horn last year: Toenail Clippers (DBL), $20; Kozy K's (DDL), $15; Charlatans (LSL), $20; Stanley's Steamers (PLL), $10; Grateful Dead (SAO), $14; Albany Machine (BWL), $10; Love It Or Leveys (BDL), $20; J.C. Pennies (TWL), $20; Burghers (WGA), $20; Elmasian's Engineers (SMS), $10.

Clearly these leagues shared our enthusiasm; they weren't much afflicted with our addiction. In fact, it's possible that only the Grateful Dead even bid on him; all other prices look like carry-over salaries (based on different league rules) from the year before.

When he had—what?—a .600 slugging percentage? Eight hundred in the minors? Didn't Ted Williams say Sam Horn reminded him of him? Wasn't Jim Rice aging rather quickly?

Well, let's see how good one-for-four is by looking up how these teams finished:

Toenail Clippers, 4th; Kozy K's, 1st; Charlatans, 8th; Stanley Steamers, 9th; Grateful Dead, 7th; Albany Machine (Mario Cuomo's team?), 8th; Love It or Leveys, 6th; J.C. Pennies, 8th; Burghers, 3rd; Elmasian's Engineers, 4th.

An utterly useless bit of research that will discourage me from wasting much more time on *that*.

AL PITCHERS

DOYLE ALEXANDER	IP	W	S	ERA	RATIO	$
1986 (TOR+)/ATL	228	11	0	4.14	12.21	**4**
1987 (ATL+)/DET	206	14	0	3.01	12.36	**28**
1988 DET	229	14	0	4.32	11.87	**5**

Doyle's considered steady; his numbers, just glanced over, seem steady. And then you check his salaries.

ALLAN ANDERSON	IP	W	S	ERA	RATIO	$
1986 MIN	84	3	0	5.55	14.51	**−4**
1987 MIN	12	1	0	5.42	21.90	**−3**
1988 MIN	202	16	0	2.45	10.50	**26**

The ERA champion! You've got to love it. Has a hitter ever done anything like it? Not near-rookies winning a batting title—there are many of those—but has any hitter who was so terrible while losing his rookie status become suddenly so terrific? His batterymate, Tim Laudner, was inspired, too—enough to bring mention of Tony Gwynn in his comment. But to keep pace with Anderson's ERA improvement, Laudner would have had to bat .422.

SCOTT BANKHEAD	IP	W	S	ERA	RATIO	$
1986 KC	121	8	0	4.61	11.75	**4**
1987 SEA	149	9	0	5.42	12.36	**0**
1988 SEA	135	7	0	3.07	10.20	**13**

Was pitching better than Tartabull was hitting before he was hurt.

FLOYD BANNISTER	IP	W	S	ERA	RATIO	$
1986 CHI A	165	10	0	3.54	11.43	11
1987 CHI A	229	16	0	3.58	10.43	25
1988 KC	189	12	0	4.33	11.88	5

Bannister, until last year, looked as though he was going to be another of those older lefties who all of a sudden have pinpoint control (maybe because the fastball goes where they aim it now). But increased walks account for his rise in ratio; since he still gave up fewer hits than innings, and was much better about gopher balls, the big jump in ERA is rather baffling, like the whole team.

JOSE BAUTISTA	IP	W	S	ERA	RATIO	$
1988 BAL	172	6	0	4.30	11.32	3

Steve Levy of the American Dreams intrepidly set sail with both Bautista and Peraza on his pitching staff and finished second in wins, first in ratio.

JUAN BERENGUER	IP	W	S	ERA	RATIO	$
1986 SF	73	2	4	2.70	13.26	5
1987 MIN	112	8	4	3.94	11.81	12
1988 MIN	100	8	2	3.96	12.15	6

Juan is so good at subduing—literally cowing—hitters in the middle of the game that Kelly can't resist wearing him out, which means you should enjoy him thoroughly right up until the trade deadline.

BERT BLYLEVEN	IP	W	S	ERA	RATIO	$
1986 MIN	272	17	0	4.01	10.60	18
1987 MIN	267	15	0	4.01	11.80	16
1988 MIN	207	10	0	5.43	12.63	−7

If we scan the pitchers in the appendix the ghoulish way, bottom up, his is the first big name we see. (We pretend not to see Lefty, whom I probably should have left out, for decency's sake.)

MIKE BODDICKER	IP	W	S	ERA	RATIO	$
1986 BAL	218	14	0	4.70	11.89	7
1987 BAL	226	10	0	4.18	11.55	11
1988 BAL/BOS	236	13	0	3.39	11.86	12

Soon it's not going to be how life imitates the World Series, but how general managers imitate Rotisserie owners; did they dump on Baltimore or what in Detroit and New York?

TODD BURNS	IP	W	S	ERA	RATIO	$
1988 OAK	103	8	1	3.16	11.13	11

A great person to gamble on next year if you're in a cynical league (see Mike Campbell comment). If you're in a league that bid Al Leiter to $20, nominate Todd in the first round. But I should lay my reputation—just not my money—on the line sometime, and here's how I see it: Oakland was winning easily but, with Curt Young's problems, was still acutely in need of another starter. They bring up Burns; he's much more than a stopgap measure. Now he's got a hundred innings in the Show behind him—the one worry is, does he think it's this easy? If he doesn't, playing on a team loaded with talented players who have themselves just learned how hard the game is, Burns will win many games this year.

CHRIS BOSIO	IP	W	S	ERA	RATIO	$
1986 MIL	35	0	0	7.01	14.02	−4
1987 MIL	170	11	2	5.24	12.55	4
1988 MIL	182	7	6	3.36	11.27	15

Looked great, then terrible, then scarce, and then was great again. Fine job taking up Plesac's slack, although he would seem destined to be a starter. Very important fellow to follow in the spring.

OIL CAN BOYD	IP	W	S	ERA	RATIO	$
1986 BOS	214	16	0	3.78	11.23	15
1987 BOS	37	1	0	5.89	13.75	−3
1988 BOS	130	9	0	5.34	13.05	−4

Unless he was as good as he used to be, if he said those things about me, I wouldn't employ him.

MIKE CAMPBELL	IP	W	S	ERA	RATIO	$
1987 SEA	49	1	0	4.74	12.04	0
1988 SEA	115	6	0	5.89	13.42	−8

He—along with Stottlemyre, Sellers, et al.—is the perfect reason why so many Rotisserie owners will just plain never buy a rookie. They buy him now.

TOM CANDIOTTI	IP	W	S	ERA	RATIO	$
1986 CLE	252	16	0	3.57	12.14	**14**
1987 CLE	211	7	0	4.78	12.20	**2**
1988 CLE	217	14	0	3.28	11.55	**15**

If he really has found the plate, that jump will hold.

JIM CLANCY	IP	W	S	ERA	RATIO	$
1986 TOR	219	14	0	3.94	10.87	**14**
1987 TOR	241	15	0	3.54	11.71	**19**
1988 TOR	196	11	0	4.49	11.64	**4**

It can't have helped his ERA that so few of his teammates gave a damn.

TERRY CLARK	IP	W	S	ERA	RATIO	$
1988 CAL	94	6	0	5.07	14.46	**−5**

He's included because he's an interesting counterpoint to Burns: also brought up to fill in (for McCaskill), and for a while he he held his own. Rotisserie owners whose staffs had been decimated found him a rather jolly replacement. In the end they would have been better off without him. Does the experience help him? Shatter his confidence? I suspect neither. He's got plenty of confidence—but no talent.

ROGER CLEMENS	IP	W	S	ERA	RATIO	$
1986 BOS	254	24	0	2.48	8.72	**37**
1987 BOS	281	20	0	2.97	10.60	**35**
1988 BOS	264	18	0	2.93	9.51	**32**

All summer long, I kept looking for the evidence of the new strike zone they were supposed to call—remember, the one with the higher strike that was going to help the power pitchers? I didn't see it, despite the drop in offense; I attribute that, as you may have guessed by now, to the ball. Strikeouts, instead of rising along with those fastballs, dropped significantly: more than 1,000 fewer in the AL, more than 600 fewer—the exact same proportion—in the NL. Even more important, the batting averages didn't drop that much. They look like they did in the NL, but that's an illusion I'll get to in the masochist notes.

One other thing was worth noting; walks were also down. It may be that the umps, in trying to carry out this weird business of widening the strike zone by narrowing its definition, made an honest effort to enforce this fuzzy edict, and batters became defensive, just trying to put the ball in play.

Through all this change for change's sake, one guy just kept rearing back and humping up that heater. Strike zone? Why worry about it; umps can't call balls they can't see at all, and hitters keep swinging at it out of some primitive instinct. Roger Clemens struck out 291 batters last year and would have gone well over 300 if not for his midseason injury problems. To one side stands Roger, topping his career best in Ks by nearly fifty; to the other is everybody else, striking out more than a thousand fewer times. It may just be—on a sort of Patton $ basis—Mr. Clemens, while no one was paying much attention, had the greatest strikeout season in history.

CHUCK CRIM	IP	W	S	ERA	RATIO	$
1987 MIL	130	6	12	3.67	11.91	20
1988 MIL	105	7	9	2.91	10.54	19

A nine-man pitching staff of Chuck Crims, which, judging by the market prices I see would cost around $45, in a typical league last year would have been first in three categories and ninth in wins: 38 points.

STORM DAVIS	IP	W	S	ERA	RATIO	$
1986 BAL	154	9	0	3.62	12.56	7
1987 SD/OAK	93	3	0	5.23	14.03	−5
1988 OAK	202	16	0	3.70	13.48	5

If you picked him up in the crapshoot, as I expect, get on the phone now, try to trade him for some dependable offense, then roll the dice again.

RICH DOTSON	IP	W	S	ERA	RATIO	$
1986 CHI A	197	10	0	5.48	13.48	−3
1987 CHI A	211	11	0	4.17	12.24	9
1988 NY A	178	12	0	4.80	13.45	−3

The difference between you and the Yankees is that you can drop him *and* his salary.

DENNIS ECKERSLEY	IP	W	S	ERA	RATIO	$
1986 CHI N	201	6	0	4.57	12.04	−2
1987 OAK	116	6	16	3.03	9.03	34
1988 OAK	73	4	45	2.35	7.80	50

If the Eck was a company, what an annual report!

STEVE FARR	IP	W	S	ERA	RATIO	$
1986 KC	109	8	8	3.13	10.65	17
1987 KC	91	4	1	4.15	13.95	1
1988 KC	83	5	20	2.50	11.32	25

Suppose you had stock in *this* company. You bought it last April for $2, and realized a good profit. Now should you dump it? Trade it in for maybe three blue chips? You can't! The management of the company predicts a new role and greatly reduced earnings! Couldn't they at least have kept it to themselves?

JOHN FARRELL	IP	W	S	ERA	RATIO	$
1987 CLE	69	5	0	3.39	11.74	7
1988 CLE	210	14	0	4.24	12.11	6

If you forecast his ERA based on his four years in the minors, as James described how to do a couple of years ago, it would come out somewhere around 25.00. And he's a right-hander.

MIKE FLANAGAN	IP	W	S	ERA	RATIO	$
1986 BAL	172	7	0	4.24	12.82	3
1987 BAL/TOR	144	6	0	4.06	12.44	5
1988 TOR	211	13	0	4.18	12.80	3

It's interesting the way two people interpret the same evidence. When Bruce Buschel in my league was scratching his head at the season's end over why the crapshoot hadn't worked for him, I said, "What do you mean?" The pitcher we both brought up first was Mike Flanagan.

WILLIE FRASER	IP	W	S	ERA	RATIO	$
1987 CAL	177	10	0	3.92	11.36	13
1988 CAL	195	12	0	5.41	13.08	−7

It's amazing the way the argument can continue. Bruce asked what the difference was between his buying Flanagan for $6 and my reserving Fraser for $2. (When we argue, he spares no feelings.) I answered that when you reserve a guy, you're showing faith; when you wait for the crapshoot you're asking for mercy. By the end, Flanagan was Bruce's most expensive starter, Fraser my least. (Fraser was also someone I could have traded in March for Doug Jones at $6; as I say, I had faith.)

WES GARDNER	IP	W	S	ERA	RATIO	$
1987 BOS	90	3	10	5.42	14.05	5
1988 BOS	149	8	2	3.50	11.05	11

Boston's the kind of town that says very funny things about Darryl Strawberry and Jose Canseco—once people find out they exist. They know who backed up Johnny Pesky in 1947 and know that Pesky played 155 games that year. Pesky committed some sin or another (I forget what, I'm not from Boston), and they'll never forgive him. Wes Gardner's victory against the Yankees in the second game of their seven-game series in September, after Clemens had lost the first game, has earned him a warm spot in New England forever.

TOM GORDON	IP	W	S	ERA	RATIO	$
1988 KC	16	0	0	5.17	13.22	−1

Rose like the *Challenger* through the minors last year, to explode in Kansas City. But he did strike out 18 in 16 innings (263 in 186 in Double A and Triple A) and is the reason you can't get much for Steve Farr right now. And thanks to *Baseball America,* which named him Player of the Year, he'll cost plenty.

CECILIO GUANTE	IP	W	S	ERA	RATIO	$
1986 PIT	78	5	4	3.35	10.85	8
1987 NY A	44	3	1	5.73	12.68	0
1988 NY A/TEX	80	5	12	2.82	10.51	19

Guante was a seriously injured player in 1987, obviously almost out of baseball. One year later he's getting the call ahead of Dave Righetti.

Gratifying, no? Big paychecks coming, *sí?* But he's getting the call, and getting the call, and getting the call. . . . There's no way he was going to tell Billy Martin to stuff it. And now he's on the scrap heap in Texas. It's not called the Bronx Zoo for nothing, and this one was straight out of Animal Farm.

MARK GUBICZA	IP	W	S	ERA	RATIO	$
1986 KC	181	12	0	3.64	11.88	11
1987 KC	242	13	0	3.98	13.05	8
1988 KC	270	20	0	2.70	10.68	29

Schuerholz to his tape recorder: "The real reason I just traded Danny Jackson is that Gubicza will stop trying to beat him on the gun, start trying to beat Saberhagen in the ratio category . . ."

RON GUIDRY	IP	W	S	ERA	RATIO	$
1986 NY A	192	9	0	3.08	11.23	14
1987 NY A	118	5	0	3.67	11.40	8
1988 NY A	56	2	0	4.18	11.57	1

I know he really belongs in Pitcher Z, but I can't bring myself to do it to him.

JOSE GUZMAN	IP	W	S	ERA	RATIO	$
1986 TEX	172	9	0	4.54	13.53	1
1987 TEX	208	14	0	4.67	12.01	9
1988 TEX	207	11	0	3.70	11.41	10

If you bought—and suffered with—the Texas trio of Guzman, Correa, and Witt in '86, your ship's coming in—with one casualty to the seas—about on schedule.

BRYAN HARVEY	IP	W	S	ERA	RATIO	$
1988 CAL	76	7	17	2.13	9.36	28

Another reason that people should, and do, pay attention to winter ball. He got cut the weekend before the season started, so Everybody's Secret had to be aired at drafts. If the decision was to bid on him anyway, he went for big money. If not, if it went to a vote whether to throw him in the reserve draft, the team with the first pick (which tends to be the team that hasn't heard of Bryan Harvey) both knew how to vote and whom to pick.

ANDY HAWKINS	IP	W	S	ERA	RATIO	S
1986 SD	209	10	0	4.30	12.60	0
1987 SD	118	3	0	5.05	13.77	−6
1988 SD	218	14	0	3.35	11.25	9

Up and down, up and down. Hope he's compared notes with Eddie Lee Whitson.

TOM HENKE	IP	W	S	ERA	RATIO	S
1986 TOR	91	9	27	3.35	9.40	34
1987 TOR	94	0	34	2.49	8.33	49
1988 TOR	68	4	25	2.91	11.12	27

The Toronto management decided it really didn't like Henke and/or his bonus clauses—the same with Steib—and was willing to lose some ballgames as a result.

MIKE HENNEMAN	IP	W	S	ERA	RATIO	S
1987 DET	97	11	7	2.98	10.76	23
1988 DET	91	9	22	1.87	9.46	36

There now is a fine reliever named Mike . . .

GUILLERMO HERNANDEZ	IP	W	S	ERA	RATIO	S
1986 DET	89	8	24	3.55	10.92	28
1987 DET	49	3	8	3.67	13.41	10
1988 DET	68	6	10	3.06	10.77	16

. . . where there once was a great reliever named Willie.

TEDDY HIGUERA	IP	W	S	ERA	RATIO	S
1986 MIL	248	20	0	2.79	10.87	26
1987 MIL	262	18	0	3.85	11.11	22
1988 MIL	227	16	0	2.45	8.99	34

Do you know those boys at "Baseball Notebook" in *USA Today?* Do you like them? I don't. I suffer them and their newspaper during the baseball season, but I wish they'd refrain from addressing us directly, because they're lamebrains. They ran a column last summer on what all the great pitching meant to Rotisserie leagues. Can you guess? You needed great pitchers now. The year before, the thing was to go for home runs, really go for them, since there were so many of them you really needed them. Two thirty-homer hitters just weren't cutting it. But now, with the pitching so excellent, you needed twenty-game winners, and two of *them* weren't enough. So try to get three.

And don't bother with Teddy Higuera.

CHARLIE HOUGH	IP	W	S	ERA	RATIO	$
1986 TEX	230	17	0	3.79	10.84	17
1987 TEX	285	18	0	3.79	11.43	22
1988 TEX	252	15	0	3.32	11.71	15

Or Charlie Hough.

MIKE JACKSON	IP	W	S	ERA	RATIO	$
1987 PHI	109	3	1	4.20	11.89	3
1988 SEA	99	6	4	2.63	10.60	15

Do Tell Us Department from *USA Today:* One of the boys noted that Mike Jackson was turning out to be a pretty good throw-in in the Phil Bradley-for-Glenn Wilson trade. The trade was *for* Jackson; Wilson was the throw-in.

DOUG JONES	IP	W	S	ERA	RATIO	$
1986 CLE	18	1	1	2.50	12.00	2
1987 CLE	91	6	8	3.15	12.36	16
1988 CLE	83	3	37	2.27	9.18	42

Some market prices for Doug Jones: $5, Great Expectorations (BDL); $9, Statesboro Blues (BWL); $5, Little Bigman (SAO); $5, Mud City Manglers (PLL); $2 Levin Thour (SGL); $5, Little D-Aitches (LSL); $9, Fuckkowee Indians (DDA); $5, Charlie's Angels (BLA); $8, Cadre Elite (DBL); $1, Nova (ADL). . . . According to the Heath rosters, once you bought him, you couldn't finish last (i.e., no team in Heath's leagues did). Does it make you hate him? It did me. I couldn't stand him, particularly after I finally saw him in September on TV and realized he was like Eckersley—here for good. Old guy, bouncing around the minors forever, pretty good movement but no fireballer—what the heck did he learn? Could he unlearn it again, please? And then I noticed a tiny item in *The Sporting News:* Instructional league had started already for the Indians. A bunch of bushers—every one of whose sole ambition was to take his place—were learning the change-up from Doug

Jones. If I was sentimental, and if I had any good keepers, I'd call the team that owns him up right now and start trying to get him.

JIMMY KEY	IP	W	S	ERA	RATIO	$
1986 TOR	232	14	0	3.57	11.48	15
1987 TOR	261	17	0	2.76	9.52	39
1988 TOR	131	12	0	3.29	10.76	14

Walter Shapiro of the Nattering Nabobs, who's got to buy Key back this year, has asked me not to say anything nice about him, and I'm certainly not going to say anything not nice.

MARK LANGSTON	IP	W	S	ERA	RATIO	$
1986 SEA	239	12	0	4.85	13.44	0
1987 SEA	272	19	0	3.84	11.78	20
1988 SEA	261	15	0	3.34	11.43	17

Was the American League's Hershiser in September.

DAVE LAPOINT	IP	W	S	ERA	RATIO	$
1986 DET/(+SD)	129	4	0	5.72	14.51	−5
1987 (STL+)/CHI A	99	7	0	6.75	11.91	8
1988 CHI A/(+PIT)	213	14	0	3.25	11.05	17

The gibberish notations for the teams he's been on remind me of the way he pitches. But I'd take him seriously. That is, there's no way I'd bid more than $5 for him, but I would put him on my team. (To decipher the gibberish: For the last three years LaPoint has managed to spend more than half the season in the American League, no matter which direction he's traveling.) With his coming to the Yankees, to be accompanied by an "obvious" leap in wins, $5 won't get him. And everyone who overpays for him can take comfort in knowing that they're playing the game just like the major leaguers do.

CHARLIE LEIBRANDT	IP	W	S	ERA	RATIO	$
1986 KC	231	14	0	4.09	11.73	11
1987 KC	240	16	0	3.41	11.59	21
1988 KC	243	13	0	3.19	11.33	17

If you traded for him in June, you had an Orel for the rest of the season.

AL LEITER	IP	W	S	ERA	RATIO	$
1988 NY A	57	4	0	3.92	12.87	1

Market prices: $16, Odd Couple (BDL); $16, Say It Ain't So's (BWL); $9, Iced Broilers (SAO); $10, Melon Collies (PLL); $15, River Rats (SGL); $13, Charlatans (LSL); $10, B&M Brookers (DDA); $18, Anderson Littles (BLA); $28, Johnson's (DBL); $12, Veecks (ADL).

KIRK MCCASKILL	IP	W	S	ERA	RATIO	$
1986 CAL	246	17	0	3.36	10.94	20
1987 CAL	75	4	0	5.67	14.22	−4
1988 CAL	146	8	0	4.31	13.29	−1

Make him an early reserve list pick.

LANCE MCCULLERS	IP	W	S	ERA	RATIO	$
1986 SD	136	10	5	2.78	10.65	15
1987 SD	123	8	16	3.72	12.73	18
1988 SD	98	3	10	2.48	11.48	12

The Yankees, after trying to do exactly what we do—play Jack Clark and Ken Phelps in the same game—made the right move.

JACK MCDOWELL	IP	W	S	ERA	RATIO	$
1987 CHI A	28	4	0	1.93	7.07	9
1988 CHI A	159	5	0	3.97	12.20	2

Had to return in April the Rookie of the Year trophy he was conceded in March.

BOB MILACKI	IP	W	S	ERA	RATIO	$
1988 BAL	25	2	0	0.72	6.48	8

I *really* want Milacki this year; in fact, I can keep him at $20. To restrain myself, all I need do is look at the 1987 line for the guy above. I sort of skipped right past McDowell in my haste to talk about Milacki, but McDowell's a good pitcher who dealt extremely well with the first rough times on the mound he's ever had. (It must be much worse than your first dance, when you've just been cut in on and you know she's glad.) If I had to set my prices right now, I'd pencil $9 for McDowell, $6 for Milacki, and in my league I might get one of them.

GREG MINTON	IP	W	S	ERA	RATIO	$
1986 SF	69	4	5	3.93	12.71	7
1987 CAL	99	6	11	3.17	12.69	19
1988 CAL	79	4	7	2.85	11.51	12

The Moon Man, Quiz—these relievers are definitely their own breed. They seem loose but hang on like pit bulls when it's time to go.

DALE MOHORCIC	IP	W	S	ERA	RATIO	$
1986 TEX	79	2	7	2.51	11.51	11
1987 TEX	99	7	16	2.99	9.73	32
1988 TEX/NY A	75	4	6	4.22	13.50	4

Complements McCullers nicely.

MIKE MOORE	IP	W	S	ERA	RATIO	$
1986 SEA	266	11	1	4.30	12.62	6
1987 SEA	231	9	0	4.71	13.71	−3
1988 SEA	229	9	1	3.78	10.19	15

The cynics say ballplayers play well going into free agency because they want to be rich, and then play badly because they are rich. The shrinks would have it the reverse: The pressure's much greater after they're rich. Either way, buyer beware.

JACK MORRIS	IP	W	S	ERA	RATIO	$
1986 DET	267	21	0	3.27	10.48	25
1987 DET	266	18	0	3.38	10.83	28
1988 DET	235	15	0	3.94	11.80	10

Speaking of free agents, I would have thought that Tiger Jack would have been one five times over by now.

JAMIE MOYER	IP	W	S	ERA	RATIO	$
1986 CHI N	87	7	0	5.05	15.36	−4
1987 CHI N	201	12	0	5.10	13.34	−4
1988 CHI N	202	9	0	3.48	11.90	2

Moyer, like quite a few other pitchers, had a problem with the gopher ball in Wrigley Field. However, since they put up a giant scoreboard a few years ago, the Arlington Stadium fences seem to have become easy targets for hitters too, and Moyer will be encountering the DH, such as it is these days in the AL.

I wouldn't hesitate to take him if he reaches the crapshoot; the question is, how far to chase him past $5? The three-year scan shows you shouldn't even have taken him in the crapshoot in the past three years, but Moyer throws hard, he's owed some luck, and the Rangers themselves are rolling craps like madmen over the winter.

I can see him earning as much as $20 next year, which to me translates into bidding him just shy of $10.

JEFF MUSSELMAN	IP	W	S	ERA	RATIO	$
1987 TOR	89	12	3	4.15	13.04	10
1988 TOR	85	8	0	3.18	11.65	8

Excellent pick if he reaches the crapshoot.

GENE NELSON	IP	W	S	ERA	RATIO	$
1986 CHI A	115	6	6	3.85	12.48	9
1987 OAK	124	6	3	3.93	11.28	12
1988 OAK	112	9	3	3.06	10.56	15

No reason he shouldn't keep it up.

TOM NIEDENFUER	IP	W	S	ERA	RATIO	$
1986 LA	80	6	11	3.71	12.94	11
1987 (LA+)/BAL	68	4	14	4.50	13.10	15
1988 BAL	59	3	18	3.51	11.90	18

If Baltimore got as many wins as the Red Sox, Niedenfuer would have gotten more saves than Lee Smith. But that is a big if. And he'll be sharing the Seattle pen with a lot of good arms.

JUAN NIEVES	IP	W	S	ERA	RATIO	$
1986 MIL	185	11	0	4.92	14.64	−2
1987 MIL	196	14	0	4.88	13.73	0
1988 MIL	110	7	1	4.08	10.93	7

The dollars don't lie; he had his best year.

JESSE OROSCO	IP	W	S	ERA	RATIO	$
1986 NY N	81	8	21	2.33	11.00	**26**
1987 NY N	77	3	16	4.44	12.74	**13**
1988 LA	53	3	9	2.72	12.06	**10**

First Davey lost confidence in him, then Tommy. Now he'll be setting up Doug Jones. It's all downhill from here, Jesse, but for one memorable October you were at the absolute top of the heap.

MELIDO PEREZ	IP	W	S	ERA	RATIO	$
1988 CHI A	197	12	0	3.79	11.79	**9**

Imagine the first Rotisserie promotional tie-in? Nationwide, every owner gets a free coffee maker with the purchase of Melido Perez. Dare to dream, folks.

Since I was sure he'd get pounded last year, I don't know what to think this year.

DAN PLESAC	IP	W	S	ERA	RATIO	$
1986 MIL	91	10	14	2.97	10.88	**23**
1987 MIL	79	5	23	2.61	9.80	**36**
1988 MIL	52	1	30	2.41	9.98	**30**

Visualize a graph that, beginning from the same point in 1986, follows his saves and innings in their separate directions; one or the other has to turn around this year.

ERIC PLUNK	IP	W	S	ERA	RATIO	$
1986 OAK	120	4	0	5.31	14.44	**−5**
1987 OAK	95	4	2	4.74	14.49	**−1**
1988 OAK	78	7	5	3.00	11.65	**12**

Heresy, but I have a hunch that if anything happened to Eckersley, they wouldn't be losing that much with this guy.

SHANE RAWLEY	IP	W	S	ERA	RATIO	$
1986 PHI	158	11	0	3.54	12.30	**6**
1987 PHI	230	17	0	4.39	13.15	**4**
1988 PHI	198	8	0	4.18	13.55	**−10**

Shane Rawley's the Steve Trout of the National League? That's what the appendix says.

JEFF REARDON	IP	W	S	ERA	RATIO	$
1986 MON	89	7	35	3.54	11.02	34
1987 MIN	80	8	31	4.39	10.98	32
1988 MIN	73	2	42	2.47	10.23	42

Another one of those complacent world champ Twins, right? And what happened to the bad arm they whispered about in Montreal as soon as they had traded him for Neal Heaton? Reardon has a history of going for dirt. The Mets could hardly contain themselves when they coaxed the Expos into letting them have Ellis Valentine. Nor could they wait to give the closer role to Neil Allen.

JERRY REUSS	IP	W	S	ERA	RATIO	$
1986 LA	74	2	1	5.84	13.74	−5
1987 (LA/CIN+)/CAL	119	4	0	5.97	15.13	−8
1988 CHI A	183	13	0	3.44	11.11	14

Gave some pretty good innings to a team that got rid of Bannister and Dotson.

RICK RHODEN	IP	W	S	ERA	RATIO	$
1986 PIT	253	15	0	2.84	10.21	19
1987 NY A	182	16	0	3.86	12.12	15
1988 NY A	197	12	0	4.20	11.97	6

Recovered pretty nicely from the shock of DHing.

DAVE RIGHETTI	IP	W	S	ERA	RATIO	$
1986 NY A	107	8	46	2.45	10.35	51
1987 NY A	95	8	31	3.51	13.17	38
1988 NY A	87	5	25	3.52	12.72	23

Walter Shapiro gets credit for this notion: Assuming Righetti is slated as a starter this spring, how much will the likelihood that the Yankees will switch him back to the bullpen in a month push his price up?

JEFF ROBINSON	IP	W	S	ERA	RATIO	$
1987 DET	127	9	0	5.37	13.15	−1
1988 DET	172	13	0	2.98	10.10	20

Walter also reports that there is not a scintilla of evidence anywhere to augur the way this Jeff Robinson threw the ball last year. I believe him.

NOLAN RYAN	IP	W	S	ERA	RATIO	$
1986 HOU	178	12	0	3.34	10.16	13
1987 HOU	212	8	0	2.76	10.23	22
1988 HOU	220	12	0	3.52	11.17	6

Had a 1.00 ERA in September; the guy has no quit. I think he'll be able to handle the climate outdoors in his home state. But there's no question he'll miss the Astrodome, where his ERA in each of the last three years has been more than a run lower than on the road.

BRET SABERHAGEN	IP	W	S	ERA	RATIO	$
1986 KC	156	7	0	4.15	11.19	7
1987 KC	257	18	0	3.36	10.47	29
1988 KC	261	14	0	3.80	11.39	12

Some things in the appendix drive even me nuts. Paul Mirabella ranked over Bret Saberhagen? Makes me want to see what Rotisserie basketball is like.

MIKE SCHOOLER	IP	W	S	ERA	RATIO	$
1988 SEA	48	5	15	3.54	12.85	15

The value of a good reserve list. Whatever round you took him in, as soon as you uttered his name, you had raised your budget to $275.

LEE SMITH	IP	W	S	ERA	RATIO	$
1986 CHI N	90	9	31	3.09	11.10	33
1987 CHI N	83	4	36	3.12	12.58	34
1988 BOS	84	4	29	2.80	11.73	30

He lowered his ERA and ratio in the American League in Boston; he should get some of the credit, along with the baseball. Very much like

Reardon, as soon as his team had traded him they were chortling—in this case, about his knees. The more I watch real general managers, the more I think they resemble us.

BOB STANLEY	IP	W	S	ERA	RATIO	$
1986 BOS	82	6	16	4.37	14.38	14
1987 BOS	153	4	0	5.01	14.12	−7
1988 BOS	102	6	5	3.19	10.54	14

I'd explain '87 by noting that it's tough to get booed as the Opening Day starter at home for the defending league champions.

DAVE STEWART	IP	W	S	ERA	RATIO	$
1986 (PHI+)/OAK	161	9	0	3.97	12.35	6
1987 OAK	261	20	0	3.68	11.34	24
1988 OAK	276	21	0	3.23	11.43	22

I've switched from thinking that he's one of the biggest fools and most wasted talents in the game to one of the finest gentlemen and biggest overachievers. Am I a front-runner? Of course. But it also happens that when a player does well, he gets a forum, and Stewart just always seems to have something interesting and generous to say. He's even generous about Clemens, really; he simply doesn't like the racism, implied in the disproportionate praise.

DAVE STIEB	IP	W	S	ERA	RATIO	$
1986 TOR	205	7	1	4.74	14.31	−3
1987 TOR	185	13	0	4.09	12.21	11
1988 TOR	207	16	0	3.04	10.24	23

He was stiffed even worse than Henke by the Toronto brass. Whatever his innings bonus, it was easily attainable; Jimy Williams would just switch to a seven-man pitching rotation from time to time. I think their dislike of Stieb was so great that his furious finish, even though it gave him some trade value, yielded no pleasure. Every single Blue Jay must have hated Williams by the end. But Gillick had gotten to dislike almost every single Blue Jay so much that he rehired him.

GREG SWINDELL	IP	W	S	ERA	RATIO	$
1986 CLE	62	5	0	4.23	11.97	3
1987 CLE	102	3	0	5.10	13.15	−3
1988 CLE	242	18	0	3.20	10.38	24

In all the leagues I looked at, the prices ran from $6 to $13 (with one league abstaining).

FRANK TANANA	IP	W	S	ERA	RATIO	$
1986 DET	188	12	0	4.16	12.49	7
1987 DET	219	15	0	3.91	11.18	18
1988 DET	203	14	0	4.21	12.28	5

There aren't any other sports in which you can do what Tanana did—carve out a useful career after losing your main talent to injury—are there? Gale Sayers couldn't become Larry Csonka. But Tanana has persevered, and for that reason the season-ending shutout to clinch the '87 pennant would have been one of the great moments in the history of sport, if the Blue Jays had had any fight left in them at all.

BOBBY THIGPEN	IP	W	S	ERA	RATIO	$
1986 CHI A	36	2	7	1.77	9.59	11
1987 CHI A	89	7	16	2.73	11.12	29
1988 CHI A	90	5	34	3.30	12.90	31

Here's a case where you go with a guy with guts; gives up hits, but they don't seem to faze him, and he gets the save.

STEVE TROUT	IP	W	S	ERA	RATIO	$
1986 CHI N	161	5	0	4.75	14.65	−8
1987 CHI N/(+NY A)	121	6	0	4.39	14.65	−4
1988 SEA	56	4	0	7.83	18.69	−14

When I was talking about Flanagan and Fraser, this was the pitcher I couldn't wait to get to. Here, in front of, I hope, millions of people, I tell the world that Bruce Buschel neglected to say he picked up Steve Trout in his crapshoot. *For $2.* That means someone else nominated him, and all he had to do was keep his lips zipped.

FRANK VIOLA	IP	W	S	ERA	RATIO	$
1986 MIN	246	16	0	4.51	12.44	**8**
1987 MIN	252	17	0	2.90	10.57	**32**
1988 MIN	255	24	0	2.64	10.22	**34**

It's not worth listing Viola's market prices; a look at his three-year scan above shows why he was so rarely available at auction last season. It's partly a fluke owing to his off year in 1986, but the end result is that he, not any reliever—or, for that matter, any hitter—is the "winningest" player in the Heath leagues: 13–0. (Thirteen teams that bought him won; none finished last.) I admit that I really enjoy seeing this starting pitcher, who has followed a great year with a greater year, leading the pack, even as I know I'd *never* spend $34 for him. I enjoy it because I like the illusion that we're somewhat in contact with real baseball, and in my opinion, over the last two years, including the furnace of the postseason, Viola's been the best.

DUANE WARD	IP	W	S	ERA	RATIO	$
1988 TOR	112	9	15	3.30	12.98	**18**

Get out your Henke hankies and welcome Ward.

BILL WEGMAN	IP	W	S	ERA	RATIO	$
1986 MIL	198	5	0	5.13	11.82	**−1**
1987 MIL	225	12	0	4.24	11.28	**14**
1988 MIL	199	13	0	4.12	11.62	**8**

An okay gamble for the crapshoot, but I wouldn't look for much more from him.

BOB WELCH	IP	W	S	ERA	RATIO	$
1986 LA	236	7	0	3.28	10.75	**9**
1987 LA	252	15	0	3.22	10.36	**25**
1988 OAK	245	17	0	3.64	11.70	**14**

Just glancing through the rosters of various leagues, it looks as if the average market price for Welch was about $25.

BOBBY WITT	IP	W	S	ERA	RATIO	$
1986 TEX	158	11	0	5.48	15.55	−5
1987 TEX	143	8	0	4.91	15.99	−9
1988 TEX	174	8	0	3.92	12.13	4

Does seem to have turned it around. The sight of Oklahoma City must, as Samuel Johnson commented, concentrate the mind wonderfully.

MIKE WITT	IP	W	S	ERA	RATIO	$
1986 CAL	269	18	0	2.84	9.74	29
1987 CAL	247	16	0	4.01	12.24	14
1988 CAL	250	13	0	4.15	12.62	3

Who'd have thought we'd see Mike outWitted?

CURT YOUNG	IP	W	S	ERA	RATIO	$
1986 OAK	198	13	0	3.45	10.59	16
1987 OAK	203	13	0	4.08	10.55	18
1988 OAK	156	11	0	4.15	12.20	5

He turned it around, also, after reacquaintance with the minors. Together, C. Young and B. Witt make very interesting bets for next year. Underpowering lefty with great control; overpowering right-hander who doesn't just miss but destroys the catcher in the process. Lefty seems crafty, righty seems dumb. Lefty plays on a team that might win even more games next year, it's got so much to prove. Righty plays on a team that has never proved anything.

So who would you take?

I'd take righty.

Pitcher Z

The same warning about minor leaguers in the National League Pitcher Z comment naturally applies here. Dozens of pitchers in the International League and American Association had what appeared to be great seasons; that doesn't tell us much about their futures.

Look at what happened to Drew Hall. Highly touted, he had a 2.34 ERA for Iowa in the American Association, notched 19 saves, had a ratio of just a little over 9 in 65 innings, struck out 75—was promoted to the Cubs, got a win and a save in 22 innings, and hurt any Rotisserie team that picked him up very badly. You will find him in the appendix at minus $4.

So who's fooling whom in the trade that brought him to the Rangers? My guess is the Rangers think they're getting, along with all the other nice things, a healthy Mitch Williams. My hunch is they're wrong. We'll know by May, because, as they say in Massachusetts elections, Valentine's going to be voting for Drew early and often.

Interesting stuff. Really. I can't say I read every word (but I'm going to!), yet I read enough to see that you talk about a little bit of this, a lot of that, without actually making any predictions if you can help it. So what I want to know is, what good is it really? What am I supposed to do with all this stuff?

Make your own predictions, based on it.

However, if you have the time, there's much, much more you can do.

I've got plenty of time. I told my wife she'll see me again in April.

Well, first of all you should analyze your team from last year. I realize that hearing about other leagues is like listening to people's dreams, yet it's sometimes instructive. In order to avoid, for now, the weighty business of "keepers"—players carried over from the previous season at clearly bargain prices—I'll take a start-up league.

Here are El Sobrante Muskrats of the Babi-NL:

		PAID	EARNED	NET
B SANTIAGO	c	31	15	−16
M SASSER	c	3	4	1
G PERRY	1b	23	30	7
D CONCEPCION	2b	1	−1	−2

		PAID	EARNED	NET
T FOLEY	ss	1	10	9
D MAGADAN	3b	6	7	1
K OBERKFELL	1b/3b	1	10	9
J LIND	2b/ss	4	13	9
A PEDRIQUE	ut	1	−2	−3
K DANIELS	of	36	31	−5
A DAWSON	of	34	34	0
B BONDS	of	31	29	−2
J CANGELOSI	of	8	4	−4
S JEFFERSON	of	2	−1	−3
		182	183	1
O HERSHISER	p	31	34	3
S GARRELTS	p	14	12	−2
A MCGAFFIGAN	p	12	8	−4
F WILLIAMS	p	7	1	−6
P PEREZ	p	7	24	17
J PRICE	p	3	1	−2
V PALACIOS	p	2	−5	−7
L ANDERSEN	p	1	7	6
R MURPHY	p	1	3	2
		78	85	7
		260	**268**	**8**

How does it look?

Just glancing, some good ballplayers and some major turkeys.

And the interesting thing is, they basically got what they paid for. Injuries or shockingly good or bad performances didn't really figure into their season. In fact, this is one of the soberest drafts I've ever seen.

Something I didn't mention in the earlier discussion is that team budgets follow from the precepts of the average hitter's and pitcher's worth. You multiply $13 times fourteen hitters and get $182, $8.67 times nine pitchers and get $78. Hitting, I'm always a little chagrined to observe, is 70 percent of this game.

The reason is not that pitchers are unreliable, although they are; the reason is the game's rules. Without fail, when the last baseball has been pitched in October, 70 percent of every league's total budget will have been earned by hitters (and their three cumulative categories), the other 30 percent by pitchers (and their two categories).

However, you certainly don't have to budget your money in those proportions. The whole object is to get more for it than anyone else, so you should grab bargains wherever you find them. Perhaps by sheer coincidence the Muskrats hit these numbers right on the nose.

Well, how did they do?

Fourth. That is, they had the fourth-best draft according to Heath's hypothetical final standings (assuming no changes after opening day). When the dust settled, El Sobrante Muskrats were in the second division, sixth.

Without knowing anything more about this team (in this case I am indebted to both Jerry Heath and Roger "Jock Strapp" Neiss for the numbers), can't we easily see what its problems were?

Number one, no upside; out of twenty-three players, they only really hit it big with Pascual Perez. That was a good pick. Particularly if it was getting late in the draft, $7 should fetch that sort of starting pitcher.

They knew talent, betting the bank on Hershiser, but all you can reasonably hope for when you go into the thirties for a starting pitcher is to avoid disaster.

They went after hitters who combined power and speed; unfortunately, so did the people they were bidding against. Gibson, Daniels— these guys weren't going to bring them a pennant. To win, they needed help from the likes of Cangelosi and Jefferson, and they didn't get it.

They were only moderately enthusiastic about relief pitching and got middling results.

They didn't have any fat anywhere—nothing to trade to cover their mistakes. And then, of course, there's Santiago.

He screwed them but good, didn't he?

I would argue they screwed themselves. They fell in love with the idea of owning the best player at a rotten position—a common fallacy. To me, a home run is a home run; it doesn't matter where it comes from. Paying for "position scarcity" makes no sense. Oh, it may be worth a dollar or two, but clearly there was frenzied bidding on Benito: "Please, God, don't leave me with Junior Ortiz." Well, Ortiz went to the Busch Leaguers for $1, earned $4, and the Busch Leaguers finished in first.

Santiago was clearly their second-biggest tactical error.

What was the first?

Hershiser.

Out of curiosity, let's see what the Babi-NL spent as a league on pitching:

	$ SPENT ON PITCHING
All Talk and No Shows	59
Busch Leaguers	107
El Sobrante Muskrats	78
Marv's Boys	96
Merry Larrys	139
ProCrastinators	88
Sacred Vessels	37
Three Blind Squid	4
Triple Headers	75
Vodka Forevers	121
total	884
average	88

The first thing to notice is that the budgets do vary widely. The Merry Larrys (who ended up in fourth in the actual final standings) just poured their money into pitching; the Sacred Vessels were at the other extreme (and finished seventh).

Neither team is "right"; the only thing that matters is, did you get what you paid for? If the average pitcher earns $8.67 and hence the average team $78, then the league as a whole earns $780. But they spent $884. Somewhere spread around among these ten teams there must be more than $100 in losses.

Can we check this out?

Sure, why not? Just do what you did for the Muskrats for the other nine teams. What did you find out?

Well, I was kind of pressed for time, yet that's precisely the way to do it for your own league.

You didn't do it? You're expecting me to?

If you're curious enough, yes. You don't have to. There is another way to do it, and it's much faster than adding up each player one by one. You've got your league's final totals, correct? However your stats are done, you know each team's final totals. All you have to do is take a peek at the Masochist Notes—go ahead, it won't kill you—see what my formulas are, set them up on a spreadsheet, and plug in whole teams.

Spreadsheet, huh?

Well, you could do it by hand, I guess. Seems awfully quaint, though. (Your partner does the stats by hand?)

The Muskrats, for all their problems, still ended up $8 to the good, slightly ahead of $260. That's the dividing line, and they were in fact a fourth-place team coming out of the draft. Teams that buy $280 or more are solid; teams that buy $300 and up are almost guaranteed winners.

What happens when four other teams buy $350?

They can't. This isn't Scrabble we're playing: "I had a lot of neat words, but shucks, hers were even better." This is poker or backgammon, a zero-sum game. I allocate $2,600 to the NL draft populations, $3,120 to the AL drafts. That's all there is.

Does it sound like I'm repeating myself?

No, but you're wandering around, kind of pissing me off. I want to start learning how to earn $300.

Of course. So let's run through it quickly and see whether there's time left for other things.

People who are new at the game think Rotisserie baseball resembles real baseball, which it does only vaguely. Real baseball games are decided by which team scores more runs, and the players most responsible for deciding that are the power hitters and starting pitchers. However, they do not drive the Cadillacs in Rotisserie baseball. Rather, on many teams they do—and those teams lose.

The eight categories we use have two enormous warps in them: steals and saves. They have equal footing with the other six, which is obviously a distortion of their value in real baseball.

But it doesn't stop there. Not only does Team A not get more credit for winning home runs and wins than Team B for winning stolen bases and saves, Team A gets no more credit for utterly dominating these categories than for winning by a whisker. The Sacred Vessels of the Babi-NL hit 63 more homers than the next-best team and had *126* more RBIs—and were quite respectable in wins with 77; hell, their ERA (3.42) was also respectable—and finished seventh.

The Busch Leaguers, with one more win, 63 fewer homers and (yes) 126 fewer RBIs, didn't just finish first; they finished first by sixteen points.

The Busch Leaguers bought $375 worth of performance at the draft; the Sacred Vessels, $242.

Three hundred-and-what?

I'm kind of shocked myself. I just worked it out. The second-best team, All Talk and No Shows, earned $294. A $34 profit. That's not bad— but it's not so hot when another team got out of the draft with $81 more dollars.

This isn't America, you know; somebody has to pay for this.

The worst team was the Triple Headers. They bought $200 worth of value in the draft. They frittered away $60. And, rest assured, they had plenty of company.

Can I see those Heath "hypothetical final standings" that you're basing this on?

Why didn't you ask sooner? You could have read me the numbers.

Just what I thought. Not only does this show the Busch Leaguers first both in the hypothetical and actual final standings, it shows the All Talks finishing second both times and the Triple Headers finishing last both times.

Those are a *couple* of things I glance at. Patton $, after all, are supposed to have some correlation with whether your team is any good or not. But I also look at such items as the steals and saves categories.

Patton $ are often better predictors than Heath's hypothetical final standings. That's because my prices weigh all eight commodities on scales; they give a more accurate index of the assets a team has for the long and treacherous pennant race that's about to begin.

Mind if I write that down? I might have to run that one by my partner.

Let's do a league as a whole, and it'll be clear. Hand me one of those ALRs—American League Rotisseries.

SOUR GRAPEFRUIT LEAGUE: PATTON $ DRAFT WORTH

HYP. FINAL	ACT. FINAL		$H	$P	$ TOTAL	PROFIT OR LOSS
3	1	Swansongs	198	146	344	84
1	2	Big Sticks	225	94	319	59
2	3	O'Dingers	199	102	301	41
5	7	Poetic Justus $ Co.	179	98	277	17
6	9	Pace-Sos	217	56	273	13
4	4	Levin Thour	109	146	255	−5

HYP. FINAL	ACT. FINAL		$H	$P	$ TOTAL	PROFIT OR LOSS
8	6	Dave's Lettermen	199	54	253	−7
10	8	Hall Stars	202	44	246	−14
9	5	Big Red Toadstools	175	68	243	−17
11	11	Master Batters	164	63	227	−33
7	10	Bunsen Byrners	133	73	206	−54
12	12	River Rats	175	18	193	−67
		league total	2175	962	3137	17
		average team	181	80	261	1

The numbers on the left are how they finished (1) in Heath's hypothetical final standings, and (2) actually. Under the "$H" column is what the drafted hitters earned all told (whether they were traded to another team is irrelevant); "$P" shows what all the drafted pitchers earned. Then we total these. And finally we subtract the amount of money that was available to spend ($260) to determine the overall profit or loss of the players a team bought in the draft when we close the books at the end of the season. If my prices are valid for individual players, then they must be valid for whole teams. Or, I suppose, we could argue it the other way.

Whatever, they look great for these Sour Grapefruits.

Don't they? See, Heath's hypothetical final standings declare twelve points and no more for winning a category. They give the pennant to the Big Sticks and tell the O'Dingers they're coming in second.

After the season, when these two teams receive this information from Jerry Heath, what are they to think? Jerry at least has his priorities straight; he mails them the actual final standings first.

And if they don't open their mail, you know the Swansongs have gotten the word to them already that they've passed them both.

So, what do the Big Sticks and O'Dingers say? "It was injuries"?

Probably. That's what we all say.

However, hypothetical final standings include injuries. Teams down in the hypothetical final standings, like Dave's Lettermen, probably had injuries that they compensated for through waiver picks or their reserve list, or even trades.

Aren't trades the likely other excuse for the decline of the Big Sticks and O'Dingers?

Sure. The Swansongs screwed the Pace-Sos or the Bunsen Byrners, and the Big Sticks and O'Dingers didn't.

I wouldn't put it past them. But isn't there a chance that the Swansongs, with their $84 profit in the draft, were in a better position to deal?

As for the victims, the Bunsen Byrners, with their $54 deficit, were out of it from the start. They either actively (through a fire sale) or passively sought their own level.

There's no question, in any case, that ranking the drafts in Patton dollars—as we have here—more closely resembles the final results than the hypothetical final standings do.

Look at that $300 dividing line.

I'm looking at the River Rats. They didn't make it to $200. They got burned so bad, you wonder if they could even have a fire sale.

You've learned to read this stuff pretty well. But I can't help pointing out one other thing: Notice how closely the Sour Grapefruit as a whole fits the "typical draft" that I base my prices on. The average team earns $261 instead of $260.

I'll get my partner to kiss you.

I didn't know she was your wife.

I got news for you. My wife is going to hate you. And my partner's wife—mention Elias in her house, and you better duck.

Yes, well—where were we?

It would be interesting to total up how these teams allocated their budgets in the draft. We could compare the market prices, in other words, to these Patton $ earnings. It's a tedious process, adding up player after player's salary, but I would definitely do that for my own league.

My partner most definitely will.

And, of course, I'm not suggesting at all that there's going to be a correlation. The only prediction I'll make is that teams with lots of home runs and RBIs spent a lot of money on hitting. That's not necessarily bad—in fact, just as you *don't* want the double whammy of bad ratio and ERA, you're in bad shape if you're deficient in these two other linked categories—it's just that it's hard to get profits there. To some extent, veteran owners put extra money into power hitters just because it's a safer place.

The main thing, though, is to grab anything anywhere that you think is underpriced. If you have any faith in your ability to make trades (and who doesn't?) and you're in a league that is willing to make trades (and if you're not, I feel sorry for you), then don't worry about coming out of the draft "balanced." Come out with profits.

So that's what we should talk about. Where do we get 'em?

Anywhere! I hear what I'm saying: Why can't *you* hear it?

When it's as important as I think this is, I want to hear it again.

How can I tell you where the profits are if I'm not in your league? Each league has its own market prices. Learn the true value of players' performances, and in your draft exploit the hell out of any and all phony market prices.

I'll tell you one person who knew that already. His name is Jeff Busch, and as he reads this, he's going to be gritting his teeth.

You no doubt know who Jeff Busch is.

Sure, the Busch Leaguers.

The reason the Busch Leaguers got $375 at the draft was that they scooped up all the scarce commodities; 264 stolen bases and 90 saves. Eventually they made 13 trades, hearing bids from groveling also-rans, to end up with 217 stolen bases and 74 saves—both still good for first.

Jeff Busch was a ringer.

What were some of his good buys? See over there? Doesn't that folder say "Babi-NL"?

Oh? By God, you're right!

Brett Butler, $17; Randy Myers, $16; Lance McCullers, $7; Chris Sabo, $4; Paul O'Neill, $1—and don't forget Junior Ortiz.

Paul O'Neill a dollar? I give that league an F. Where the hell is this Babi-NL? I want to join.

There are probably a few openings. I think it's in the Bay Area; somehow, that's what the name is trying to tell us, I think.

Damn. Too far. Well, at least the Busch Leaguers have already lost McCullers.

Right. Justice, as usual—too late.

We were talking, though, about the illusions you mustn't get caught up in. Do you think Jeff Busch cares that if you ran his players onto an actual field with the Sacred Vessels (Dale Murphy, Andy Van Slyke, Glenn Davis) they'd get their butts kicked?

Which brings up another way that we misperceive the game. Fourteen players go up to the plate, not nine, and none of them take the field. Far too often, owners get three outfielders in the draft and then start coasting, concentrating on other positions. Oh, they'd be happy to have Butler fall their way—a terrific fourth outfielder—but they won't pursue him as aggressively; they think they need to save that money to buy a first baseman.

What difference does it make? Would you rather have Keith Hernandez as your starting first baseman or Butler as your spare outfielder?

Who'd they have at first?

Who? The Busch Leaguers? You still hung up on them?

Yes. When a team buys $375 with $260, the answer is yes. Also I figure since you happen not to have lost this league's market prices, we might as well hear them.

I haven't lost anything! Just takes a little while to find them.

But all right: at first base for the Busch Leaguers, Mike Aldrete. You can't win them all. At $11 (his salary, are you satisfied?) you can't lose much. In fact—let's look in the appendix . . . they didn't lose anything.

Their outfield was Vince Coleman, $33; John Kruk, $22; Brett Butler, $17; Dave Martinez, $14; and Rafael Palmeiro, $9. O'Neill was their utility man.

San-Fran-cisco, here-I-come . . .

You call that a voice?

Look, this was a start-up league, so all these prices are last year's market prices. Coleman is explained by the fact that the Babi-NL didn't understand that he was a better Rotisserie ballplayer than Dale Murphy ($34); he was better in 1987, too, when both were outstanding. I don't have the order of the draft, but I'm sure Palmeiro is explained by money running out—

And O'Neill by ignorance.

I agree. Read the player comment on O'Neill, and you'll see other, more alert market prices. I think we've kicked the Babi-NL around enough so that I'm not going anywhere near San Francisco for a while.

The point I'm trying to make is, just the way Santiago's home runs don't count extra because he also throws base runners out, your team isn't any better if your "starting" first baseman is worse than the other team's "spare" outfielder. So what if you end up with a funny-looking team? You can't see it, anyway.

The key to success is not so much pursuing the best players at a position as avoiding the worst. That's why the appendix is so important. When you're studying it position by position, your first concern is the overall strength of the position—which is what the average shows— and your second is the depth, which is what the worst player shows.

If you look carefully, you'll see you could very well get better results, with two dollars to spend at the end, from your third middle infielder than your fifth outfielder.

Are you sure?

Yes. It comes from our peculiar supply and demand:

	PLAYERS NEEDED	REGULARS AVAILABLE	IRREGULARS ON ROSTERS	%
OF-NL	50	36	14	.28
2B/SS-NL	30	24	6	.20
OF-AL	60	42	18	.30
2B/SS-NL	36	28	8	.22

The percentages are the odds of getting a bench warmer. Every Rotisserie team has nine decent hitters; your draft is won or lost, on offense, as you battle for those other five.

By the way, the percents also give an indication of the slimmer pickings in the ALRs.

First and third, I take it, is the same as the middle infielders?

Same math, and so the same amount of depth; there's more strength but not as much more as you might think. And if you shuffle someone like Todd Benzinger or Chris James into the outfield, both strength and depth take serious nose dives.

AVERAGE PLAYERS ($ EARNED)

	NL	AL
OF	19.60	18.72
3B	13.81	13.81
1B	19.03	18.70
SS	13.48	10.84
2B	15.24	10.96

	NL	AL	
C	7.44	8.05	
DH		7.85	
Average	14.66	14.71	(without DH)
		14.21	(with DH)
P	12.47	12.01	

Both sets of middle infielders in the National League last year, particularly the second basemen, were better than the third basemen. That's on the basis of the strength of the average player. As far as depth goes, only with the catchers is there any danger of not getting a dollar for your dollar. The math on them is grim: In the American League you need twenty-four and only fourteen can start, so 42% of the catchers ride the pines every day.

Does that mean you're hedging on what you said about Benito?

Not at all. I'd rather get no dollars of performance for my one dollar spent than $15 for my $31.

The lesson I draw from the charts in the appendix is to try to get five *good* outfielders, because that's where far and away the best strength is, and there really isn't more depth; my prospects in the one-dollar endgame just aren't that good anywhere. (However, it's certainly true that in the waning stages of every draft all scrub position players left only cost a dollar or two. In that sense, no matter what my charts say, they aren't worth more.)

You make me nervous. I keep thinking you're telling me to buy Benito.

Relax. We've got a long way to go. We haven't even mentioned how woeful the DH has become; it's as if Darwin were somehow phasing it out. The average designated hitter (after I barely scraped together 12) earned less than the average pitcher's salary last year! Nevertheless, it's a great place to look for profits, thanks to the simple math: 12 players needed, 168 available.

But wait a minute. Aren't the overall averages a far cry from what you say the averages should be, especially for the pitchers—$12, not $8.

They are, because this is a retrospective list: the fifty best producers in the National League outfield, for example, at the season's end. How many people had Otis Nixon and his 46 steals in their plans? That's why it's not valid to base salaries on final NL and AL totals, or even on your league's final totals.

You're right, though: especially pitchers. Let's just scan down the AL pitcher list in the appendix: Bryan Harvey, $28; Allan Anderson, $26; Mike Schooler, $15; Craig McMurtry, $15; Todd Burns, $11— all sorts of major contributions coming out of nowhere.

That's why you keep mocking Hershiser?

I don't mock him! He was awesome. It's just that the math on pitching shows the reverse situation, a glut. Teams come up from Florida with about ten on their rosters.

	PITCHERS NEEDED	PITCHERS AVAILABLE	PITCHERS LEFT OVER	%
NL	90	120	30	25
AL	108	140	32	23

One out of four *not taken*—which means there's even more to choose from.

Suppose you didn't fill a single pitching spot throughout the draft. The auction is over; people are looking at you. You've got $9 left. In the NL you'd have a choice of 39 pitchers, *33 percent* of the original pool.

The result is a huge $1 crapshoot. As I said earlier, the last move made in the American Dreams draft (at that point it is a draft instead of an auction) was the nomination of Doug Jones for $1. Bingo: $41 profit. If they had bought exact value with their $259 to that point, that pick alone made them a contender.

Isn't that luck?

Only if it's accidental.

No, of course it's luck. This is a game of luck; we kid ourselves that we're in control. Bad luck will sink anybody, and good luck consists mainly of avoiding it. But by taking a few $1 pitchers at the end, you're acknowledging that there is still a vast number to choose from and you *could* get lucky. If you don't, it's like passing up a free raffle ticket.

What if you get a stiff?

Then it's not free, quite true. If your league doesn't allow you to drop pitchers, you've got to be more careful. Frankly, I don't understand those leagues. Every Rotisserie League in the country should be required by law to change that rule, before a distraught owner shoots someone like Steve Trout in an airport.

Or the Mexican. I like the guy, but I admit it crossed my mind.

How much did you pay for him?

None of your bleeping business.

Hey, no problem; let me just look through some of this stuff I've got.

PRICE PAID FOR FERNANDO VALENZUELA IN 1988
(AND WHERE THE TEAM FINISHED)

Triple Headers, Babi-NL	$19 (10th)
K-Marks, Crabhouse	$21 (9th)
Bobby Sox, Beanhead	$32 (7th)
Alibis, Hot Pepper	$18 (8th)
Beer and Pirogis, Money-Is-No-Object	$34 (5th)
Bert's Sognatores, W.O.R.L.D.	$25 (9th)

Well, we bought him for less than any of these guys, and we didn't even want him; we were just trying to chase his price up. Minus $8 to go with the $16 we paid, a $24 beating; that hurt. Hey, let's do Hershiser.

Okay. This should be interesting.

PRICE PAID FOR OREL HERSHISER IN 1988
(AND WHERE THE TEAM FINISHED)

El Sobrante Muskrats, Babi-NL	$31 (6th)
Tapers, Crabhouse	$17 (1st)
Anteaters, Beanhead	$10 (1st)
Alibis, Hot Pepper	$26 (8th)
Beer and Pirogis, Money-Is-No-Object	$25 (5th)
Glassmen, W.O.R.L.D.	$18 (1st)

Now you've got to admit, Orel was worth it; he delivered the bacon three times. Pitching for sure counts.

For sure. It counts half. I trust *you* noticed, though, that there was no bacon for anyone who paid more than $20 for him.

But he earned, according to you, $34!

They made a profit on *him;* overall, I'll bet you anything their approach was shaky. Let's zero in on those two teams that had both Fernando and Hershiser. Would you mind reading me their entire pitching staffs? (Thanks. It's a big help.)

BEER AND PIROGIS		ALIBIS	
VALENZUELA	$34	MATHEWS	$10
HERSHISER	$25	DUNNE	$10
BROWNING	$21	R. ROBINSON	$12
MARTINEZ	$10	CONE	$12
RASMUSSEN	$10	D. ROBINSON	$ 5
KRUKOW	$15	HERSHISER	$26
ST. CLAIRE	$ 1	D. JACKSON	$16
PENA	$ 6	VALENZUELA	$18
SUTTER	$ 5	LEACH	$ 4
TOTAL	$127	TOTAL	$113

I can tell you all about these owners, just from the totals. They know baseball, but they either haven't played or still don't understand Rotisserie baseball. One team has the Cy Young Award winner, the other has the two runner-ups, and they finished fifth and eighth. Why? Because they way overspent on pitching. You shouldn't follow my proportions exactly, but any time you go over $100 on pitching, you're asking for trouble; and if you do it while mostly ignoring relief pitching, you're ensuring disaster.

Would you mind reaching over there—yes, I think it's that pile—and getting Heath's hypothetical and actual final standings? Thanks.

Beautiful. Pirogis, coming out of the draft: ninth in home runs, last in RBI. Alibis: last in both. Alibis were also last in steals and last in saves. Pirogis were ninth in saves. They both were first or almost first in ERA, ratio and wins—and had no chance.

Now the actual final standings. Pirogis improved a little in saves, were still last in homers and RBIs. Holding onto their pitching, they climbed from ninth, their hypothetical finish, to fifth. The Alibis faded in pitching and slightly improved in hitting—probably making perfectly fair trades—and remained eighth all the way.

The whole idea is to be strong in the cumulative categories, really strong, because that's stuff you can trade. Of all the cumulative items, wins have the least currency, because they carry with them the double jeopardy of those vexing, usually redundant, qualitative categories,

ERA and ratio. Pluses in those averages can and do disappear in the carnage of one weekend.

If you don't want to take that chance, you don't have to. One way or another, you can put pitchers on ice, giving up or quasi-giving up on wins. This is frowned on in real baseball. And even if it's not, someone's got to start every game, someone's got to finish it, and someone's got to pitch all the innings in between. At the end of the season, every team has well over 1,400 innings; the few Rotisserie teams that do are normally losers. The long and short of it is that the market for starting pitchers in Rotisserie baseball is not what it is in real baseball.

You've convinced me.

Luckily for you, not everyone knows. The reason the Busch Leaguers had such an easy time of it was that someone else bid Hershiser to $30; *they* didn't, you know that. While someone else was bidding $20 for Browning, they sat there quietly, watching money vanish.

I'm really getting excited about the crapshoot. What would you say to spending $18 on pitchers, just so you have a choice?

I don't recommend it. What you need is an extremely deep list of starters, and don't be picky. Once prices fall to the $5 to $15 range, you'll still have a wide choice. However, if your league's any good, there won't be many solid starters left below $5. In the American Dreams, we have two teams, the Palukas and BB Guns, who just love the crapshoot, and they always get hammered.

Money spent on pitching by the BB Guns last year: $37. By the Palukas: $34. Final ERA and ratio: BB Guns 4 points, Palukas 2 points. Overall pitching points: BB Guns 16.5, Palukas 7. Overall finish: BB Guns eighth, Palukas twelfth.

And, finally, that $18 of yours isn't going to buy you one first-class relief pitcher.

I was just kidding you. See if I could get a rise.

I'm glad you're having fun.

Let's talk about relievers. My prices for them, they don't bother you?

Nope. We pay through the nose for them.

Well, you should. Everything I've been saying just now applies to starters *only*. Everything that drives market prices for starters down in veteran leagues makes relievers expensive.

The Mahatma Ghumbies of the Hot Pepper League spent $88 on pitching, over half on relief pitching. They were in the happy position of having Dave Smith as a $9 keeper, but they weren't complacent: They bought Tim Burke for $29 and Craig Lefferts for $7. Burke earned an astonishing $37 the year before, and I don't blame them for chasing him; however, last year he only earned $15. A Fernando type of mistake? Not at all. He had a much better chance than Fernando to go over thirty, and a much smaller chance of going under zero. In all events, the Mahatma Gumbies finished first.

The Swansongs of the Sour Grapefruit League spent $84 on pitching, and $69 of it went to Jeff Reardon, Dennis Eckersley, and Bobby Thigpen. They finished first.

The Semi-Conductors of the Bos-Wash League spent $95, $38 of it precommitted to Reardon, and they won.

In the American Dreams, the Hackers froze Righetti at $40 and still came in second.

The Wssox, a squad I envied in my guide last year for its overpowering freeze list—among others, Eckersley for $1 and Mitch Williams for $3—still proceeded to buy Gene Garber for $4, Don Aase for $4, Willie Hernandez for $10, and Lee Smith for $45.

And, yes, they did win.

So you didn't, huh?

Guess not.

Didn't come in second either.

What can I tell you? It's a tough league.

I think I have heard you say that before.

Shall we get on?

The hardest thing to comprehend about relievers is their four-category impact. Time and again, I run into people who can't or won't believe that their best reliever often helps them more in ERA and ratio than their best starting pitcher. The thing is, some of what I do is definitely arguable; it can be attacked at its premise. The math in each points column in the appendix, however, is exactly that—math. If one player—

Are we getting into something for the masochists?

Not really. If one player gets more points in a category than another player, he's better in that category, it's that simple.

I believe you.

John Franco's ERA helped more than Mike Scott's; so did Randy Myers's. Whether ten saves or ten wins help more, that's another matter; that you can argue, that's where I'll listen to—

Save it for my partner, I know he's going to be real interested.

All right. I guess that's it, then. I don't know what else there is to talk about.

That's it?

I think so. For now.

I now know how to buy me $300?

Don't you?

I'll tell you what. Let me keep reading this book of yours. But I want a last shot at you when it's all over. You make sure you save time for it. Don't go off on a hundred tangents with my partner and then not let me get the last crack.

Fine. Now I really do have to get started on the minor leagues.

Want me to help? We won't talk. I'll just read you the numbers.

Really? I'd appreciate that.

Yeah, maybe I'll spot some good rooks. Where's the stuff?

See that stack of *Baseball Americas?* Right. It's on the top; says "Final minor-league statistics."
   Okay, try the second one.

Got it. What do you think of Sandy Alomar? No, shh, no talking. Where do we start?

The International League. Hitters. Whoever looks like he's any good at all. . . .

If there's any doubt that they were making different baseballs last year, this should dispel it:

AMERICAN ASSOCIATION AVERAGE TEAMS

	HR	RBI	SB	BA	ERA
1987	134	746	132	.282	4.91
1988	79	549	131	.258	3.64

The only other possible explanation for such a huge shift from offense to defense would be a huge turnover of personnel: all the great 1987 hitters going to the majors, all the terrible 1987 pitchers going back to school. But this didn't happen. The only 1987 big bopper that comes to mind who got any significant playing time in the majors was the much-touted (by me) Joey Meyer, and he turned out to be not great.

The Denver team that Meyer played on had much the same cast both years. It would seem that hitter after hitter just about completely lost it. Billy Bates went from .316 to .258, Brad Komminsk from 32 homers and .298 to 16 homers and .239, Steve Kiefer from 31 and .330 to 10 and .214.

On the other hand, if the object is for a team to get more homers than anyone else—an area in which real baseball and Rotisserie baseball more or less agree—then Denver did all right. They won the home run category in 1987 with 192; they tied for first last year with 108.

Bates, Komminsk, and Kiefer did lose something; even a little banjo hitter like Billy missed the rabbit, and even in Denver's thin air, the new ball just didn't race away the way it did in that fun '87. These guys never hit like that before in their lives, and hopefully never will again now that Ubie's gone.

Joey Meyer, Sam Horn, Dave Clark, Randy Milligan—in Rotisserie Leagues all around the country last April, we fell for it. I paid $13 for Joey. What the heck. I'd stumbled on McGwire and Nokes the year before, and even though I ranted and raved in my 1988 price guide how their home runs had about as much value as a peso, it never occurred to me it was going to *stop*.

But it did. So the obvious lesson is, beware of all those fine-looking flingers now.

I try to accomplish two things with these charts. First, to show players in the contexts of their leagues. Second, to project them so they have all played the same amount.

To establish the context, I figure out the average player, just as I do with the majors. I make the average pitcher worth $8.67 and the average hitter $13. I use denominators that roughly express the same proportions as those in the majors. In other words, if the average hitter in the Southern League gets fewer homers than the average hitter in the National League, he gets a smaller denominator than the National League denominator of four. I won't plague you with all the denominators, but you can easily infer them by glancing at the average player, which I list.

For pitching, since what we're interested in are the ERA and ratio contexts, they are all that change; I stick with the major-league wins and saves denominators of three and 2.5. (Look at the Eastern League average hitter; no wonder his homer denominator is under three!) The dollars that the players are projected to have earned last year, in essence, are strong approximations of what they would have earned if their minor league had a Rotisserie league. (That's a strange idea. Does anyone want to start one? The perpetual bummer of a minor-league Rotisserie League would be, of course, losing all your best players.) Most don't come close to even 500 at bats, so I stretch them all out to 500 (the few who go over 500 get shrunk) and show what their earnings would be then. I stretch starting pitchers out to 220 innings pitched and relievers to 60 games, and give those earnings.

Don't take the totals seriously. This is just a useful way of ranking the players—it amounts to their production per at bat or inning or game. Indeed, it was the only viable way of ranking them I could think of.

Here's what may seem like a digression: Can you rank the leagues themselves?

No, of course not, because they don't play each other. At least that was my impression.

Quite belatedly, in putting together the numbers for this section, I decided to double-check a few figures, and in the course of checking the wins denominator (I'm the original masochist) I found out that the International League had 538 wins while the American Association had 595. Curious, I thought, since both are eight-team leagues playing 142-game schedules. I first thought that the Howe News Bureau, the Elias of the minors, was being a bit cavalier with its numbers. So I added up the loss columns. The International League, it seemed, went 538–594 against itself, while the American Association was 595–539.

When I combined the two and got a record of 1133–1133, I had an inkling of what had happened, and a call to *Baseball America* confirmed it. Almost entirely without the notice of fans in major-league cities, these two leagues played an experimental (read, promotional) stretch of forty games against each other. Evidently, it was a good promotion. It also did wonders for the prestige of the AA, which won 188 of the 320 games played. That .413 winning percentage for the IL would have put it behind Seattle in the AL West.

When you're studying rookies this spring, as if you don't have enough to keep in your mind, factor in the indisputable fact that hitters or pitchers from the American Association played 102 of their 142 games at a higher level of competition than at least one of the other leagues in Triple A.

How would I use the charts? Sparingly. I'd hunt around for familiar faces like Lonnie Smith or Ken Howell to get my bearings in each league. (Good lord, there's old Rupe Jones still? The rest of these guys, forget it.) I wouldn't get too excited over Pete Harnisch, after the way he was pounded in the majors, but I wouldn't write him off, either. I'd give, and expect the Blue Jays to give, Todd Stottlemyre another chance.

I would give Rick Rodriguez a lot of credit, even though I picked him up late in the season a couple of years ago and it completed my ruin. I know: He was brought up last year and ruined some more people. But in the Pacific Coast League, the one place they didn't change the baseballs, in Colorado Springs, which must be a mile higher than Denver—where Joe Skalski's ERA was 6.55 and Mike Brown's was 6.12 (the only other pitchers with more than a hundred innings), where the team ERA was 5.23—Rick Rodriguez had a 3.06 ERA.

I'd watch out for the PCL in general. Eric Hanson got pounded, and he looked pretty good in the majors. Luis Medina looked good when he wasn't looking awful (in fact he looked a bit like McGwire, I'm here to say), but remember, he played in Colorado Springs. Mike Devereaux, Edgar Martinez—I'd like to see them get demoted to the Eastern League and have those batting averages.

(I know what happened: Ubie's so cheap he couldn't bear to throw away the old balls; they're all in the PCL, while they last.)

If I didn't have the time to cross-check players against *Baseball America,* the Bill Mazeroski annual, on-site inspections in Florida, etc., I could probably do worse in the reserve-pick portion of the draft than to just take fliers. Who's Mark Gardner? I have no idea. But man, oh man, could he pitch in Double A. Unlike the majors, such matters as hits, walks, and strikeouts are presented for you to ponder. A dagger indicates the player is considered hot stuff by *Baseball America,* one of the ten best prospects in his league.

It will be interesting to see if I've missed anyone. There were no set criteria. I probably included all pitchers with ten or more wins or saves, for instance, but I certainly didn't only include them.

So . . . now can I get excited? *Gary Sheffield.*

Gregg Jefferies, you'll notice, really wasn't so bad in the International League; Sheffield was dynamite at both El Paso (AA) and Denver (AAA). Both are notorious hitters' ballparks, and at El Paso two teammates appear to have done better than him (really only because he didn't bother to run the bases), but any way you look at it he was in a class by himself in the minors.

What's impressive is that the promotion to Triple A only made him better. Nine home runs may not knock your eyes out, yet his stats for 500 at bats are 21 HR, 127 RBI, and 47 SB. They may not add up to $65 in the American League (they don't), but against the puny average player of the American Association, that's what they're worth. Just in actual earnings, not projected, he racked up $55 in the minors last year, and then for the Brewers he earned $4. *He was better than Henderson and Canseco.*

No, wait. I'll be sued if people take that seriously. He outearned those two. He was worth more in these three leagues he played in, in their Rotisserie Leagues—which in two cases don't even exist—than Henderson and Canseco were worth in American League Rotisserie Leagues. He's going to be a fine ballplayer, probably better than Jefferies.

Who the thunder is Mitch Lyden? I'm looking in my *Baseball America,* my Mazeroski, my *Sporting News Register,* and I can't find him.

Whoever he is, he's a real pain. What he did in the Eastern League, even if it's only 78 at bats, is indeed quite remarkable, but it escaped my notice. I had everybody projected out to 550 at bats, closer to a full major-league season, when I pressed the sort key of Lotus—blam, there he was: $106. I had to go back and do every chart over again at 500 at bats.

I have some shame.

INTERNATIONAL LEAGUE (AAA)

		HR	RBI	SB	BA	AB	S*
Average Player		6	33	8	.244	324	**20**
ROBERTO KELLY of	(NY A)	3	16	11	.333	120	**58**
LONNIE SMITH of	(ATL)	9	51	26	.300	290	**50**
KEVIN ROMINE of	(BOS)	4	26	3	.358	148	**44**
TONY BROWN of	(PHI)	3	21	6	.299	127	**39**
RON JONES of	(PHI)	16	75	16	.267	445	**35**
JIM TRABER 1b	(BAL)	6	23	2	.285	144	**34**
KEN LANDREAUX of	(BAL)	7	23	6	.272	173	**34**
KEITH HUGHES of	(BAL)	7	49	11	.270	274	**34**
BRADY ANDERSON of	(BOS)	4	19	8	.287	167	**33**
JAY BUHNER of	(NY A)	8	18	1	.256	129	**33**
DAVE GRIFFIN 1b	(ATL)	21	72	0	.289	453	**33**
GREGG JEFFERIES 3b†	(NY N)	7	61	32	.282	504	**32**
MARK CARREON of	(NY N)	14	55	11	.263	365	**32**
PHIL LOMBARDI of	(NY N)	9	44	2	.308	292	**32**
JEFF STONE of	(BAL)	3	27	20	.277	267	**32**
STEVE FINLEY of†	(BAL)	5	54	20	.314	456	**32**
TOMMY DUNBAR of	(ATL)	4	33	4	.291	189	**32**
SCOTT LUSADER of	(DET)	4	46	22	.261	329	**31**
RICKY JORDAN 1b†	(PHI)	7	36	10	.308	338	**30**
KELLY HEATH dh	(TOR)	5	41	5	.310	287	**30**
ALEX INFANTE ss	(TOR)	2	28	21	.300	340	**30**
ERIC YELDING 2b†	(TOR)	1	38	59	.250	556	**29**
CARLOS QUINTANA of	(BOS)	16	66	3	.285	471	**28**
DANNY SHEAFFER c	(BOS)	1	28	20	.274	299	**27**
CRAIG WORTHINGTON 3b	(BAL)	16	73	3	.244	430	**25**
BOB GREEN of	(PHI)	4	30	7	.251	207	**25**
TURNER WARD of	(PHI)	7	50	28	.251	490	**25**
OTIS GREEN 1b	(TOR)	10	41	13	.266	410	**25**
TOM BARRETT 2b	(PHI)	1	33	21	.285	390	**25**
KEITH MILLER 2b	(NY N)	1	15	8	.281	171	**24**
MARCUS LAWTON of	(NY N)	0	17	35	.233	335	**24**
RANDY VELARDE ss	(NY A)	5	37	7	.270	293	**24**
ROB DUCEY of	(TOR)	7	42	7	.256	317	**23**
JEFF BLAUSER ss†	(ATL)	5	23	6	.284	271	**23**
HECTOR DELACRUZ	(TOR)	4	27	16	.202	228	**22**
PAT DODSON 1b	(BOS)	7	28	3	.228	197	**22**
GLENALLEN HILL of	(TOR)	4	19	7	.233	172	**22**
GERONIMO BERROA of†	(TOR)	8	64	7	.260	470	**21**
SAM HORN dh	(BOS)	10	31	0	.233	279	**17**
HENSLEY MEULENS 3b	(NY A)	6	22	2	.230	209	**16**

*Projected to 500 AB

INTERNATIONAL LEAGUE (AAA)
ERA 3.47   RATIO 11.57

STARTING PITCHERS		W	S	ERA	Rto	IP	H	BB	SO	S*
TODD STOTTLEMYRE	(TOR)	5	0	2.05	8.25	48	36	8	51	50
PETE HARNISCH	(BAL)	4	0	2.16	9.00	58	44	14	43	39
SCOTT NIELSEN	(NY A)	13	1	2.40	9.63	172	142	42	62	33
DAVID WEST†	(NY N)	12	0	1.80	11.42	160	106	97	143	27
LEE GUTTERMAN	(NY A)	9	0	2.76	10.04	121	109	26	49	27
JOSE NUNEZ	(TOR)	5	0	2.90	9.89	71	62	16	67	26
RICK LANGFORD	(NY A)	9	0	3.13	9.71	127	109	28	84	25
PAT CLEMENTS	(NY A)	6	5	2.75	10.63	144	136	34	69	25
JOHN SMOLTZ†	(ATL)	10	0	2.79	10.33	135	118	37	115	25
WALLY WHITEHURST	(NY N)	10	0	3.05	9.65	165	145	32	113	24
JOHN MITCHELL	(NY N)	10	0	2.84	9.90	190	164	45	65	22
STEVE SEARCY†	(DET)	13	0	2.59	11.12	170	131	79	176	22
DICKIE NOLES	(BAL)	10	1	3.12	10.73	130	124	31	59	21
ERIC KING	(DET)	3	0	3.26	10.04	69	54	23	51	18
DON SCHULZE	(DET)	10	0	3.11	11.09	185	172	56	107	14
BOB MILACKI	(BAL)	12	0	2.70	12.15	177	174	65	103	14
STEVE CURRY	(BOS)	11	0	3.08	11.96	146	125	69	110	13
DEREK LILLIQUIST	(ATL)	10	0	3.38	11.32	171	179	36	80	11
MARK BOWDEN	(BAL)	9	0	3.38	12.28	96	80	51	94	11
STEVE DAVIS	(TOR)	10	0	3.29	11.73	178	166	66	130	9
DAVE MILLER	(ATL)	11	0	4.12	11.48	116	128	20	67	9
STAN CLARKE	(TOR)	12	0	3.48	11.67	189	184	61	133	9
ALEX SANCHEZ	(TOR)	4	0	3.59	13.97	58	47	43	57	−5
MARVIN FREEMAN	(PHI)	5	0	4.62	13.14	74	62	46	37	−10

*Projected to 220 IP.

RELIEF PITCHERS		W	S	ERA	Rto	IP	H	BB	SO	S**
DANNY CLAY	(PHI)	5	10	0.99	8.60	45	24	19	41	50
JOE BOEVER	(ATL)	6	22	2.14	8.75	71	47	22	71	41
DOUG BAIR	(TOR)	3	14	2.34	8.45	65	41	20	59	35
MARK HUISMANN	(DET)	4	21	1.87	10.09	58	50	15	61	34
TODD FROWIRTH	(PHI)	7	13	2.44	10.14	63	52	19	39	26
JACK SAVAGE	(NY N)	5	13	3.16	10.64	88	67	37	46	25
JUAN EICHELBERGER	(ATL)	2	5	3.14	10.14	63	58	13	44	22
MITCH JOHNSON	(BOS)	4	11	2.92	9.73	74	61	19	60	22
COLIN MCLAUGHLIN	(TOR)	9	7	2.88	10.96	69	47	37	62	19
ROB WOODWARD	(BOS)	1	13	3.86	13.91	44	44	24	53	10
MIKE KINNUNEN	(NY A)	4	13	3.98	15.11	81	78	58	73	6
MIKE RACZKA	(BAL)	1	10	5.94	14.58	50	57	24	35	−1

**Projected to 60 G.

150

AMERICAN ASSOCIATION (AAA)

		HR	RBI	SB	BA	AB	$*
Average Player		6	39	9	.258	337	**19**
GARY SHEFFIELD 3b†	(MIL)	9	54	20	.344	212	**65**
OTIS NIXON of	(MON)	0	19	40	.285	235	**42**
REX HUDLER of	(MON)	7	25	20	.303	234	**41**
PHIL STEPHENSON 1b	(CHI N)	22	81	9	.293	426	**40**
GERMAN RIVERA 3b	(MIL)	21	87	6	.300	436	**40**
JOHNNY PAREDES 2b†	(MON)	4	46	43	.295	400	**38**
ROLANDO ROOMES of	(CHI N)	16	66	15	.301	419	**38**
DAVE MEIER 3b	(CHI N)	20	83	5	.305	456	**37**
RUPPERT JONES of	(TEX)	7	30	8	.253	154	**37**
JOHN CANGELOSI of	(PIT)	0	10	14	.331	145	**35**
DARRYL HAMILTON of	(MIL)	0	32	20	.325	277	**33**
DENNY GONZALES 3b	(PIT)	8	39	9	.296	267	**33**
LAVELL FREEMAN of	(MIL)	5	59	15	.318	384	**32**
TIM JONES ss	(STL)	6	38	39	.257	370	**32**
JIM EISENREICH of	(KC)	4	14	9	.289	142	**32**
VAN SNIDER of†	(CIN)	23	73	5	.290	525	**31**
NICK CAPRA of	(KC)	1	43	28	.289	346	**30**
BILLY MOORE of	(MON)	17	80	4	.285	467	**30**
BARBERO GARBEY of	(TEX)	5	41	6	.308	263	**30**
BILLY JOE ROBIDOUX 1b	(MIL)	8	42	1	.292	240	**29**
LENNY HARRIS 2b	(CIN)	0	35	45	.277	422	**29**
ORESTES DESTRADE 1b	(PIT)	12	42	2	.271	273	**28**
TIM PYZNARSKI dh	(MIL)	10	66	4	.291	381	**28**
DOUG DASCENZO of	(CHI N)	6	49	30	.295	505	**28**
DWIGHT SMITH of	(CHI N)	9	48	25	.293	505	**28**
BRAD KOMMINSK of	(MIL)	16	57	7	.239	348	**27**
TOM PRINCE c†	(PIT)	14	42	3	.260	304	**27**
TOMMY GREGG of	(PIT)	6	27	7	.294	252	**26**
RAZOR SHINES 1b	(MON)	12	55	7	.263	358	**26**
JIM REBOULET 2b	(PIT)	0	13	26	.280	264	**25**
JACK DAUGHERTY 1b	(MON)	6	67	18	.285	481	**25**
BENNY DISTEFANO of	(PIT)	19	63	6	.263	482	**25**
AL PEDRIQUE 3b	(PIT)	1	22	10	.307	218	**25**
LARRY SEE 1b	(TEX)	12	55	1	.261	329	**25**
BILL BATHE c	(CHI N)	8	49	0	.312	385	**24**
CHARLIE O'BRIEN c	(MIL)	4	25	1	.281	153	**24**
LUIS DE LOS SANTOS 1b†	(KC)	6	87	2	.307	535	**24**
MARK RYAL of	(STL)	11	62	1	.256	336	**24**
GARY THURMAN of	(KC)	3	40	35	.251	422	**24**
ODDIBE MCDOWELL of	(TEX)	1	6	4	.286	70	**23**

*Projected to 500 AB.

AMERICAN ASSOCIATION (AAA)
ERA 3.64   RATIO 11.94

STARTING PITCHERS		W	S	ERA	Rto	IP	H	BB	SO	S*
VICENTE PALACIOS	(PIT)	3	0	1.99	8.72	32	26	5	23	51
TOM GORDON	(KC)	3	0	1.33	11.70	20	11	15	29	48
MIKE HARKEY†	(CHI N)	7	0	3.23	9.64	70	47	28	57	33
BRIAN HOLMAN†	(MON)	8	0	2.36	10.68	91	78	30	70	33
JEFF FISHER	(MON)	13	0	2.69	9.86	177	162	32	110	31
DORN TAYLOR	(PIT)	10	0	2.14	10.94	139	125	44	65	30
RICK ANDERSON	(KC)	7	0	2.62	10.35	100	92	23	54	30
JACK ARMSTRONG	(CIN)	5	0	3.00	9.15	120	84	38	116	28
MIKE JEFFCOAT	(TEX)	9	0	2.80	10.20	157	137	41	95	26
RANDY KRAMER	(PIT)	10	0	3.13	9.59	198	161	50	120	25
NORM CHARLTON	(CIN)	11	0	3.02	10.14	182	149	56	161	24
CHRIS CARPENTER†	(STL)	6	0	2.87	10.94	88	81	26	45	24
LUIS AQUINO	(KC)	8	0	2.85	10.88	129	106	50	93	23
BOB SEBRA	(MON)	12	0	2.94	11.02	174	154	59	126	22
BILL SWAGGERTY	(KC)	10	1	3.43	11.16	121	123	27	30	21
SCOTT MAY	(TEX)	8	0	2.97	11.19	152	132	57	103	18
JOSE DEJESUS	(KC)	2	0	3.44	10.44	50	44	14	57	17
ZIP SANCHEZ	(KC)	7	0	2.91	12.18	102	102	36	85	16
RANDY JOHNSON†	(MON)	7	0	3.00	12.26	105	79	64	102	14
DAVE JOHNSON	(PIT)	15	0	3.51	12.61	192	213	56	90	10

*Projected to 220 IP.

RELIEF PITCHERS		W	S	ERA	Rto	IP	H	BB	SO	S**
JEFF MONTGOMERY	(KC)	1	13	1.91	8.36	28	15	11	36	50
JOHN COSTELLO	(STL)	1	11	1.84	7.45	29	17	7	34	48
ROBBIE DIBBLE	(CIN)	2	13	2.31	9.00	35	21	14	41	34
DREW HALL	(CHI N)	4	19	2.34	9.28	65	41	26	75	33
RICH SAUVEUR	(MON)	7	10	2.43	9.78	81	60	28	58	31
GARY MIELKE	(TEX)	6	13	2.87	10.80	60	50	22	42	30
SCOTT MEDVIN	(PIT)	5	12	2.41	10.13	56	38	25	49	30
RANDY ST. CLAIRE	(CIN)	0	13	2.68	9.90	40	35	9	27	25
STEVE SHIRLEY	(MON)	3	9	2.86	10.44	50	34	24	56	23
BOB BUCHANAN	(KC)	5	6	2.37	11.72	76	70	29	44	17
DICK GRAPENTHIN	(STL)	3	10	3.63	11.48	69	67	21	30	15
TIM WATKINS	(MIL)	6	7	4.10	12.84	68	62	35	50	9

**Projected to 60 G.

PACIFIC COAST LEAGUE (AAA)

		HR	RBI	SB	BA	AB	S*
Average Player		7	46	10	.278	341	**18**
BRIAN HARPER c	(MIN)	13	42	2	.353	170	**50**
JOHN RABB of	(SEA)	13	44	6	.309	181	**45**
SHANE MACK of	(SD)	10	40	7	.347	196	**44**
MIKE DEVEREAUX of†	(LA)	13	76	33	.340	423	**44**
BIP ROBERTS 2b	(SD)	7	51	29	.353	343	**42**
JOSE GONZALES of	(LA)	5	22	44	.306	288	**42**
LUIS POLONIA of	(OAK)	2	27	31	.335	254	**40**
EDGAR MARTINEZ 3b	(SEA)	8	64	9	.363	331	**37**
CAMERON DREW of†	(HOU)	4	70	18	.356	354	**37**
LUIS MEDINA of	(CLE)	28	81	1	.310	406	**37**
DAVE GALLAGHER of	(CHI A)	4	27	5	.336	131	**36**
TRACY WOODSON 1b	(LA)	17	73	1	.319	313	**36**
GEORGE HINSHAW of	(LA)	13	94	15	.340	470	**36**
ROD ALLEN dh	(CLE)	23	100	1	.324	469	**34**
MARIANO DUNCAN ss	(LA)	0	25	33	.286	227	**34**
ERIC BULLOCK of	(MIN)	2	46	51	.309	434	**34**
LANCE JOHNSON of†	(CHI A)	2	36	49	.307	411	**33**
GREG BRILEY of	(SEA)	11	66	27	.313	444	**33**
MIKE SHARPERSON 2b	(LA)	0	30	19	.319	210	**31**
MIKE BRUMLEY ss	(SD)	3	41	41	.315	425	**31**
CHICO WALKER of	(CAL)	7	39	25	.289	304	**31**
CRAIG BIGGIO c	(HOU)	3	39	19	.320	281	**30**
STANLEY JEFFERSON of	(SD)	4	33	19	.317	278	**30**
BRIAN GILES ss	(SEA)	13	56	26	.272	383	**30**
MIKE BROWN of	(CAL)	3	21	1	.347	118	**29**
SANDY ALOMAR c†	(SD)	16	71	1	.297	337	**29**
FELIX JOSE of	(OAK)	12	83	16	.317	504	**29**
BRUCE FIELDS of	(SEA)	4	19	8	.321	168	**28**
REGGIE WILLIAMS of	(CLE)	6	58	36	.294	456	**28**
FRANCISCO MELENDEZ 1b	(SF)	4	58	5	.361	368	**28**
JOHN FISHEL of	(HOU)	18	68	11	.261	360	**28**
DARRELL MILLER of	(CAL)	4	19	3	.317	123	**28**
JIM WEAVER of	(HOU)	8	73	30	.272	423	**28**
LANCE BLANKENSHIP 2b	(OAK)	9	52	40	.265	437	**28**
JUAN BELL ss†	(LA)	8	45	7	.300	257	**27**
JESSE REID of	(SF)	18	72	5	.276	381	**26**
GILBERTO REYES c	(LA)	12	66	2	.292	318	**26**
BRIAN DORSETT c	(CAL)	11	31	0	.262	164	**26**
EVERETT GRAHAM of	(SF)	3	11	7	.303	119	**26**
ROB NELSON 1b	(SD)	23	77	0	.260	388	**25**
DAVE CLARK of	(CLE)	4	31	4	.297	165	**25**

*Projected to 500 AB.

PACIFIC COAST LEAGUE (AAA)
ERA 4.47   RATIO 13.32

STARTING PITCHERS		W	S	ERA	Rto	IP	H	BB	SO	S*
DAN SCHATZEDER	(MIN)	6	0	2.60	10.97	87	82	24	55	**42**
RAMON MARTINEZ†	(LA)	5	0	2.76	11.44	59	43	32	49	**41**
ED WOJNA	(CHI A)	10	1	3.27	10.74	124	112	36	73	**40**
KEN HOWELL	(LA)	10	0	3.27	11.27	107	92	42	95	**37**
SHAWN HILLEGAS	(LA)	6	0	3.49	10.25	101	93	22	65	**36**
RICK RODRIGUEZ	(CLE)	8	0	3.06	10.98	127	112	43	55	**36**
RICH BORDI	(OAK)	7	3	3.48	11.72	119	120	35	81	**32**
BILL KRUEGER	(LA)	15	0	3.01	12.28	173	167	69	114	**32**
JACK LAZORKO	(CAL)	11	0	3.87	11.42	149	156	33	59	**27**
ADAM PETERSON	(CHI A)	14	0	3.32	12.74	171	161	81	103	**26**
DENNIS COOK	(SF)	11	0	3.88	12.06	141	138	51	110	**24**
JOE BITKER	(SD)	8	0	3.63	11.93	178	195	41	106	**22**
ANTHONY KELLY	(HOU)	13	0	3.96	12.24	186	210	43	93	**21**
BILL BRENNAN†	(LA)	14	0	3.82	12.99	167	185	56	80	**20**
GREG HIBBARD	(CHI A)	11	0	4.12	12.44	144	155	44	65	**20**
DENNIS BURT	(LA)	12	0	3.83	12.99	167	185	56	80	**19**
ERIK HANSON	(SEA)	12	0	4.23	12.44	162	167	57	154	**18**
RAY SOFF	(MIN)	8	2	3.97	13.03	134	149	45	61	**18**
BALVINO GALVEZ	(MIN)	11	0	3.77	13.34	143	149	63	60	**18**
ED VOSBERG	(SD)	11	2	4.15	13.57	128	137	56	75	**18**
JEFF SHAVER	(OAK)	7	0	4.48	11.63	147	151	39	93	**17**
GREG HARRIS†	(SD)	9	0	4.11	12.66	160	160	65	147	**16**
MANNY HERNANDEZ	(HOU)	10	0	4.24	12.36	185	210	44	122	**16**
DAVE OTTO	(OAK)	4	0	3.52	13.08	128	123	63	80	**15**
TERRY CLARK	(CAL)	7	0	4.51	12.71	114	128	33	59	**13**

*Projected to 220 IP

RELIEF PITCHERS		W	S	ERA	Rto	IP	H	BB	SO	S**
HECTOR HEREDIA	(CHI A)	4	11	2.32	10.36	66	55	21	38	**36**
DONN PALL	(CHI A)	5	10	2.23	9.99	73	61	20	41	**35**
MIKE SCHOOLER	(SEA)	4	8	3.21	10.32	34	33	6	47	**33**
KARL BEST	(SF)	0	21	4.32	11.36	42	36	17	34	**31**
KEITH COMSTOCK	(SD)	5	17	3.14	12.25	72	67	31	78	**29**
KEN PATTERSON	(CHI A)	6	12	3.23	10.47	86	64	36	89	**28**
JIM CORSI	(OAK)	2	16	2.75	12.66	59	60	23	48	**25**
JAY BALLER	(SEA)	10	10	3.75	11.39	98	91	33	82	**21**
LUIS DELEON	(HOU)	4	14	5.23	12.46	65	68	22	59	**18**
JEFF KAISER	(CLE)	3	6	3.74	12.74	53	56	19	47	**16**
MIKE COOK	(CAL)	5	10	4.65	13.25	91	93	41	84	**13**

**Projected to 60 G.

EASTERN LEAGUE (AA)

		HR	RBI	SB	BA	AB	S*
Average Player		4	33	11	.249	314	**21**
MITCH LYDEN dh	(NY A)	8	21	0	.410	78	**98**
DELWYN YOUNG of	(DET)	11	49	20	.315	302	**52**
BILL MCGUIRE c†	(SEA)	5	24	23	.206	136	**51**
HOWARD NICHOLS 3b	(PHI)	4	13	6	.322	118	**46**
CHRIS HOILES c	(DET)	17	73	4	.283	360	**46**
TONY BROWN of	(PHI)	8	39	18	.280	243	**46**
KEN GRIFFEY of	(SEA)	2	10	4	.279	61	**45**
ROB RICHIE of†	(DET)	14	82	24	.309	501	**44**
JEROME WALTON of†	(CHI N)	3	49	41	.331	414	**43**
BRYAN HOUSE of	(CHI N)	8	50	34	.316	430	**42**
JAMES WILSON dh	(SEA)	17	73	11	.282	439	**41**
HECTOR VILLANUEVA 1b	(CHI N)	10	75	5	.314	436	**37**
KEVIN MAAS 1b	(NY A)	16	55	5	.263	372	**36**
TOREY LOVULLO 3b	(DET)	9	50	2	.274	270	**36**
SAM KHALIFA ss	(PIT)	2	15	5	.331	142	**36**
SCOTT LITTLE of	(PIT)	6	52	26	.290	410	**34**
HENSLEY MEULENS 3b†	(NY A)	13	40	3	.245	278	**34**
JOHN ROBERTS of	(BOS)	0	26	39	.299	335	**34**
CED LANDRUM of	(CHI N)	1	39	69	.245	445	**33**
PATRICK LENNON 3b	(SEA)	9	40	15	.259	320	**32**
JOSE BIRRIEL 1b	(BOS)	9	43	0	.280	289	**32**
JEFF KING 3b	(PIT)	14	66	5	.255	411	**32**
DAN DIMASCIO c	(DET)	6	31	1	.280	211	**31**
LANCE HUDSON of	(DET)	1	23	15	.289	211	**30**
TOMMY SHIELDS ss	(PIT)	2	21	7	.308	198	**30**
DOUG STRANGE 3b	(DET)	1	36	11	.280	218	**29**
PAT AUSTIN 2b	(DET)	1	29	24	.297	337	**28**
SHANE TURNER 3b	(PHI)	3	21	14	.298	295	**27**
JOE GIRARDI c†	(CHI N)	7	41	7	.272	357	**25**
OSCAR AZOCAR of	(NY A)	6	66	21	.273	543	**25**
OMAR VIZQUEL ss†	(SEA)	2	35	30	.253	375	**24**
JEFF COOK	(PIT)	1	29	45	.257	490	**22**
TIM BECKER ss	(NY A)	0	16	13	.281	217	**22**
SCOTT JORDAN of	(CLE)	4	33	33	.254	481	**21**
MILT HARPER 1b	(CLE)	12	50	3	.225	404	**21**
LANCE BELEN	(PIT)	11	62	5	.231	472	**20**
ED ESTRADA 3b	(BOS)	2	38	5	.303	456	**20**
TOM LAMPKIN c†	(CLE)	3	23	1	.270	263	**17**
TODD PRATT c	(BOS)	8	49	1	.225	395	**16**

*Projected to 500 AB

EASTERN LEAGUE (AA)
ERA 3.33   RATIO 11.88

STARTING PITCHERS		W	S	ERA	RTO	IP	H	BB	SO	S*
MIKE HARKEY†	(CHI N)	9	0	1.37	10.57	86	66	35	73	42
LADDIE RENFRO	(CHI N)	9	1	1.96	10.31	110	102	24	57	36
DAVE EILAND	(NY A)	9	0	2.56	8.85	119	95	22	66	36
PAUL WENSON	(DET)	8	5	2.04	11.43	115	112	34	95	33
CESAR MEJIA	(DET)	14	0	2.43	10.05	163	132	50	99	31
GREG BRINKMAN	(SEA)	11	0	2.46	9.97	157	136	38	72	29
MIKE CHRIST	(SEA)	6	0	2.37	9.93	106	88	29	52	29
LUIS VASQUEZ	(BOS)	3	0	2.48	9.24	112	87	28	97	27
TONY GHELFI	(CLE)	7	0	2.76	10.74	88	83	22	62	24
CURT SCHILLING	(BOS)	8	0	2.97	11.12	106	91	40	62	19
DAVE MCCORKLE	(SEA)	7	0	3.00	11.05	114	116	24	46	17
JIM NEIDINGER	(PIT)	5	2	2.82	11.52	125	135	25	88	16
JACKIE DAVIDSON	(CHI N)	10	0	2.99	11.92	145	149	43	81	14
SCOTT SERVICE	(PHI)	3	0	2.86	11.68	57	52	22	39	14
MIKE CARISTA	(BOS)	8	0	3.45	10.83	162	147	48	76	12
CHARLIE SCOTT	(CLE)	5	0	3.26	11.08	108	108	25	50	12
KRIS ROTH	(CHI N)	6	0	2.90	12.02	143	128	63	77	10
CLINT ZAVARAS	(SEA)	10	0	3.92	11.79	129	115	54	120	7
DARYL IRVINE	(BOS)	5	0	3.09	12.17	125	113	56	82	7
MIKE CHRISTOPHER	(NY A)	13	0	3.83	12.35	153	166	44	67	6
MIKE WALKER	(CLE)	15	0	3.72	12.95	164	162	74	145	5
LARRY MELTON	(PIT)	7	0	3.66	12.45	120	111	55	93	3
MIKE CURTIS	(PIT)	6	0	3.28	12.90	143	148	57	81	1
CHUCK MALONE†	(PHI)	12	0	3.91	13.82	127	107	88	117	− 2
KEN WILLIAMS	(DET)	11	0	3.61	14.27	135	132	82	86	− 3

*Projected to 220 IP

RELIEF PITCHERS		W	S	ERA	RTO	IP	H	BB	SO	S**
KEVIN WICKANDER†	(CLE)	1	16	0.63	7.14	29	14	9	33	54
MARK WOODEN	(SEA)	8	21	3.36	10.07	59	55	11	28	36
DEAN WILKINS	(CHI N)	5	26	1.63	10.38	72	53	30	59	34
PAUL WILMET	(PIT)	8	6	1.98	10.98	41	34	16	31	31
BRETT GIDEON	(PIT)	3	6	1.36	10.80	40	27	21	30	29
DANA RIDENOUR	(NY A)	5	14	3.92	11.86	44	29	29	56	28
SHAWN HOLMAN	(DET)	8	10	1.87	10.57	92	82	26	44	27
KENT MURPHY	(CLE)	6	4	2.24	11.00	72	57	31	58	24
BILL MENDEK	(SEA)	2	9	2.23	11.22	65	54	27	42	24
BRAD MOORE	(PHI)	4	18	3.06	11.41	71	57	33	39	21
MIKE DALTON	(BOS)	6	8	2.24	11.14	84	65	39	61	19
PAUL KUZNIAR	(CLE)	7	3	1.14	11.86	63	46	37	65	19
ROBERT LINK	(DET)	5	13	2.81	11.71	83	81	27	64	18
ROB RUSSELL	(PIT)	5	10	2.65	12.04	71	65	30	61	16
CARL KELIIPULEOLE	(CLE)	1	8	2.56	14.63	32	35	17	28	13

**Projected to 60 G

SOUTHERN LEAGUE (AA)

		HR	RBI	SB	BA	AB	S*
Average Player		6	37	10	.244	333	**20**
MARK DAVIS of	(CHI A)	6	27	32	.290	248	**47**
BUTCH DAVIS of	(BAL)	13	82	15	.301	412	**41**
MARK GILLASPIE of	(KC)	10	41	1	.284	204	**39**
JOSE TOLENTINO 1b	(HOU)	9	53	1	.305	259	**38**
STEVE HOWARD of	(OAK)	17	78	29	.247	461	**37**
HEDI VARGAS 1b	(CIN)	12	61	1	.291	309	**36**
MATT WINTERS of	(KC)	25	91	1	.275	488	**36**
GLENALLEN HILL of	(TOR)	12	38	10	.264	269	**35**
CORNELIO GARCIA 1b	(CHI A)	2	25	22	.284	229	**35**
CARLOS MARTINEZ of	(CHI A)	14	73	24	.277	498	**34**
FRANCISCO CABRERA c†	(TOR)	20	54	4	.284	429	**33**
ED WHITED 3b	(ATL)	16	62	18	.252	428	**32**
KASH BEAUCHAMP of	(ATL)	5	33	6	.292	226	**31**
RANDY BRAUN of	(MON)	15	76	3	.284	461	**31**
MARK LEMKE 2b†	(ATL)	16	80	18	.270	567	**30**
JUNIOR FELIX of	(TOR)	3	25	40	.253	360	**29**
BRIAN FINLEY of	(CIN)	1	25	30	.273	315	**29**
CARLOS COLOMBINO 3b	(HOU)	8	62	10	.285	417	**29**
DREW DENSON 1b	(ATL)	13	78	11	.268	507	**28**
MATT STARK dh	(TOR)	11	54	1	.266	334	**27**
JEFF HUSON ss	(MON)	0	34	55	.251	471	**27**
BERNARDO BRITO of	(MIN)	24	76	2	.240	508	**27**
JOE JARRELL of	(BAL)	16	52	4	.228	334	**27**
RAFAEL DELIMA of†	(MIN)	3	46	29	.286	500	**26**
TROY AFENIR of	(HOU)	16	66	11	.247	494	**25**
GERRY HOLTZ of	(BAL)	1	39	17	.281	349	**24**
MIKE BLOWER 3b	(MON)	15	60	6	.250	460	**24**
KEITH LOCKHART 3b	(CIN)	12	68	7	.266	515	**24**
CHITO MARTINEZ of	(KC)	13	65	20	.225	485	**23**
TOM FORRESTER dh	(CHI A)	13	72	4	.240	446	**23**
DOMINGO MARTINEZ 1b	(TOR)	13	70	2	.264	516	**22**
SHERWIN CIJNTJE of	(BAL)	1	27	20	.260	304	**22**
OZZIE CANSECO of	(OAK)	3	12	3	.222	99	**21**
SCOTT HEMOND 3b	(OAK)	9	53	28	.220	482	**21**
DEREK PARKS c†	(MIN)	7	42	1	.235	400	**13**
WILLIE MAGALLANES of	(CHI A)	9	40	7	.193	400	**10**

*Projected to 500 AB

SOUTHERN LEAGUE (AA)
ERA 3.54   RATIO 11.88

STARTING PITCHERS		W	S	ERA	RTO	IP	H	BB	SO	S*
MARK GARDNER	(MON)	6	0	1.60	8.68	112	72	36	130	46
CHRIS HAMMOND†	(CIN)	16	0	1.72	10.03	183	127	77	127	40
HUGH BRINSON	(TOR)	8	1	2.18	10.92	103	76	49	79	33
GENE HARRIS	(MON)	9	0	2.56	9.92	127	95	45	103	32
JOE LAW	(OAK)	9	0	2.56	10.32	116	100	33	67	31
ALEX SANCHEZ†	(TOR)	12	0	2.53	10.51	149	100	74	166	30
RUSTY RICHARDS	(ATL)	10	0	2.63	10.22	147	125	42	96	29
GORDON DILLARD	(BAL)	7	2	2.19	11.25	132	98	67	98	28
KEVIN BLANKENSHIP	(ATL)	13	0	2.35	10.99	176	132	83	127	28
PETE HARNISCH†	(BAL)	7	0	2.58	11.25	132	113	52	141	22
CHUCK STANHOPE	(BAL)	7	0	3.01	10.44	144	127	40	97	22
MATT CROUCH	(KC)	8	0	2.92	11.29	114	107	36	110	21
STEVE CUMMINGS	(TOR)	14	0	2.75	11.41	213	206	64	131	21
JOE LAZOR	(CIN)	11	0	3.51	10.51	161	119	69	133	20
TOM DREES	(CHI A)	9	0	2.79	11.45	158	149	52	94	19
GRADY HALL	(CHI A)	9	0	3.02	11.43	137	132	42	69	19
GARY BLOUIN	(KC)	7	0	2.87	12.16	94	94	33	83	18
LARRY CASIAN	(MIN)	9	0	2.95	11.74	174	165	62	103	15
MIKE SMITH	(CIN)	9	0	3.20	11.97	194	160	98	141	11
JOSE DEJESUS†	(KC)	9	0	3.88	12.26	116	88	70	149	8
KEN SPRATKE	(KC)	11	4	4.18	12.86	140	149	51	105	8
TONY MENENDEZ	(CHI A)	6	0	3.94	11.47	153	131	64	111	6
JEFF BUMGARNER	(MIN)	3	0	3.84	14.23	117	129	56	67	−11
YORKIS PEREZ	(MON)	8	0	5.82	16.27	130	142	93	105	−34

*Projected to 220 IP.

RELIEF PITCHERS		W	S	ERA	RTO	IP	H	BB	SO	S**
GERMAN GONZALES†	(MIN)	2	30	1.02	8.71	62	41	19	67	47
TIM PETERS	(MON)	1	8	1.27	10.61	28	20	13	26	41
KIRK KILLINGSWORTH	(OAK)	3	8	1.77	9.59	46	30	19	42	36
LUIS ENCARNACION	(KC)	4	22	2.77	10.15	78	60	28	64	34
DARREN HALL	(TOR)	3	17	2.23	10.13	40	28	17	33	34
BRIAN MEYER	(KC)	4	25	2.27	10.63	83	60	38	68	31
EDDIE MATHEWS	(ATL)	10	15	1.70	10.96	69	56	28	42	29
JOE KLINK	(OAK)	1	3	0.78	10.03	35	25	14	30	28
JIM JEFFERSON	(CIN)	3	10	2.95	12.65	37	31	21	33	22
KEVIN PRICE	(BAL)	6	11	3.84	12.15	80	83	25	47	16
TIM DEITZ	(CIN)	3	12	2.31	12.89	74	59	47	75	16
PAUL THORPE	(BAL)	6	12	2.87	12.78	88	80	45	89	14
BRYAN FARMER	(ATL)	3	7	2.60	11.60	52	45	22	29	13
EDDIE DICKSON	(MON)	7	4	2.74	11.84	92	79	42	52	12

**Projected to 60 G.

TEXAS LEAGUE (AA)

		HR	RBI	SB	BA	AB	S*
Average Player		6	40	8	.261	324	**20**
TODD BROWN of	(MIL)	2	16	5	.393	89	**55**
DEE DIXON of	(SF)	3	36	72	.290	455	**48**
GREG VAUGHN of†	(MIL)	28	105	22	.301	505	**47**
GARY SHEFFIELD ss†	(MIL)	19	65	5	.314	296	**47**
JEFF MANTO 3b†	(CAL)	24	101	7	.301	408	**45**
JIM MCCOLLOM 1b	(CAL)	20	75	13	.343	452	**44**
ALAN HAYDEN of	(NY N)	1	48	64	.297	525	**41**
JAVIER ORTIZ of	(LA)	8	33	6	.291	182	**38**
DOMINGO MICHEL of	(LA)	7	50	15	.330	352	**37**
MIKE HUFF of	(LA)	2	40	33	.304	395	**35**
MARCUS LAWTON of	(NY N)	2	20	16	.298	205	**34**
MARIO MONICO dh	(MIL)	8	52	8	.342	386	**34**
C. L. PENIGAR of	(CAL)	2	45	47	.269	454	**33**
MIKE WISHNEVSKI 1b	(SF)	4	26	2	.294	126	**33**
FRANK MATTOX 2b	(MIL)	5	51	24	.290	379	**33**
KEVIN REIMER dh	(TEX)	21	76	4	.302	486	**32**
TOM HOWARD of	(SD)	0	16	6	.301	103	**31**
JOHN SKURLA of	(SF)	11	51	12	.301	392	**31**
TODD ZEILE c†	(STL)	19	75	6	.270	430	**30**
JUAN BELL ss†	(LA)	5	21	11	.279	215	**28**
RICK LOCKWOOD 3b	(STL)	6	32	0	.290	186	**26**
KEVIN BOOTAY of	(TEX)	3	25	23	.274	325	**26**
JEFF YURTIN of	(SD)	16	77	1	.287	512	**24**
WALT MCCONNELL 3b	(LA)	11	53	4	.268	354	**23**
GARY ALEXANDER 1b	(TEX)	17	78	0	.265	464	**23**
BILL SPIERS ss	(MIL)	3	21	4	.280	168	**22**
SCOTT COOLBAUGH 3b	(TEX)	13	75	2	.270	470	**22**
ANGELO CUEVAS of	(NY N)	8	42	0	.296	355	**21**
CRAIG SHIPLEY ss	(NY N)	6	41	6	.263	335	**18**
TOM BAINE of	(STL)	1	40	8	.307	482	**18**
MONTY FARISS ss	(TEX)	3	31	2	.224	165	**15**
CHAD KREUTER c	(TEX)	3	51	2	.265	358	**14**

*Projected to 500 AB

TEXAS LEAGUE (AA)
ERA 3.98   RATIO 12.42

STARTING PITCHERS		W	S	ERA	Rto	IP	H	BB	SO	S*
TREVOR WILSON†	(SF)	5	0	1.86	9.62	73	55	23	53	**48**
BLAINE BEATTY	(NY N)	16	0	2.46	9.69	209	191	34	103	**39**
RAMON MARTINEZ†	(LA)	8	0	2.46	10.71	95	79	34	89	**37**
MICKEY WESTON	(NY N)	8	0	2.23	10.58	125	127	20	61	**36**
MIKE COSTELLO	(SD)	8	0	2.7	10.35	107	87	36	70	**35**
SCOTT ARNOLD	(STL)	10	0	2.55	10.99	131	108	52	103	**33**
STEVE WILSON	(TEX)	15	0	3.16	10.91	165	147	53	132	**30**
DAVE OSTEEN	(STL)	9	0	3.46	10.10	156	153	22	103	**26**
KYLE HARTSHORN	(NY N)	11	0	3.29	11.50	151	135	58	82	**22**
GREG LAFEVER	(LA)	9	0	3.49	11.14	147	148	34	82	**21**
DAVE EICHHORN	(LA)	5	0	3.51	10.71	105	99	26	43	**22**
JOHN BARFIELD	(TEX)	9	0	2.88	11.98	169	159	66	125	**20**
JOE OLKER	(SF)	15	0	3.40	12.81	151	152	63	94	**18**
JEFF OYSTER	(STL)	3	0	3.04	11.82	83	82	27	50	**18**
DEAN FREELAND	(SF)	11	0	3.38	12.17	176	162	76	101	**16**
KEVIN BROWN†	(TEX)	12	0	3.52	12.16	174	174	61	118	**16**
PAUL MCCLELLAN	(SF)	10	0	4.04	11.21	167	146	62	128	**15**
MATT MAYSEY	(SD)	9	0	3.71	11.94	187	180	68	120	**12**
JOHN WETTELAND	(LA)	10	0	3.88	12.11	162	141	77	140	**12**
DAN SCARPETTA	(MIL)	11	0	4.45	13.46	113	119	50	79	**5**
GREG HARRIS	(SD)	5	3	4.68	12.93	110	112	46	86	**3**

*Projected to 220 IP

RELIEF PITCHERS		W	S	ERA	Rto	IP	H	BB	SO	S**
DARRELL WHITAKER	(TEX)	2	6	2.32	9.18	50	38	13	39	**42**
RICK RAETHER	(TEX)	4	16	0.96	10.13	56	35	28	40	**36**
JOSE DOMINGUEZ	(SF)	3	22	2.71	9.56	80	65	20	67	**32**
MIKE MUNOZ	(LA)	7	14	1.00	10.88	72	63	24	71	**31**
ED PUIKUNAS	(SF)	7	7	2.78	10.04	78	62	25	62	**26**
MIKE MILLS	(SD)	7	13	2.47	11.81	77	76	25	41	**26**
TONY MACK	(LA)	6	4	2.95	11.67	64	57	26	69	**19**
ED PUIG	(MIL)	8	12	4.39	12.03	92	92	31	62	**17**
HOWARD HILTON	(STL)	8	7	2.65	12.09	102	91	46	90	**17**
KURT WALKER	(CAL)	3	12	3.66	12.52	64	71	18	60	**17**
BARRY BASS	(MIL)	9	11	3.99	14.66	70	77	37	44	**14**
RICH RODRIGUEZ	(NY N)	2	6	2.87	12.46	78	66	42	68	**13**
JEFF FASSERO	(STL)	5	17	3.58	15.81	78	96	41	72	**10**
TODD WELBORN	(NY N)	0	10	6.00	16.00	63	49	63	63	**−4**

**Projected to 60 G.

This will be brief, for there really is a wealth of material about actual leagues that I hope to get to.

The profiles of National and American League Rotisserie drafts look as follows:

MASOCHISTS CHART I

PITCHERS	IP	ER	H + BB	W	S	ERA	Rto	
NL DRAFT	12032	4430	14739	700	370	3.31	11.02	
AVG TEAM	1203	443	1474	70	37	3.31	11.02	
AVG PLAYER	86	32	105	7.8	4.1	3.31	11.02	1.22

	IP	ER	H + BB	W	S	ERA	Rto
AL DRAFT	14121	6048	18622	840	444	3.85	11.87
AVG TEAM	1177	504	1552	70	37	3.85	11.87
AVG PLAYER	84	36	111	7.8	4.1	3.85	11.87

HITTERS		AB	H	HR	RBI	SB	BA
NL DRAFT		49587	12867	1075	5706	1493	.259
AVG TEAM		4959	1287	108	571	149	.259
AVG PLAYER		354	92	8	41	11	.259

HITTERS	AB	H	HR	RBI	SB	BA
AL DRAFT	63656	16742	1677	7870	1294	.263
AVG TEAM	5305	1395	140	656	108	.263
AVG PLAYER	379	100	10	47	8	.263

When you apply the denominators to these figures to determine the total points available, this is what you get:

MASOCHISTS CHART II
TOTAL POINTS AVAILABLE

PITCHERS	W+	S+	ERA+	Rto+	Pts	$
NL DRAFT	233.3	148.0	0.0	0.0	381.3	780
AVG TEAM	23.3	14.8	0.0	0.0	38.1	78
AVG PLAYER	2.6	1.6	0.0	0.0	4.237	8.67

	W+	S+	ERA+	Rto+	Pts	$
AL DRAFT	280.0	177.6	0.0	0.0	457.6	936
AVG TEAM	23.3	14.8	0.0	0.0	38.1	78
AVG PLAYER	2.6	1.6	0.0	0.0	4.237	8.67

HITTERS	HR+	RBI+	SB+	BA+	Pts	$
NL DRAFT	268.8	372.2	248.8	0.0	889.8	1820
AVG TEAM	26.9	37.2	24.9	0.0	89.0	182
AVG PLAYER	1.9	2.7	1.8	0.0	6.356	13.00

	HR+	RBI+	SB+	BA+	Pts	$
AL DRAFT	335.4	444.6	287.6	0.0	1067.6	2184
AVG TEAM	28.0	37.1	24.0	0.0	89.0	182
AVG PLAYER	2.0	2.6	1.7	0.0	6.355	13.00

NL total hitting $ + pitching $ = $2600
AL total hitting $ + pitching $ = $3120

And the denominators themselves, the secret ingredients that maybe two people in America can't wait to see each year, are:

MASOCHISTS CHART III

NL & AL PITCHERS:
W+ = W/3
S+ = S/2.5

NL PITCHERS:

ERA+ = (typing this is almost as hard as reading it) $(3.31 - ((386 + ER) \div ((1050 + IP)/9)))$
$\div 0.05$

Ratio+ = $(11.03 - ((1286 + H + BB) \div ((1050 + IP)/9))) \div 0.08$

AL PITCHERS:

ERA+ = $(3.85 - ((449 + ER) \div ((1050 + IP)/9))) \div 0.05$

Ratio+ = $(11.87 - ((1385 + H + BB) \div ((1050 + IP)/9))) \div 0.08$

NL HITTERS:

HR+ = HR/4

RBI+ = RBI/15.3

SB+ = SB/6

BA+ = $((1217 + H)/(4700 + AB) - 0.259) \div 0.0015$

AL HITTERS:

HR+ = HR/5

RBI+ = RBI/17.7

SB+ = SB/4.5

BA+ = $((1289 + H)/(4900 + AB) - 0.263) \div 0.0015$

Except in two cases, I wouldn't pay any attention to decimals. (If you're one of those two people, you're going to be mad, because I don't even show *all* the decimals. They're everywhere—the average NL player got 10.642857 steals last year—but who cares? Despite how casual I try to seem to my interlocutor, I'm obviously crazy.) The two cases are the 2.5 of the saves denominator and, believe it or not, all those decimals for the average player's points.

I'll go over the three charts in order.

Masochists Chart I is the composite of all the leagues that Jerry Heath sends me. Figure out your own draft, if you want (do *not* merrily add up your final standings—that's the whole point of my prices; I measure what was available for our bucks in April), but you needn't bother. A draft is a draft is a draft.

In fact, if my editor doesn't mind all this junk for two people, why not? This stuff is already in Lotus and takes no time. Here are the draft-day totals for hitters for twelve American League Rotisseries. The letters are Heath's codes, so if you're a Heath user, maybe you'll spot yourself.

AL DRAFT POPULATIONS

	AB	H	HR	RBI	SB	BA
ADL	64500	16963	1683	7933	1350	.263
TWL	64174	16896	1707	7949	1316	.263
DBL	64527	16961	1692	7983	1318	.263
BLA	63815	16789	1679	7912	1310	.263
WGL	63571	16704	1705	7904	1285	.263
SMS	63715	16713	1675	7903	1307	.262
BWL	63734	16756	1682	7896	1283	.263
PLL	63906	16763	1688	7893	1275	.262
SGL	63530	16744	1689	7896	1245	.264
BDL	63342	16666	1647	7790	1283	.263
DDA	62120	16300	1616	7653	1306	.262
LSL	62935	16505	1657	7726	1244	.262
AVG LEAGUE	63656	16730	1677	7870	1294	.263
AVG TEAM	5305	1394	140	656	108	.263

The best home run league got 2 percent more than the average league, and the worst got 4 percent less—trailing the next worst by quite a bit, you'll notice.

It would be sort of interesting (wouldn't it, both of you?) to have mammoth *league* races. Maybe Jerry will do that next year; as it is, he does riffs like which leagues are the most competitive as judged by the closeness of the standings, but it would be a simple matter to rank whole leagues in all the categories.

It's *very* simple in Patton dollars, so simple I've done it.

PATTON $ WORTH OF AL DRAFT POPULATIONS

	HR+	RBI+	SB+	BA+	PTS	$	PROFIT OR LOSS
ADL	336.6	448.2	300.0	0.0	1084.8	2219	35
TWL	341.4	449.1	292.4	0.2	1083.1	2216	32
DBL	338.4	451.0	292.9	−0.1	1082.2	2214	30
BLA	335.8	447.0	291.1	0.1	1074.0	2197	13
WGL	341.0	446.6	285.6	−0.1	1073.0	2195	11
SMS	335.0	446.5	290.4	−0.4	1071.5	2192	8
BWL	336.4	446.1	285.1	−0.1	1067.6	2184	0
PLL	337.6	445.9	283.3	−0.4	1066.4	2182	−2
SGL	337.8	446.1	276.7	0.3	1060.9	2170	−14
BDL	329.4	440.1	285.1	0.1	1054.7	2158	−26
DDA	323.2	432.4	290.2	−0.4	1045.4	2139	−45
LSL	331.4	436.5	276.4	−0.5	1043.9	2135	−49
AVG. LEAGUE	335.3	444.6	287.4	0.0	1067.4	2184	0

ADL stands for the American Dreams League. That's us, you two: number one.

Masochists Chart II has got some serious questions in it. Just as it's hard to understand how Henderson can gain more points in a category than there are teams in a league, it doesn't seem to make much sense that leagues can gain more points in one category than they can in another. The zero gain of the qualitative categories is fairly obvious, but how does the NL draft produce 233 win points and only 148 save points?

It goes back to scarcity. If I made the saves denominator 1.5 instead of 2.5, to reflect how much scarcer saves are than wins, then the saves points and win points would come out the same. That would send relievers' prices rocketing even higher, which might be all right, except we then would have to completely ignore the qualitative categories: How scarce is the average player's batting average? How abundant is Boggs's?

And, as I said before, saves don't seem to be twice as valuable as wins, regardless of the math. Every September there's a large crowd of teams climbing the escalator in the wins category, practically on the same step. By contrast, many teams have given up on saves. In Peter Golenbock's book, I used this reasoning to flip-flop the denominators, actually making the wins denominator smaller than the saves.

Since then, it's apparent that I've flip-flopped. Oh, I did okay in Peter's book, but I hate to think that I made Clemens and Righetti the same in 1986; Clemens did have the better year in real baseball, and there's no doubt I was happy to find our game giving him his due. And also, frankly, I probably wanted to avoid being too radical myself, out there in public; that probably entered in. But since then I've found out that, more than anything, people like to *win*.

The points totals in Chart II, consequently, are a blend. The rule now is that when the theory of scarcity and the reality of the standings collide, both get dented. You can see by the proportions what gets played up and what doesn't. Essentially, the very things that I've been accused of overvaluing—steals and saves—get played down; steals don't get as many points as home runs in either league.

Finally, why do I like the decimals for the average player's points? Two reasons. First, it can be no accident that the average pitcher in both leagues is the same to three decimals, and it's not. I fiddled (ever so slightly, I promise) with the draft populations in both leagues so that the average pitcher got exactly the same number of wins and saves in each league. This seemed reasonable, since wins and saves count exactly the same in each league, wins have exactly the same scarcity

165

in each league (one per game), and last year, unlike 1987, saves appeared in roughly the same proportion to wins in each league. We want a pricing system that removes any phony distinctions between the two major leagues and hence emphasizes the true distinctions, which are ratio and ERA.

Secondly, I like all these decimals because they are what finally bring you the average player's exact price. Isn't it plain when, looking at the total points chart (one more time, my two bleary friends), you see the two 0.0 columns for the pitcher and the one 0.0 column for the hitter— isn't it obvious that the hitter is worth more than the pitcher? When you look at the hitter's three columns *with* points, versus the pitcher's two, doesn't he suddenly announce that he's worth exactly 50 percent more?

That's what I see, anyway. It is, of course debatable. Between seasons. Now, in order to spew forth price after price for player after player, I want two of the simplest formulas in the world—(1) each hitter's salary divided by his points equals the average hitter's salary divided by his points; (2) each pitcher's salary divided by his points equals the average pitcher's salary divided by his points—and I want them to be the same.

What?

Yes, even you two are probably scurrying on to the next chapter. That's all right. If there's *anybody* who's still interested (we know that real sabermetricians don't go near this game; I wouldn't be surprised if they don't go to real baseball games), the reason the formulas must be the same, as in mean the same, as in be interchangeable, is that it would be silly for a pitcher with exactly the same point contribution to a team not to have exactly the same salary. We want to be fair here.

Perhaps this shows what I'm talking about more successfully:

$$\$8.67/4.237 = \$13.00/6.355$$

Well, not exactly. But close enough for our purposes.

That's the American League. With a microscope you can see in the National League:

$$\$8.67/4.237 = \$13.00/6.356$$

Even I don't worry about the difference. I just thought I would confess—here, where I don't have an audience—that I screwed up somewhere.

If I'm wrong, though, if people *are* reading this—and remember, I didn't recommend it—I should try to bring us all back to relative sanity. How the whole thing works is really quite simple. To begin with, let's zap the decimals entirely. You take the average pitcher and put him on your team, and you should discover, more or less, that he contributes four points to your team in the final standings: His eight wins and four saves, in a typical Rotisserie League, do that. Add the average hitter, and your final standings should gain around six points. Pay these dudes $8.67 and $13.00, respectively, for their efforts.

Subtract the average hitter from your team (8 HR, 41 RBI, etc.): Temporarily delete his stats from your final totals. (Check to see how many points it drops you; it should also be around six, but of course it might be different, depending on the specific context of your team and league. Your mileage may vary.) Now pretend you had had the two more bucks you needed to get Kirk Gibson in April. Plug his numbers in. Those twenty-five homers move you past *six* teams? Great, I got lucky; that's what happens to my typical team. (It might be four, it might be seven, it might be three; but there's something seriously amiss in your offense if he doesn't take you around a few teams.) Seventy-six RBI—you were expecting him to knock in more for the Dodgers, but the RBI category was so squeaky this year that you actually go around five teams (or three teams or six). His 31 stolen bases, you discover, don't bump you up as much as the 25 home runs did; still, a five-point gain in the standings, you'll take it. Batting average . . . you get out your pencil and subtract the average player's at bats (you skipped that before, because you didn't think you'd have to) and you add Kirk's at bats; after a while, you've got the new AB and hit totals and begin your long division (because you're trying to do this while your wife's asleep, and the night light doesn't run your solar calculator, and this is getting *tedious*) and you learn Kirk's kind of so-so-looking .290 brings you past two teams. Interesting.

You add this up, all the points that your team now has, compared with how many it had when you subtracted the average player, and, hmmm, there's an 18.5 point improvement (must have been a tie you missed). If you're paying that average player $13, as you're supposed to (this is Karl Marx speaking, hired by the owners to enforce their salary cap), you pay Kirk Gibson $38.

He thinks he did pretty much what he did the year before in Detroit, and now here comes this big raise, so he'll be ecstatic. And that's fair, too, after the way he and so many other hitters were gypped by Patton prices following the 1987 season.

I've gone on at perhaps too much length about the way the quantities of things have fluctuated over the last three years; accordingly, I'll go on just a little bit more about the way averages have as well. Gibson gets two points in BA+ with his .290 batting average this year because the NL Rotisserie batting average was .259, down from .273 the year before.

I *am* in danger of digressing; the next few observations have very little connection with Rotisserie baseball, but if I don't get to blurt them here, I won't get to. First, why did the NL hitters crash even more precipitately than the AL hitters. Second, did they?

Only a few National Leaguers batted over .300, and the best one hit only .313. But the Rotisserie batting average of .259 is only four points below the AL Rotisserie average. I think it was a fluke that could almost have been avoided by Tony Gwynn alone, if his hand wasn't hurt, that the top of the heap in the NL showed such poor averages. I can remember not so long ago when Rod Carew covered for similar AL sins. Take the period after the notorious 1968 season, the culmination of the last strike-zone change, which Bill James investigated at length last year. Nineteen sixty-nine, second-best AL hitter—Reggie Smith, .309 (Carew, .332), 1973, second-best AL hitter—George Scott, .306 (Carew, .350). I'm convinced that what made the pitchers so dominant in the NL last year—in addition to the new baseball, of course—was the pitchers. *At the plate.*

Up there taking their hacks, they have gone way past just abysmal. Atrocious? Frightened to death inside those earmuffs?

Rotisserie baseball gets the credit for bringing to light the disgrace pitchers have become. Since we've always just ignored their woeful efforts, batting Omar Moreno before we'd let one of them try, we show that the NL hitter-hitters batted that quite respectable .259, not the anemic .248 the league reports. That eleven-point spread is the biggest yet. For an NL Rotisserie league draft to end up with a .248 batting average, the hitters would have to go 0-for-5,296.

Bill, do us a favor. Number one, come back. And then make as your first exploration what it means never to face a pitch since high school and then suddenly walk up to the plate in Shea Stadium. How about a pitch count on how many it takes to be punched out? (Get out the decimals, for you know it's less than five.) How about a comparison of Mike Scott's 190 strikeouts to Dave Stewart's 192? This will be easy: What did Welch get for the Dodgers in 1987? 196 in 252 innings. Last year in Oakland? 158 in 245 innings. Not too bad at all; for sure, he struck out *more* hitter-hitters.

When the complete final statistics come out, how about a comparison of how many fewer sacrifice hits there were in the National League last year? These clueless ninth-place batters can't even bunt anymore. Instead of staying out of the double play, the bunt is more likely to produce one; managers are becoming reluctant even to try it. (Soon the only pitchers who bunt at all will be the only ones who can hit a little bit.) If the seventh-place hitter gets on, and there are no outs, the eighth-place hitter is liable to bunt—especially now that they call bunting for a hit a sacrifice, if it's not a hit (those are great odds; you know, I don't think I could resist them)—to give the leadoff hitter a crack at driving in the run.

Where have you gone, Don Newcombe?

And then it's true that Newk could probably come out today and do better than Don Baylor. Strange things are happening; the DH getting phased out in the American League, the bottom third of the order getting phased out in the National. (Bill? Would you mind giving us a run-through on the runs produced by the bottom three batters in 1950, as opposed to today? Wouldn't be hard. . . . No, it would be hellishly hard, of course; I have no idea how he did it.) Meantime, we Rotisserie sorts will just take what's given to us—and try to get most of it.

Okay, fire away. Last chance.

What did you call me? Your intercom or something?

Pardon?

Interlocking door?

Good God! *You* read the masochist notes?

I was sitting right here, remember, flipping through the Baseball Americas.

Oh, yeah—you were quiet, thanks.

Don't tell anybody, but I like this guy Biggio better than Sandy Alomar. Anyway, it was good for me to have some time when you weren't talking. No offense, but sometimes it's like I'm being pushed around, and what I did was make a list of my own questions, really getting down to strategy.

We haven't talked about strategy?

I knew you weren't going to like this. Yes, we've talked about it. But the next thing I know, you're piling the numbers on. A lot of us don't keep our calculators next to our night tables. We play this game to

*have some fun duking it out with our buddies, and we buy a book like
this to help us get psyched.*

So can we talk strategy?

Yes! Let's hear the first question.

I suppose the biggest one is, how do you get the bargains in the draft?

I can answer that. But you *have* to let me lay a few numbers on.
Otherwise it isn't any different from you and your partner sitting together in a bar, trying to bludgeon each other with your reasons for
buying the players you like.

The first thing you have to do is set your prices. I mean *really* set
them. None of this $25 to $35 for Jack Clark. And not $25 to $30, or
$30 to $35. Not $20 to $25, either, if you're as suspicious of him as
I am. Setting prices means penciling in a single dollar value.

You're kidding.

I am not kidding, at least not about hitters. With pitchers, of course
I'm kidding. Because there are so many of them, and because their
performances fluctuate so much, the best you can do is rank them in
separate groups, within price ranges. Clemens, Higuera, Viola,
Hershiser, maybe Danny Jackson—these are Grade A starting pitchers.
What's Grade A worth? What's venture capital worth? The reason you
can get oil wells cheap these days isn't that oil's not worth it; lots of
oil is still worth lots of money, and Grade A pitchers are definitely
worth pennants. But there are so many wells just sitting there and so
many that are empty.

Braver souls might spend between $20 and $30 for Grade A wells.
Grade B—this group should have at least ten pitchers and run from $10
to $20. Grade C—this group is huge and runs from $5 to $15.

Notice the overlap? No one says pitching is logical. Under $5 is the
crapshoot.

Rank relievers separately, and don't look for any logic in their ranges.
Grade A: $40 to $45. Grade B: $20 to $30. Grade C (good middle
relievers who might end up working the ninth inning, and bad ones
who might have to): $5 to $15. Grades D through F: the crapshoot.
Have many, many more to choose from on your list than there are
openings. At the end, this mangled document with checks and circles
and pencil holes will come in handy in the reserve phase of the draft.
There will be pitchers there worth a hell of a lot more than Robin
Ventura.

For the auction itself, the reason you need a huge list, and small
preference, is that pitching is where you can make adjustments during

the draft. You don't shed a tear when Orel goes for $35; you look for this year's Orel, who's still there, still beckoning, just at a lower price.

However, if the draft is hitter-crazy, as it is getting to be in some leagues, *you* start taking the pitchers. Go ahead, indulge your preferences, and buy them cheap. You *must* swim against the current. If pitching is being trashed at ridiculously low prices, pay just slightly more respectful prices; you'll still have enough money left for an adequate offense, and people will be coming to you in June, trying to gain some respectability in half the categories.

With hitters, the worry is *getting caught in the current.* That's why you must set your prices exactly. You've got to know when to grab land and get out.

How can you price exactly? Aren't there a lot of factors, just like with pitchers, that can change things?

There are hundreds of factors involved. I'm going to cover as many of them as I can right now. But the thing is, you figure out those factors *ahead* of time. If you start trying to figure them out in the auction, when you're already cascading toward Niagara Falls—well, that's when people walk out, shaking their heads, looking at this crumpled roster in their trembling hands, staring at twenty-three players that they're going to have to live with for the next six months.

Is the price you set what you think they're going to earn or the tops you're willing to pay?

A very good question. It's the one consideration that tempts me into having a double standard. The price I set is what I think they're going to earn; it's the one number in front of me. I don't want to be confused by even one other number near it. However, let's say I set a price of $31 for Ruben Sierra this year. If you read my comment, you know that I think he's capable of having that kind of year, but you also could tell that I'm not as wild about him as some people.

The bidding goes $20 . . . $25 . . . $28 . . . $29 . . .

Unexpectedly, it seems to be ending.

Do I say $30 and grab my anticipated $1 profit?

I would.

Then do. I might not. It's not that I'm greedy, but that I'm satisfied that Sierra's being charged the full freight. I list my prices down to the dollar, but they're fuzzy all the same—these are not Patton $ in front of me, they're Patton guesses—so if I'm not in love with a player, I might drop out a dollar or two early. I don't let the bidding end on

Sierra in the low twenties—if I think he's no better than that, then why on earth do I have $31 on the paper in front of me?

You get everyone onto one sheet of paper?

No, I have a sheet for the outfielders, a sheet for first and third, a sheet for second and short, a sheet for catchers and the DH-only players, and several sheets for the pitchers.

That's in one hand, or on my knees, or falling on the floor. . . . It was so much simpler when Dollar Bill was around—

Who's he?

My partner, if you read the acknowledgments. In my other hand—

You had a break-up?

Read the acknowledgments! Now, in my other hand is the master list. I assume you know what that is?

I ask you just one little personal question, and you get huffy. Sure, the master list is who's got what and needs what, every team. What they've spent, what they've got to spend.

Correct. So if there are thirty-five outfield positions to fill, you sure as hell better have forty outfielders listed, to be safe. Carmelo Martinez may be grabbed by somebody for first base. Someone might have filled his outfield positions, not like it when Roberto Kelly is about to go for $4, and make him his DH.

The first rule in finding bargains is to fight for a bargain *twenty-three* times. Never chase anyone out of love or panic.

Tell me someone you love.

Huh?

Who's your favorite player.

You're not going to put my name in this, right? Or my league?

Not even in the acknowledgments.

Kruk of San Diego. I spotted him right away in '86, and he earned us second place two years ago. Last year was a wipeout, but he'll come back.

173

To what?

Twenty-five.

So if you're going against me, you've got him, because I don't think so. If you're going against yourself, what are you going to do?

Twenty-six.

To how far?

Thirty-one.

That's interesting: Why not thirty or thirty-two?

Because thirty-one's my limit.

Well, at least you have a limit; that's the main thing. The next question is, when do you plan to put his name in? You don't want to have to bid on him early, because that's when people's pockets are full. How often in the first round do people nominate a player they want? The first round is a sucker's round.

Everyone knows this. Painful experience just doesn't seem to be much help here. The veteran owners show up with their pages of charts, their vials of pills that are only supposed to be taken before airplane flights, their ''do you mind if my friend sits in?''—someone who knows nothing about baseball, whose sole assignment as to kick them in the shins when they overcome their pills and ignore their charts.

It doesn't work. In my guide last year, after comparing the salaries for the first-rounders in my league and the Virginia Gentlemen in a National League Rotisserie against what they earned at season's end, I found that we were getting not much more than fifty cents on our dollar. Out of twenty-two first-round picks in both leagues, one player made a profit—of $2.

My advice was to send your friend to keep the records for you and show up after the first round.

I hear you—but who wants to miss the most fun fifteen minutes of the year?

Not me. So we keep bidding and losing. Still, we did manage to clean up our acts slightly in the American Dreams last year: Instead of losing $15 per player, we lost $10 per player. Here are the details—they're pretty grim:

	PLAYER	PAID	EARNED	NET
1	DAN PLESAC	37	30	−7
2	RICKEY HENDERSON	64	56	−8
3	HAROLD REYNOLDS	33	25	−8
4	DAVE PARKER	26	11	−15
5	MIKE STANLEY	10	2	−8
6	ROGER CLEMENS	37	32	−5
7	RICKY HORTON	10	2	−8
8	DEVON WHITE	38	18	−20
9	LEE SMITH	45	30	−15
10	MIKE WITT	24	3	−21
11	GLENN WILSON	15	5	−10
12	DAVE BERGMAN	2	9	7
	TOTAL	341	223	−118
	AVERAGE	28	19	−10

What I get out of this is the only reason you didn't lose fifteen bucks per player again is that your last player in the round was Bergman. What's he doing there? Somebody trying to clear out someone else's first base slot?

Precisely. Which is why that second dollar was the big excitement of the first round. People burst out laughing; I'm not kidding.

You guys are a riot. But then I see Rickey there—and I say you guys are insane.

Maybe yes, maybe no. You really don't have enough information here to judge. It's posted as a warning. A red flag saying, First round! Thin ice! Don't you come here if you're looking for bargains!

So the idea is to wait?

Wait for bargains. Waiting by itself can backfire. A lot of people group hitters the way I do pitchers. These are the six Type A outfielders available, they say; should be able to get one of them for $30 to $35. They sit there patiently, crossing each one off that creeps past $35, until there's one left.

Unfortunately, three other teams still don't have *their* Grade A outfielder—thirty-five, thirty-six . . . forty, forty-one, forty-two. . . . This can be well along in the draft, money is getting scarce, and at least two teams engage in what can only end in Pyrrhic victory, all because they feel they must have *one* top-notch player in their outfield.

Didn't you say before that the outfield was a position where you had to be strong?

Yes, but I meant strong deep, as opposed to strong pretty. Put five Rob Deers out there instead of three Dave Winfields. I've had literally dozens of leagues to browse through this year, and it's all served to confirm what I already knew: The secret to Rotisserie baseball is winning ugly.

Have you figured out when these ugly ones come up? I mean, from all this browsing, can you give me a general hint when I'm supposed to be on the edge of my seat?

No, I can't. I have scores of rosters and price lists, not just from Jerry Heath but from people all over who sent me stuff after their drafts. However, only a minority listed the prices round by round, and fewer still listed them through the last round. There are too many other things to worry about in a draft.

The impression I get from what I have seen is that there are mysterious lapses in each auction, sort of Bermuda Triangles, in which lots of damage gets done by a few people. I don't know whether they just have super endurance, or whether they happen to be the lucky recipients of a general siesta, or what.

Therefore, for me to say the "sweet spot" of the draft is in the sixth round—which is what you would like me to say, isn't it?—

That would be nice.

—would be bogus. I *can* say that there are three distinct periods in the draft:

(1) The early rounds—certainly the first three—when the whole object is to drain other people's money. You are not trying to obtain Don Mattingly. You are trying to make somebody else obtain him for more than he's worth.

(2) The middle rounds—from round 4 on, until you get to the crapshoot. This is a long, grueling stretch, the key to the entire draft, during which bizarre things happen. Dave Winfield should go for $22 at this point; instead, two owners freak out, and he goes for $40. You sit there, opening your third can of Jolt, waiting for a Bermuda Triangle.

(3) The crapshoot.

When does that occur? About what round are we at?

The crapshoot isn't a round, it's a price. *Anybody* can be had for under $5.

In the middle rounds, you'll see people going for cheap prices, but that's not the crapshoot yet, because there's still money around. In the middle rounds, you'll hear Steve Jeltz nominated for a dollar and then—

You keep your mouth shut; The Dave Bergman Memorial Silence.

See? You're an old hand at this.

But I never had your prices before. I want to see where they kick in.

I'll tell you what. Let's run through a league that I do have round-by-round prices for, and look for what I've just described. Dave Peregrim, who published the *Baseball Dream Report,* sent me his Jersey Beer Barrel draft with no team names attached. He just listed the players they bought in order, numbers one through 131.

No team names attached? How do they remember who's got who?

Oh, he sent me the rest, I'm sure. I just filed it somewhere and now can't find it. But I've got his prices right here, round by round. In a way it's a blessing. We can just zero in without the distraction of personalities getting in the way. Take a look at the first two rounds:

	ROUND 1	PAID	EARNED	NET		ROUND 2	PAID	EARNED	NET
1	STRAWBERRY	45	45	0	11	DURHAM	17	2	−15
2	SAMUEL	38	24	−14	12	MARSHALL	24	25	1
3	BUTLER	29	28	−1	13	COLES	19	17	−2
4	K. GROSS	13	3	−10	14	CARMAN	18	−6	−24
5	ELSTER	9	5	−4	15	OBERKFELL	7	10	3
6	DAWSON	43	34	−9	16	MILLIGAN	8	2	−6
7	WALLACH	39	16	−23	17	GOTT	17	33	16
8	HERR	18	9	−9	18	D. JACKSON	25	28	3
9	P. PEREZ	17	24	7	19	LARKIN	20	33	13
10	HAYES	31	17	−14	20	D. ROBINSON	20	20	0
	TOTAL	282	205	−77		TOTAL	175	164	−11

I knew Milligan was a bum.

I didn't (and am still not so sure; I'd give him as many at bats as Traber got last year before I platooned). But the big difference between them and us so far is the first *two* rounds have gone by, and there's only $88 in losses—who are these skinflints?

They're trying to avoid the early wipeout; I mean, what else?

It would seem so. But there are signs, too, that they might not know what they're doing. Study it carefully. We've reached the stage where you should be able to anticipate what I'm going to say, even if you don't agree with it.

Durham? People didn't know about his coke problem, but everyone knew Grace was coming along.

So did they. That's why he's only $17—the fear of his going over to the AL.

You don't mean Strawberry, just because you blew it in your prediction last year?

Nope. They started as we did with Plesac and Rickey, by letting loose the biggest fish in the pond, and showed considerably more restraint. Then begins the long string of minuses—but lesser minuses—that we saw in the American Dreams.

(The earnings for both Herr and Coles, by the way, include what they made after they were traded. An owner continues to follow his lost player in the other league's box scores, thinking, "Those are stats *I* deserve." A player who gets traded is called bad luck, yet one who goes into rehab a bad choice, as if the former isn't and the latter is our fault.)

My objection to the Beer Barrels is that they spent more on Dawson and Wallach than on Samuel and Hayes. All four were losses, we now know, but last April, why did Dawson and Wallach cost more? They fell into the trap of rewarding the great real baseball players with impossible salaries. If Dawson couldn't break the $40 barrier with his MVP season in 1987, how on earth was he going to earn $43 last year? It's irrelevant that Samuel fell further short; he had a much better chance of earning $38.

My next criticism is a compliment to the nominating teams, as long as they aren't the buyers. Kevin Gross, Pascual Perez, Don Carman, and Danny Jackson are, I'm quite sure, being proposed by teams who think they're good pitchers, who think other people think so too, and who, therefore, look forward to watching money disappear *without fail,* if the bidding averages more than $15 on them.

Fifteen dollars doesn't seem like much, but remember, that's almost twice what the average pitcher earns ($8.67), and the average pitcher's price *includes* what relief pitchers earn. Fifteen dollars is well over double what the average starter earns—and even more important, you don't have to pay that much for promising starters in market prices.

I'm making two assertions. The first is not the smug view of hindsight. If I'm at the draft, and I watch $60 go to form a starting pitching staff of Jackson, Perez, Gross, and Carman, I worry less about that team. It can win the pennant, of course, but its overall profits won't be coming from those four.

Next, hindsight. Four reasonably hopeful starting pitchers out on the table early, four reasonably hopeful market prices—the hopes, in sum, dashed. Seventy-three dollars spent on them, more than $18 each. Forty-nine dollars earned by them; $24 gone from the Beer Barrels, on four good players.

What's sad is that even Carman did his job last year. If he came before me in arbitration, I'd give him a raise.

What grade would you have given D Jax?

B. The $10 to $20 range.

Would you have followed him all the way to the top?

Probably not. I probably would have been in there making loud noises at $13, $16, but then faded away.

You've never spent $20 on a starter?

No. I'm not sure I've spent $15.

What happens when Clemens comes up?

Oh, I *would* spend it. I've tried to. When Clemens comes up I can just as well save my breath, but last year I think I shouted, "Twenty-nine dollars!"—just to see what it felt like.

Shall we check out the next two rounds?

ROUND 3					ROUND 4			
		PAID	EARNED	NET			PAID	EARNED	NET
21	PALACIOS	5	−5	−10	31	TEUFEL	11	4	−7
22	VAN SLYKE	30	41	11	32	K. HERNANDEZ	25	15	−10
23	L. RIVERA	8	4	−4	33	TREADWAY	8	4	−4
24	SABO	7	29	22	34	C. JACKSON	1	1	0
25	LAVALLIERE	8	9	1	35	HORNER	23	6	−17
26	O. SMITH	19	29	10	36	GIBSON	27	38	11
27	RASMUSSEN	16	9	−7	37	BROWNING	19	18	−1
28	OROSCO	18	10	−8	38	GOSSAGE	17	9	−8
29	BRADLEY	24	18	−6	39	FROHWIRTH	8	−4	−12
30	G. DAVIS	30	32	2	40	G. CARTER	24	10	−14
	TOTAL	165	176	11		TOTAL	163	101	−62

Look at that! The Bermuda Triangle, and so soon!

Where?

Round three!

Sabo? That's just lucky.

It's *not* just Sabo! It's Ozzie Smith and Andy Van Slyke! There is no excuse for those prices on those players this early in the game! The sharks are circling. If I could just find Dave Peregrim's number, I'd call him up right now and ask him how those two owners did. I'll lay you a side bet they finished in the money.

As for Sabo, I didn't say the Bermuda Triangle was a place for sharks only; it's just the place *where these things happen.*

Considering that Sabo was a spring sensation, considering that if you don't let his hair fool you, Buddy Bell isn't much younger than Pete Rose, I can see a much higher bidding war over Sabo this early in the game.

And how do you account for Gibson going for not much more than Horner in round 4?

ROUND 5		PAID	EARNED	NET
41	SANDBERG	26	33	7
42	PARRISH	24	11	−13
43	GRIFFIN	14	1	−13
44	TRILLO	5	3	−2
45	D. GARCIA	6	−1	−7
46	MAGADAN	16	7	−9
47	FERNANDEZ	18	16	−2
48	VALENZUELA	20	−8	−28
49	PETERS	7	−8	−15
50	MCGEE	22	27	5
	TOTAL	158	81	−77

ROUND 6		PAID	EARNED	NET
51	G. MADDUX	4	12	8
52	C. BROWN	18	2	−16
53	GANT	3	24	21
54	MIKE DAVIS	24	1	−23
55	O'NEILL	9	20	11
56	J. REED	3	1	−2
57	YOUMANS	13	2	−11
58	MORELAND	29	11	−18
59	ASSENMACHER	1	9	8
60	SIMMONS	1	1	0
	TOTAL	105	83	−22

Round 5 is obviously a disaster. Some rounds just seem to have a hex on them. If you look at the "net" column, it's as bad as the first round, though if you look at the "paid," you can see that prices are coming down considerably. The cost per player has just about been cut in half.

I don't mean to be cruel by bringing up Fernando again, so let's look at the next guy. I like that $7 spent on Steve Peters.

You do?

Sure. A lefty, 1.57 ERA in Double A, 0.95 in Triple A, 1.80 for St. Louis during his cup of coffee in '87—isn't that just about the way Fernando came along?

What you hope is to take a $2 or $3 flier on him at the end. Some spoilsport has put him on the table now. Out of the woodwork come two or three others who were planning to take that flier.

Seven dollars to catch Fernando Valenzuela or Vida Blue or Mark Fidrych in a bottle? That's what venture capital is all about.

I'm more curious about that money that's being piled into Moreland; he had a career year in 1987, but it was only worth—what?—$20; what's all the excitement? Here's a guy who had just *left* the cozy confines of Wrigley; do you suppose we might be looking at the Last Best Corner Baseman Available?

Obviously if he's your last hitting spot open, you're going to send some serious money after him; otherwise, buy your hitting elsewhere. When we get to the crapshoot, we're going to see plenty of people to plug that slot. Better to have an underpaid wimp there than Keith Moreland.

But I don't want underpaid wimps. I want underpaid Sabos. We've done six rounds, and I still don't see these obvious bargains.

Look more closely. The sharks are right there, on the edge of the reef. Sharks are very patient. Sandberg comes out in the fifth round, just peeks his head out, and *gulp*. Sharks can be poisoned, too, of course; they gulp anything that looks reasonable. Alfredo Griffin and then Mike Davis, I imagine, didn't leave them feeling too well.

Paul O'Neill—*gulp*. That one was yummy. In the comment on him, I gave many of his market prices: plenty of people were paying $9 or more. Ron Gant may be luck—in fact, I thought he started the year in the minors, so I'm not sure what he's doing there—but O'Neill is called homework.

I see Ted Simmons there. Ha, ha. No one said two.

	ROUND 7	PAID	EARNED	NET
61	SUTTER	2	9	7
62	BO DIAZ	16	6	−10
63	OQUENDO	8	13	5
64	LINDEMAN	12	1	−11
65	TEMPLETON	8	8	0
66	ABNER	11	0	−11
67	RAWLEY	11	−10	−21
68	HAVENS	1	1	0
69	BARRY JONES	1	5	4
70	JODY DAVIS	16	6	−10
	TOTAL	86	39	−47

	ROUND 8	PAID	EARNED	NET
71	MELVIN	1	6	5
72	VIRGIL	18	9	−9
73	SCIOSCIA	14	6	−8
74	SASSER	2	4	2
75	J. DELEON	3	5	2
76	M. WILSON	8	18	10
77	K. GRIFFEY	15	5	−10
78	LIND	11	13	2
79	R. J. REYNOLDS	8	14	6
80	DERNIER	8	8	0
	TOTAL	88	88	0

	ROUND 9	PAID	EARNED	NET
81	COX	10	−2	−12
82	FITZGERALD	10	7	−3
83	KNEPPER	6	9	3
84	LYONS	1	1	0
85	SHOW	4	18	14
86	LEFFERTS	10	16	6
87	L. ANDERSEN	4	7	3
88	SCHIRALDI	1	−4	−5
89	TUDOR	10	16	6
90	M. K. YOUNG	9	1	−8
	TOTAL	65	69	4

	ROUND 10	PAID	EARNED	NET
91	J. HOWELL	4	27	23
92	PAGNOZZI	7	3	−4
93	LEARY	5	19	14
94	BACKMAN	7	9	2
95	MARK DAVIS	2	33	31
96	D. HALL	1	−4	−5
97	R. MURPHY	9	3	−6
98	TEKULVE	4	2	−2
99	WALLING	9	3	−6
100	LACOSS	5	3	−2
	TOTAL	53	98	45

That rounds off the old Beer Barrels at an even 100. Since there's only ten players per round, it's easy to see the average price paid per player go down: $28, $18, $17, $16, $16, $11, $9, $9, $7, $5. This has to happen.

I see their prices going down, I see the losses getting smaller; I still kind of get the feeling I'm a long way from my $300.

Of course average earnings go down! The obvious stars are disappearing. But look at what's there! Is a $23 profit on Jay Howell too small for you? Are we looking at the same charts?

Oh, sure, I see it—now. Last April what I saw was Jay Howell's five-something ERA the year before at Oakland.

For $4, how bad can he be? He had a down year, like a lot of relievers—especially in '87—but the Dodgers gave up Bob Welch to get a short-stop and a man to pitch the ninth inning for them. He was worth more of a gamble than $4.

Leary was luck.

Leary was not luck. Leary was homework. But don't believe me, believe the price: $5. That's at least four different claims that Leary was not luck.

Eric Show. Why bid $13 for Kevin Gross when you can pay $4 for Eric Show? Frankly, why bid $25 for Danny Jackson or $19 for Tom Browning when you can buy John Tudor for $10?

Tudor was a screwup.

When the prices are too high, there *have* to be screwups. What about Mark Davis? There's another nice profit.

In the tenth round you scoop up Mark Davis, Jay Howell, and Tim Leary for a total of $11. They earn $79. If one team scooped them all, that's the match right there.

If one team can spot those three klutzes in April, they should be on Wall Street or at the tracks. They don't need this penny-ante stuff.

Mark Davis is a klutz, too? The guy is a wicked lefty! It seems to me your definition of a klutz is anyone *you* didn't spot.

Give me a break. Mark Davis had two saves the year before. He had an ERA over 4.00.

Pass me that *Who's Who,* would you? I challenge that . . .

Okay, two saves (what are you, some sort of stats freak?), but also 9 wins; also an ERA of just under 4.00 in a year when that was hard to do. Let's check him out in Patton dollars—that's what they're for, you know . . .

Here he is. Having what the world thinks is a terrible year in '87, yet earning $6. Gossage is gone; McCullers, if he can't cut it in the ninth inning, won't be the first pitcher that's happened to.

You still say risking $2 on Mark Davis is risking $2 on a klutz?

You know what you remind me of? A goddam shrink. Shrinks are always telling you why something is the way it is after it's the way it is.

Now wait a minute. I admit I'm looking over these last four rounds and picking all the big winners, but look at all the other winners.

And look at all the losers still.

Hey. It's getting late. If the league's any good, they mostly *are* losers. But look at the winners. Little winners, but making money: Jose Oquendo, Bob Melvin, Mackey Sasser, Jose DeLeon, Jose Lind, R. J. Reynolds, Bob Knepper, Craig Lefferts, Larry Andersen, Wally Backman.
   That's it through the tenth round.

You know what? This team you just named sucks.

It does, doesn't it?

There's something fishy about all this. I'm beginning to think I'd rather collect stats than Patton dollars.

We've still got the crapshoot to go; thirty-one more players. Don't forget that.

It's all going to be in the crapshoot? The last thirty-one players?

No, not all. By no means. But there should be some nice morsels here. Let's have a look.

BEER BARREL ENDGAME CRAPSHOOT

		PAID	EARNED	NET
101	JERRY MUMPHREY	4	−1	−5
102	DARREN DAULTON	2	1	−1
103	JEFF HEATHCOCK	1	−5	−6
104	MICKEY HATCHER	3	6	3
105	BOB FORSCH	1	−3	−4
106	ED WHITSON	4	7	3
107	TOM FOLEY	3	10	7
108	RAFAEL RAMIREZ	6	14	8
109	DANNY DARWIN	6	4	−2
110	BOB WALK	5	15	10
111	HERM WINNINGHAM	4	5	1
112	DARRIN JACKSON	1	7	6
113	LES LANCASTER	1	2	1
114	TIM FLANNERY	1	4	3
115	DON SUTTON	5	−2	−7
116	JEFF HAMILTON	1	6	5
117	JIM SUNDEBERG	1	2	1
118	CRAIG REYNOLDS	2	3	1

		PAID	EARNED	NET
119	MIKE DIAZ	1	0	−1
120	TERRY MCGRIFF	1	0	−1
121	WALLY JOHNSON	1	2	1
122	JOHN CANGELOSI	4	4	0
123	KEN DAYLEY	1	7	6
124	CHRIS SPEIER	2	3	1
125	AL PEDRIQUE	2	−2	−4
126	STEVE HENDERSON	1	0	−1
127	BOB MCCLURE	1	0	−1
128	DICKIE THON	1	10	9
129	GRAIG NETTLES	1	0	−1
130	TERRY BLOCKER	4	0	−4
131	JESSE REID	1	0	−1
	TOTAL	72	99	27

Well, I take it back: they didn't agree with my prices in the Beer Barrel League, but they had studied for their draft. There's not much here, is there?

There ain't bleep here, face it.

And what there is of it, they actually had some money left to pay for. That's impressive. Bob Walk, Rafael Ramirez, anyone halfway decent left, and they have quite a nice little scuffle over him.

Way to go, Beer Barrels.

It beats me how you sit there so detached, when what it means is, your prices are worth bleep.

This is going to be very simple to explain—

Sure it is. Give me your calculator, would you? You just sit there . . . only take me a second.

I think I have created a monster.

Got it! There's something fishy in the Beer Barrel.

I have.

	PAID	EARNED	NET
round 1	282	205	−77
round 2	175	164	−11
round 3	165	176	11
round 4	163	101	−62
round 5	158	81	−77
round 6	105	83	−22
round 7	86	39	−47
round 8	88	88	0
round 9	65	69	4
round 10	53	98	45
	1340	1104	−236
Crapshoot	72	99	27
Total	1412	1203	−209

There's $209 missing, mister. That's the bottom line.

I hate that expression. I've spent the whole book trying to avoid it.

I'll say it again, then. The bottom line is your prices suck in this Beer Barrel draft.

No, they don't. You asked me where the bargains were; I was trying to show you. We were talking about winning pennants the old-fashioned way, not inheriting them.

But I guess it's time to talk about your inheritances—that is, your freeze lists. This is really *the* final question.

Talk. I'm listening.

Well, first we know how many players were frozen for how much money. Since the budget is $2,600 and they spent $1,412 in the draft, they prespent $1,188. Since they need 230 players and bought 131, they froze 99.

Why do we freeze players, anyway?

Because they're cheap.

No, because we expect them to make profits. And usually they do. As a group, they always do. The Beer Barrel 99 cost $1,188; that's $12 a player. The average the budget allows per player ($11.30) is less than that, so obviously the frozen players weren't cheap in that sense.

They cost $1,188 and earned $1,397; it's in that sense they were cheap. They combined for $209 in profits.

You're sure of that. You're not playing shrink again?

Positive. Although, of course, in a way I am playing shrink. I'm looking back on the 1988 season with the knowledge of what each and every player earned. Having gone through the Beer Barrel draft, we know what the players they bought lost overall, so we know what the profits were among the players they froze overall. The average Beer Barrel frozen player cost $12 and earned $14. A profit of $2.

Doesn't seem like all that much.

Spread out equally among 10 teams, it's nothing; concentrated in a few hands, it's overwhelming.

Is there a general way you can adjust your prices to these freeze lists?

Sure there is. If we were clairvoyants instead of shrinks and knew that the average player frozen was going to claim a $2 profit, then we would know that the average player we bought was going to take a $1.50 loss. Here's the math.

$$\text{paid: } \$1,412/131 = \$10.77 \text{ per player}$$
$$\text{earned: } \$1,203/131 = \$9.25 \text{ per player}$$

So each player is going to take about a 14 percent loss; you can increase each player's Patton $ by 14 percent to set up a new salary structure.

Fourteen percent? Now it seems like a lot.

It is a lot. It creates all-new prices. If you happen to know Dawson is going to earn $34, his new price is $39. That's the amount you can afford to overpay him—with one small catch.

What's that?

If you keep doing this, your team breaks even and you finish sixth.

Remember, we're talking about the Beer Barrels as a whole. By saying they have $209 of profits already sewn up in their freezes, we're saying they have $209 extra to fling around. They can and will waste $209 before the draft is over. So each time you buy Dawson for $39 instead of the $34 he will earn, you and the league as a whole are inching back to the break-even point.

By all means, set up a new salary schedule if you want to, to learn how much you can afford to waste on Dawson. Just remember the purpose is not to have him earn more, because he doesn't: The purpose is to acquire Dawson.

If I'm getting this right, you're saying that if the Beer Barrels had spent $39 on Dawson instead of $43, you wouldn't have thought they were so cuckoo.

I didn't say I was certain whoever bought him at $43 *was* cuckoo. If he had by far the best freeze list in the league—meaning he could take a $9 loss on Dawson and still be ahead of everyone else—paying $43 for Dawson made sense. If he kept overpaying at that rate, it would soon become cuckoo.

The most important thing about your freeze list is knowing how yours ranks with everyone else's. What looks like a good freeze list is a bad freeze list if a lot of others are better.

What's the best way to rank them? With Patton $ or Patton guesses?

You know me: I love my dollars, hate my guesses. To get a general idea of where I stand, I count as "keepers" only those players who have earned more in the previous year than they are going to cost in this one. It's a method that saves time—and also the aggravation of paying too much attention to who has Jefferies or Sheffield for $15.

If a team has Tony Gwynn for $25 and he earned $35 the year before, I give that team plus $10, and so forth. Here is how the American Dreams Leagues ranked by freeze lists before last year's draft:

WSSOX	157
NOVA	101
MOOSE FACTORY	100
BAGS	71
BB GUNS	60
NABOBS	59
RESIDUALS	51
HACKERS	46
TOONERS	36
AMAROS	31
PALUKAS	29
VEECKS	25
TOTAL	766
AVERAGE	64

Am I seeing $766 as the bottom—um, as the total profits?

Total *projected* profits, based on this purely mechanical assessment of freeze lists. Throw in the Sheffields of that year, and it's no doubt worse.

So your league had much better freeze lists than the Beer Barrels, and I'm seeing Moose Factory there in pretty good shape. How'd you blow it?

In the order of the questions you've raised: (1) the Beer Barrel's projected profits might have looked every bit as good before their draft; (2) I was in relatively good shape, if you don't mind having very little hope of first; and (3) I didn't blow it. I came within an inch of blowing it, and then pulled it out.

I get the feeling I'm about to hear a dream.

I doubt it; I don't have the space. But I want to show you what happens to these projected "profits."

Three different teams, with three quite different outlooks, based on their freeze lists: the Wssox, the Moose Factory, and the Bags.

WSSOX	POS.	SALARY	PROJ. PROFIT	ACTUAL EARNINGS	ACTUAL PROFIT
GREENWELL	OF	1	22	39	38
SHEETS	OF	6	19	6	0
FRANCO	SS	21	7	28	7
SURHOFF	C	4	13	14	10
STEINBACH	C	3	9	11	8
D. STEWART	P	2	23	22	20
ALEXANDER	P	15	7	5	−10
C. YOUNG	P	7	11	5	−2
MI. WILLIAMS	P	3	12	13	10
ECKERSLEY	P	1	34	50	49
10 PLAYERS		63	157	193	130

MOOSE FACTORY					
LEMON	OF	7	8	15	8
MCGWIRE	1B	6	24	24	18
BOGGS	3B	29	1	25	−4
SVEUM	SS	2	14	8	6
FISK	C	13	0	15	2
NOKES	C	15	7	12	−3
SABERHAGEN	P	11	19	12	1
DOTSON	P	6	3	−3	−9
FRASER	P	2	12	−7	−9
BERENGUER	P	1	12	6	5
10 PLAYERS		92	100	107	15

BAGS

CALDERON	OF	8	17	8	0
BRANTLEY	OF	17	1	21	4
SEITZER	3B	13	14	19	6
BROCK	1B	13	6	6	−7
GUILLEN	SS	2	16	16	14
FLETCHER	SS	8	8	11	3
WHITT	C	10	3	15	5
BOSIO	P	2	2	15	13
CERUTTI	P	4	4	8	4
9 PLAYERS		77	71	119	42

The truly remarkable Wssox freeze list had its ups (Eckersley, Greenwell) and downs (Sheets, Alexander) during the course of the season, but came out of it only down $27 from their projected profits.

Moose Factory, which looked so strong—except in comparison to the Wssox—barely ended up with any profits from its freeze list.

Rooks and geezers—what'd you expect?

About $50. Certainly not $100, but not $15 either.

The Bags, who were behind me in projected profits, actually got more than I did from their freeze list.

They finish ahead of you?

You seem to be begging for a dream.

I just want to know the answer.

No you don't. You want to know, or should, what this all means.

First, there's a strong indication of what I believe Bill James calls the law of competitive balance at work here. By the time all twelve of the American Dreams teams had had their projected profits trimmed, who knows what the real profits from the league's freeze lists might have been down to? Perhaps to less than the $209 of the Beer Barrels.

Second, there's always hope, within a certain range. The Bags appear to be starting out $29 behind me; in actuality, they started out $27 ahead of me. A $56 swing between what we thought we had and what we had.

Third, there's no hope outside of a certain range. There was simply no way the Veecks, the Palukas, the Amaros, and even the Tooners or the Hackers were going to catch the Wssox. I say "even" because the Tooners and Hackers made a good run at it, but they simply could never quite whittle down that huge freeze list advantage.

How'd it happen? Fire sale?

Yes, the Wssox and Nova both gained their freezes through fire sales.

But not you? Not Big Time?

Not Big Time. He feels it's his moral obligation to try to win each year, with the result that he'll probably never win again.

The reason I'm dwelling on this is that there may be other leagues that are having similar problems. We have become so highly skilled at wielding the knife of underpriced players that for three years in a row now the pennant has been decided in June of the year before.

In June, if your pony is lumbering along at the back of the pack, why not drop out? Unload all your excess baggage for lean items like Greenwell and Eckersley for $1. Coast the rest of the way. Next year, you're rested, you've got a tremendous weight allowance, you rub out your nearest competitor at the starting gate, and you take off. You never look back.

I think I got all except the rubout. Who's getting rubbed out and how?

All right. Here's the dream, briefly.

Look over the freeze lists again of the Wssox, heavy favorites, and the still-dreaded Moose. The Wssox have just what the Moose have always wanted most and now are conspicuously without. The Wssox—

Excuse me, but if I have to listen to this, could you give me a better handle? I really don't like that name.

Sweeney. Call them Sweeney. Sweeney knows that I want to have two people, Rickey and Lee Smith, and I've got to have one of them. He's got lots of money to see that I don't.

Now refer back to the first round (page 175).

Plesac is a warm-up. The team that nominates him has the topper on him and takes him. Fair price.

The next team to nominate is Nova, the other fire-sale team, and they're looking for the Rickey bloodbath, since they already have speed.

Now, I still don't know how Sweeney did this, but not only did he fire out of the block with me after Rickey, he brought another horse with him. We charged into the $50 range side by side, and, by God, there were the Hackers still with us! The Hackers had plenty of money, but they had few freezes, and what freezes they did have were pitchers: small profits and shaky at that. But they kept pounding along, right into the sixties with us.

Sweeney dropped out. He was delighted. But what was I supposed to do?

I cranked it to $61. The Hackers gleefully said $62! I paused; I thought; I gave it one more try. Sixty-three dollars. Sixty-four dollars! roared the Hackers.

On to Lee Smith.

Not that it matters; can you guess who nominated him? The still-panting Hackers. Well, to make the story as short as the race was, Sweeney galloped after Lee Smith, whom he of course had no use for—but I sure did—and pretty soon we were in a game of chicken in the midforties.

Once it got to $45, I didn't *want* Lee Smith; it was a question of how much farther I could drive Sweeney—and I'll never know, will I?

Once and for all, how'd you finish? Just say it.

Third. Tied for third. The funny thing is that I went through the whole draft without ever getting one of my favorite items—stolen bases—and precious little of the other, saves.

Why not? How come you didn't get any stolen bases?

Because *the prices were too high!* Don't you see? You *can't do that!* You can't just chase things! What have we been talking about for a whole book?

You know? I'm just looking at my watch and I think I'm due some-where. Sorry that I bothered you for so long.

No, I'm sorry. Excuse me. I mean, walk out if you want to, but I've got a grip on myself. It's not you, it's the pressure.

No, really, you've told me a lot. I think I've got it.

Let me just finish the train of thought on the fire sales. We've found them to be such a scourge that we're tempted to throw everybody back in the pot each year. The trouble with that is: very boring winters and early springs that are both boring and anxiety-ridden; with no real reason to call each other, we don't know what each other is doing.

Anyway, we've tried a partial cure to fire sales: All players whose salaries are under $15 who are traded during the season have their next year's salaries automatically jump to $15. We'll see if it helps. So far, the only thing I've noticed is that Sweeney, unable to get any takers on Jay Buhner at $15, still has him at $1.

Probably a great new rule would be that the winner has to take a year off; whoever wins is always so obnoxious.

Well, that hasn't happened to me and my partner yet. We've come close . . .

I'll tell you what. Let me simplify it.

All we've been talking about from the very beginning is having an understanding of the value of ballplayers' performances. If you've got a good line on that, and you're in a room that's a little hazy on this subject—well, you've got a terrific advantage.

Make your lists, set your prices. Every so often, set fairly optimistic prices, but they must be obtainable; you have to be realistic.

Think about what everybody else will be thinking about; try to anticipate. The fewer surprises the better. But you'll never anticipate everything, so don't worry about the surprises when they happen. Be flexible.

I like this. I'm really sorry to interrupt. But does that mean I sometimes disregard my prices? Say the hell with them, it's not working?

Nope. Nope, nope, nope, nope.

Don't get mad again, please.

I'm not mad. I'm just saying, nope. Your prices are real; you've thought about them; they add up. They are, in fact, the only thing you can depend on when the shit hits the fan.

I'll give you one last snippet of a dream; very self-serving, but what the hell.

As I said, for some reason my colleagues decided to take me seriously last year. I don't know why suddenly last year, because they never had before. If they didn't want to spend $50 on Rickey Henderson, they didn't, and I got him, and I won.

Well, as you can see just from the first round, relief pitching and stolen bases were taken with extreme seriousness in the American Dreams last year. Too extreme. When I found that I had to go to $30 for the privilege of sticking my neck into a noose named Lance Johnson, I said the heck with it. Since my freeze list was a team of lead-legs and the few players I had bought so far (all terrible: Parker, Barfield) were lead-legs, I just kept buying more. Since they weren't expected to run, and they could do the other three things with varying degrees of success, they weren't such stiffs anymore. In essence, I decided to buy about three hundred home runs in the draft and—would you believe?—spend the rest on *pitching*.

And I never did get the home runs; at least not in time, which in our league means by June, when I could deal to solve my other inevitable problems.

Like stolen bases?

No, no—they were gone forever, I was never getting those back. My inevitable pitching problems.

However, as it turned out, I didn't have any problems. I mean, this league had let me buy all these great pitchers for incredible prices. Gubicza $12, Swindell $7, Mike Jackson $12, Brian Harvey $8—

I thought this was meant to be a sharp league.

So did I!

I think you see the point. If you have a strong understanding of the value of players' performances, if you set your prices accordingly, if you come well equipped with Qaaludes in one hand and Jolt in the other, if you don't lose your nerve or your concentration, if you sit there with *no plan* other than to get value for your dollar, and you succeed in doing that . . . you're going to win.

I mean, you might at least win third, ugly.

I'm psyched.

Can I add as a footnote, in case it sounds like I really do know what I'm doing in a draft?

Say it. I'm ready to go. I'm out of here. Got to go talk to my partner.

Ah, doesn't matter.

Go ahead, tell me.

Well, I was going to say, if a voice from the future had whispered in my ear in the middle of the draft, "Patton? Your freeze list? It's only worth fifteen dol-lars."

If that had happened, I think I would have fainted.

Uh-huh. And I'll bet the draft would have kept right on going; no time-out for that.

Not a chance.

Can I ask one last question? It's really been bugging me. Of all the weird names people give their teams, yours is the one I don't have a clue about. Moose Factory? What kind of name is that?

It's named after a mutt Dollar Bill found in an Indian village on James Bay. A mutt, mind, but his foot did sort of resemble a rabbit's. We used to irritate people by pressing Moose's foot on an ink pad, then on freeze lists that we distributed to the league.

As I've been saying from the beginning, it's a game of luck. After all the sweat and blood, all you can do is grab whatever talisman you can, and hope for the best.

NL CATCHERS

	HR	RBI	SB	BA	AB	HR+	RBI+	SB+	BA+	POINTS	$
B SANTIAGO	10	46	15	.248	492	2.5	3.0	2.5	−0.7	7.3	15
T PENA	10	51	6	.263	505	2.5	3.3	1.0	0.3	7.1	15
L PARRISH	15	60	0	.215	424	3.8	3.9	0.0	−2.4	5.2	11
G CARTER	11	46	0	.242	455	2.8	3.0	0.0	−1.0	4.7	10
O VIRGIL	9	31	2	.256	320	2.3	2.0	0.3	−0.1	4.5	9
D BERRYHILL	7	38	1	.259	309	1.8	2.5	0.2	0.0	4.4	9
M LAVALLIERE	2	47	3	.261	352	0.5	3.1	0.5	0.1	4.2	9
N SANTOVENIA	8	41	2	.236	309	2.0	2.7	0.3	−0.9	4.1	8
R DEMPSEY	7	30	1	.251	167	1.8	2.0	0.2	−0.2	3.7	8
M FITZGERALD	5	23	2	.271	155	1.3	1.5	0.3	0.3	3.3	7
A ASHBY	7	33	0	.238	227	1.8	2.2	0.0	−0.6	3.3	7
B DIAZ	10	35	0	.219	315	2.5	2.3	0.0	−1.7	3.1	6
J DAVIS	7	36	0	.230	257	1.8	2.3	0.0	−1.0	3.1	6
M SCIOSCIA	3	35	0	.257	408	0.8	2.3	0.0	−0.1	2.9	6
B MELVIN	8	27	0	.234	273	2.0	1.8	0.0	−0.9	2.9	6
J ORTIZ	2	18	1	.280	118	0.5	1.2	0.2	0.3	2.2	4
A TREVINO	2	13	5	.249	193	0.5	0.8	0.8	−0.3	1.9	4
M SASSER	1	17	0	.285	123	0.3	1.1	0.0	0.4	1.8	4
T PAGNOZZI	0	15	0	.282	195	0.0	1.0	0.0	0.6	1.6	3
L MCCLENDON	3	14	4	.219	137	0.8	0.9	0.7	−0.8	1.6	3
Average, top 20	6	33	2	.247	287	1.6	2.1	0.4	−0.4	3.6	7.44

CONTINUED ON NEXT PAGE

	HR	RBI	SB	BA	AB	HR+	RBI+	SB+	BA+	POINTS	$
M PARENT	6	15	0	.195	118	1.5	1.0	0.0	−1.0	1.4	3
C BIGGIO	3	5	6	.211	123	0.8	0.3	1.0	−0.8	1.3	3
K MANWARING	1	15	0	.250	116	0.3	1.0	0.0	−0.1	1.1	2
J SUNDBERG	2	9	0	.241	54	0.5	0.6	0.0	−0.1	0.9	2
B BRENLY	5	22	1	.189	206	1.3	1.4	0.2	−2.0	0.9	2
B BENEDICT	0	19	0	.242	236	0.0	1.2	0.0	−0.6	0.7	1
J RUSSELL	2	4	0	.245	49	0.5	0.3	0.0	−0.1	0.7	1
S LAKE	1	4	0	.278	54	0.3	0.3	0.0	0.1	0.7	1
D DAULTON	1	12	2	.208	144	0.3	0.8	0.3	−1.0	0.4	1
B LYONS	0	11	0	.231	91	0.0	0.7	0.0	−0.4	0.4	1
J REED	1	16	1	.226	265	0.3	1.0	0.2	−1.2	0.3	1
T MCGRIFF	1	4	1	.198	96	0.3	0.3	0.2	−0.8	−0.1	0

NL FIRST BASEMEN

	HR	RBI	SB	BA	AB	HR+	RBI+	SB+	BA+	POINTS	$
A GALARRAGA	29	92	13	.302	609	7.3	6.0	2.2	3.3	18.7	38
W CLARK	29	109	9	.282	575	7.3	7.1	1.5	1.7	17.5	36
G DAVIS	30	99	4	.271	561	7.5	6.5	0.7	0.8	15.5	32
G PERRY	8	74	29	.300	547	2.0	4.8	4.8	2.8	14.5	30
P GUERRERO	10	65	4	.286	364	2.5	4.2	0.7	1.3	8.7	18
S BREAM	10	65	9	.264	462	2.5	4.2	1.5	0.3	8.5	17
V HAYES	6	45	20	.272	367	1.5	2.9	3.3	0.7	8.4	17
M GRACE	7	57	3	.296	486	1.8	3.7	0.5	2.3	8.3	17
N ESASKY	15	62	7	.243	391	3.8	4.0	1.2	−0.8	8.1	17
R JORDAN	11	43	1	.308	273	2.8	2.8	0.2	1.8	7.5	15

CONTINUED ON NEXT PAGE

	HR	RBI	SB	BA	AB	HR+	RBI+	SB+	BA+	POINTS	$
K HERNANDEZ	11	55	2	.276	348	2.8	3.6	0.3	0.8	7.4	15
J KRUK (OF)	9	44	5	.241	378	2.3	2.9	0.8	−0.9	5.0	10
F STUBBS	8	34	11	.223	242	2.0	2.2	1.8	−1.2	4.9	10
D MAGADAN (3B)	1	35	0	.277	314	0.3	2.3	0.0	0.8	3.3	7
B HORNER	3	33	0	.257	206	0.8	2.2	0.0	0.0	2.9	6
Average, top 15	12	61	8	.276	408	3.1	4.0	1.3	0.9	9.3	19.03
M TRILLO	1	14	2	.250	164	0.3	0.9	0.3	−0.2	1.3	3
R MILLIGAN	3	8	1	.220	82	0.8	0.5	0.2	−0.5	1.0	2
W JOHNSON	0	3	0	.309	94	0.0	0.2	0.0	0.6	0.8	2
L DURHAM	4	8	0	.218	124	1.0	0.5	0.0	−0.7	0.8	2
T SIMMONS	2	11	0	.196	107	0.5	0.7	0.0	−0.9	0.3	1
R NELSON	1	3	0	.190	21	0.3	0.2	0.0	−0.2	0.2	0
H SPILMAN	1	3	0	.156	45	0.3	0.2	0.0	−0.7	−0.2	0
L MAZZILLI	0	12	4	.147	116	0.0	0.8	0.7	−1.8	−0.4	−1
M LAGA	0	4	0	.130	100	0.0	0.3	0.0	−1.8	−1.5	−3

NL SECOND BASEMEN

	HR	RBI	SB	BA	AB	HR+	RBI+	SB+	BA+	POINTS	$
R SANDBERG	19	69	25	.296	618	4.8	4.5	4.2	2.9	16.3	33
S SAX	5	57	42	.277	632	1.3	3.7	7.0	1.4	13.4	27
R GANT (3B)	19	60	19	.259	563	4.8	3.9	3.2	0.0	11.9	24
J SAMUEL	12	67	33	.243	629	3.0	4.4	5.5	−1.2	11.6	24
R ALOMAR	9	41	24	.266	545	2.3	2.7	4.0	0.5	9.4	19

CONTINUED ON NEXT PAGE

	HR	RBI	SB	BA	AB	HR+	RBI+	SB+	BA+	POINTS	$
R THOMPSON	7	48	14	.264	477	1.8	3.1	2.3	0.3	7.5	15
B DORAN	7	53	17	.248	480	1.8	3.5	2.8	−0.7	7.4	15
R HUDLER (SS)	4	14	29	.273	216	1.0	0.9	4.8	0.4	7.2	15
J LIND	2	49	15	.262	611	0.5	3.2	2.5	0.2	6.4	13
R READY (3B)	7	39	6	.266	331	1.8	2.5	1.0	0.3	5.6	11
T FOLEY (SS)	5	43	2	.265	377	1.3	2.8	0.3	0.3	4.7	10
W BACKMAN	0	17	9	.303	294	0.0	1.1	1.5	1.7	4.3	9
T TEUFEL	4	31	0	.234	273	1.0	2.0	0.0	−0.9	2.1	4
J TREADWAY	2	23	2	.252	301	0.5	1.5	0.3	−0.3	2.1	4
T FLANNERY	0	19	3	.265	170	0.0	1.2	0.5	0.1	1.9	4
Average, top 15	7	42	16	.265	434	1.7	2.7	2.7	0.3	7.5	15.24
R OESTER	0	10	0	.280	150	0.0	0.7	0.0	0.4	1.1	2
T HERR	1	3	3	.260	50	0.3	0.2	0.5	0.0	1.0	2
J PANKOVITS	2	12	2	.221	140	0.5	0.8	0.3	−0.7	0.9	2
J PAREDES	1	10	5	.187	91	0.3	0.7	0.8	−0.9	0.8	2
T LAWLESS	1	3	6	.154	65	0.3	0.2	1.0	−1.0	0.5	1
L ALICEA	2	24	1	.212	297	0.5	1.6	0.2	−1.9	0.4	1
M SHARPERSON	0	4	0	.271	59	0.0	0.3	0.0	0.1	0.4	1
K MILLER	1	5	0	.214	70	0.3	0.3	0.0	−0.4	0.1	0
M LEMKE	0	2	0	.224	58	0.0	0.1	0.0	−0.3	−0.2	0
T BARRETT	0	3	0	.204	54	0.0	0.2	0.0	−0.4	−0.2	0
D GARCIA	1	4	1	.117	60	0.3	0.3	0.2	−1.2	−0.5	−1
D CONCEPCION	0	8	3	.198	197	0.0	0.5	0.5	−1.6	−0.6	−1
C CANDAELE	0	5	1	.170	147	0.0	0.3	0.2	−1.8	−1.3	−3

NL SHORTSTOPS

	HR	RBI	SB	BA	AB	HR+	RBI+	SB+	BA+	POINTS	$
B LARKIN	12	56	40	.296	588	3.0	3.7	6.7	2.7	16.1	33
O SMITH	3	51	57	.270	575	0.8	3.3	9.5	0.8	14.3	29
H JOHNSON (3B)	24	68	23	.230	495	6.0	4.4	3.8	−1.8	12.4	25
S DUNSTON	9	56	30	.249	575	2.3	3.7	5.0	−0.7	10.2	21
A THOMAS	13	68	7	.252	606	3.3	4.4	1.2	−0.5	8.4	17
R RAMIREZ	6	59	3	.276	566	1.5	3.8	0.5	1.2	7.0	14
J OQUENDO (2B, 3B)	7	46	4	.277	451	1.8	3.0	0.7	1.1	6.5	13
J URIBE	3	35	14	.252	493	0.8	2.3	2.3	−0.5	4.9	10
D THON	1	18	19	.264	258	0.3	1.2	3.2	0.2	4.7	10
G TEMPLETON	3	36	8	.249	362	0.8	2.3	1.3	−0.5	3.9	8
K ELSTER	9	37	2	.214	406	2.3	2.4	0.3	−2.4	2.6	5
L AGUAYO	5	13	2	.247	97	1.3	0.8	0.3	−0.2	2.3	5
D ANDERSON	2	20	4	.249	285	0.5	1.3	0.7	−0.4	2.1	4
L RIVERA	4	30	3	.224	371	1.0	2.0	0.5	−1.7	1.7	4
C REYNOLDS	1	14	3	.255	161	0.3	0.9	0.5	−0.1	1.6	3
Average, top 15	7	40	15	.256	419	1.7	2.6	2.4	−0.2	6.6	13.48
C SPEIER	3	18	3	.216	171	0.8	1.2	0.5	−1.0	1.4	3
TiJONES	0	3	4	.269	52	0.0	0.2	0.7	0.1	0.9	2
F FERMIN	0	2	3	.276	87	0.0	0.1	0.5	0.2	0.8	2
J HUSON	0	3	2	.310	42	0.0	0.2	0.3	0.3	0.8	2
J BLAUSER (2B)	2	7	0	.239	67	0.5	0.5	0.0	−0.2	0.8	2
A GRIFFIN	1	27	7	.199	316	0.3	1.8	1.2	−2.5	0.7	1
J GUTIERREZ	0	9	0	.247	77	0.0	0.6	0.0	−0.1	0.5	1
R BELLIARD	0	11	7	.213	286	0.0	0.7	1.2	−1.7	0.1	0
A SALAZAR	0	1	0	.250	60	0.0	0.1	0.0	−0.1	0.0	0
A PEDRIQUE	0	4	0	.180	128	0.0	0.3	0.0	−1.4	−1.1	−2
S JELTZ	0	27	3	.187	379	0.0	1.8	0.5	−3.6	−1.3	−3

NL THIRD BASEMEN

	HR	RBI	SB	BA	AB	HR+	RBI+	SB+	BA+	POINTS	$
C SABO	11	44	46	.271	538	2.8	2.9	7.7	0.8	14.1	29
B BONILLA	24	100	3	.274	584	6.0	6.5	0.5	1.1	14.1	29
V LAW	11	78	1	.293	556	2.8	5.1	0.2	2.4	10.4	21
K MITCHELL (OF)	19	80	5	.251	505	4.8	5.2	0.8	−0.5	10.3	21
C JAMES (OF)	19	66	7	.242	566	4.8	4.3	1.2	−1.2	9.0	18
T WALLACH	12	69	2	.257	592	3.0	4.5	0.3	−0.2	7.7	16
M SCHMIDT	12	62	3	.249	390	3.0	4.0	0.5	−0.5	7.0	14
T PENDLETON	6	53	3	.253	391	1.5	3.5	0.5	−0.3	5.2	11
K OBERKFELL	3	42	4	.271	476	0.8	2.7	0.7	0.7	4.9	10
G JEFFERIES	6	17	5	.321	109	1.5	1.1	0.8	0.9	4.4	9
B BELL	7	40	1	.241	323	1.8	2.6	0.2	−0.8	3.8	8
E RILES	3	28	1	.294	187	0.8	1.8	0.2	0.9	3.6	7
J HAMILTON	6	33	0	.236	309	1.5	2.2	0.0	−0.9	2.7	6
M WILLIAMS	8	19	0	.205	156	2.0	1.2	0.0	−1.2	2.1	4
L HARRIS	0	8	4	.372	43	0.0	0.5	0.7	0.7	1.9	4
Average, top 15	10	49	6	.262	382	2.5	3.2	0.9	0.1	6.8	13.81
T WOODSON	3	15	1	.249	173	0.8	1.0	0.2	−0.2	1.6	3
D WALLING	1	21	2	.239	234	0.3	1.4	0.3	−0.6	1.3	3
R BOOKER	0	3	2	.343	35	0.0	0.2	0.3	0.4	0.9	2
C BROWN	2	19	0	.235	247	0.5	1.2	0.0	−0.8	0.9	2
T O'MALLEY	0	2	0	.259	27	0.0	0.1	0.0	0.0	0.1	0
G NETTLES	1	14	0	.172	93	0.3	0.9	0.0	−1.1	0.0	0
J MORRISON	2	13	0	.152	92	0.5	0.8	0.0	−1.4	0.0	0
K CAMINITI	1	7	0	.181	83	0.3	0.5	0.0	−0.9	−0.2	0

NL OUTFIELDERS

	HR	RBI	SB	BA	AB	HR+	RBI+	SB+	BA+	POINTS	$
D STRAWBERRY	39	101	29	.269	543	9.8	6.6	4.8	0.7	21.9	45
A VAN SLYKE	25	100	30	.288	587	6.3	6.5	5.0	2.1	19.9	41
E DAVIS	26	93	35	.273	472	6.5	6.1	5.8	0.9	19.3	39
K MCREYNOLDS	27	99	21	.288	552	6.8	6.5	3.5	2.0	18.7	38
K GIBSON	25	76	31	.290	542	6.3	5.0	5.2	2.1	18.5	38
V COLEMAN	3	38	81	.260	616	0.8	2.5	13.5	0.1	16.8	34
A DAWSON	24	79	12	.303	591	6.0	5.2	2.0	3.3	16.4	34
K DANIELS	18	64	27	.291	495	4.5	4.2	4.5	2.0	15.2	31
T GWYNN	7	70	26	.313	521	1.8	4.6	4.3	3.6	14.2	29
B BONDS	24	58	17	.283	538	6.0	3.8	2.8	1.6	14.2	29
H BROOKS	20	90	7	.279	588	5.0	5.9	1.2	1.5	13.5	28
B BUTLER	6	43	43	.287	568	1.5	2.8	7.2	2.0	13.5	28
G YOUNG	0	37	66	.257	576	0.0	2.4	11.0	−0.1	13.3	27
W MCGEE	3	50	41	.292	562	0.8	3.3	6.8	2.3	13.2	27
K BASS	14	72	31	.255	541	3.5	4.7	5.2	−0.3	13.1	27
T BRUNANSKY	22	79	16	.245	523	5.5	5.2	2.7	−1.0	12.4	25
T RAINES	12	48	33	.270	429	3.0	3.1	5.5	0.6	12.3	25
M MARSHALL (1B)	20	82	4	.277	542	5.0	5.3	0.7	1.2	12.2	25
B HATCHER	7	52	32	.268	530	1.8	3.4	5.3	0.6	11.1	23
R PALMEIRO	8	53	12	.307	580	2.0	3.5	2.0	3.5	11.0	22
L DYKSTRA	8	33	30	.270	429	2.0	2.2	5.0	0.6	9.8	20
P O'NEILL (1B)	16	73	8	.252	485	4.0	4.8	1.3	−0.5	9.6	20
J SHELBY	10	64	16	.263	494	2.5	4.2	2.7	0.3	9.6	20
DA MURPHY	24	77	3	.226	592	6.0	5.0	0.5	−2.4	9.1	19
M WILSON	8	41	15	.296	378	2.0	2.7	2.5	1.9	9.0	18
P BRADLEY	11	56	11	.264	569	2.8	3.7	1.8	0.3	8.6	18
C MALDONADO	12	68	6	.255	499	3.0	4.4	1.0	−0.3	8.1	17
DA MARTINEZ	6	46	23	.255	447	1.5	3.0	3.8	−0.2	8.1	17
O NIXON	0	15	46	.244	271	0.0	1.0	7.7	−0.6	8.1	17
C MARTINEZ (1B)	18	65	1	.236	365	4.5	4.2	0.2	−1.1	7.8	16

CONTINUED ON NEXT PAGE

	HR	RBI	SB	BA	AB	HR+	RBI+	SB+	BA+	POINTS	$
M WEBSTER	6	39	22	.260	523	1.5	2.5	3.7	0.1	7.8	16
T PUHL	3	19	22	.303	234	0.8	1.2	3.7	1.4	7.1	14
M THOMPSON	2	33	17	.288	378	0.5	2.2	2.8	1.5	6.9	14
R REYNOLDS	6	51	15	.248	323	1.5	3.3	2.5	−0.5	6.8	14
TR JONES	3	24	18	.295	224	0.8	1.6	3.0	1.1	6.4	13
M WYNNE	11	42	3	.264	333	2.8	2.7	0.5	0.2	6.2	13
K MORELAND (1B)	5	64	2	.256	511	1.3	4.2	0.3	−0.2	5.6	11
M ALDRETE	3	50	6	.267	389	0.8	3.3	1.0	0.4	5.4	11
R JONES	8	26	0	.290	124	2.0	1.7	0.0	0.5	4.2	9
D JAMES	3	30	9	.256	386	0.8	2.0	1.5	−0.1	4.1	8
B DERNIER	1	10	13	.289	166	0.3	0.7	2.2	0.7	3.8	8
D JACKSON	6	20	4	.266	188	1.5	1.3	0.7	0.2	3.6	7
A HALL	1	15	15	.247	231	0.3	1.0	2.5	−0.4	3.3	7
D NIXON	0	6	11	.346	78	0.0	0.4	1.8	0.9	3.2	6
D COLES	5	36	1	.232	211	1.3	2.3	0.2	−0.8	3.0	6
J LEONARD	2	20	7	.256	160	0.5	1.3	1.2	−0.1	2.9	6
M HATCHER (1B)	1	25	0	.293	191	0.3	1.6	0.0	0.9	2.8	6
H WINNINGHAM	0	21	12	.232	203	0.0	1.4	2.0	−0.8	2.6	5
K GRIFFEY	4	23	1	.255	243	1.0	1.5	0.2	−0.1	2.5	5
J CANGELOSI	0	8	9	.254	118	0.0	0.5	1.5	−0.1	1.9	4
Average, top 50	10	50	19	.271	413	2.6	3.2	3.1	0.6	9.6	19.60
G WILSON	2	15	0	.270	126	0.5	1.0	0.0	0.2	1.7	3
L SMITH	3	9	4	.237	114	0.8	0.6	0.7	−0.3	1.7	3
D COLLINS	0	14	7	.236	174	0.0	0.9	1.2	−0.6	1.5	3
S MACK	0	12	5	.244	119	0.0	0.8	0.8	−0.3	1.4	3
G VARSHO	0	5	5	.274	73	0.0	0.3	0.8	0.2	1.3	3
C FORD	1	18	6	.195	128	0.3	1.2	1.0	−1.1	1.3	3
J YOUNGBLOOD	0	16	1	.252	123	0.0	1.0	0.2	−0.1	1.1	2
B DISTEFANO	1	6	0	.345	29	0.3	0.4	0.0	0.4	1.0	2
G REDUS	2	4	5	.197	71	0.5	0.3	0.8	−0.6	1.0	2
T GREGG	1	7	0	.295	44	0.3	0.5	0.0	0.2	0.9	2

CONTINUED ON NEXT PAGE

	HR	RBI	SB	BA	AB	HR+	RBI+	SB+	BA+	POINTS	$
D DASCENZO	0	4	6	.213	75	0.0	0.3	1.0	−0.5	0.8	2
D HEEP	0	11	2	.242	149	0.0	0.7	0.3	−0.4	0.7	1
M CARREON	1	1	0	.556	9	0.3	0.1	0.0	0.4	0.7	1
M YOUNG	1	14	0	.226	146	0.3	0.9	0.0	−0.7	0.5	1
V SNIDER	1	6	0	.214	28	0.3	0.4	0.0	−0.2	0.5	1
J LINDEMAN	1	7	0	.209	43	0.3	0.5	0.0	−0.3	0.4	1
MI DAVIS	2	17	7	.196	281	0.5	1.1	1.2	−2.4	0.4	1
J MORRIS	0	3	0	.289	38	0.0	0.2	0.0	0.2	0.4	1
M DIAZ	0	5	0	.230	74	0.0	0.3	0.0	−0.3	0.0	0
S HENDERSON	0	5	1	.217	46	0.0	0.3	0.2	−0.3	0.2	0
G ROENICKE	1	7	0	.228	114	0.3	0.5	0.0	−0.5	0.2	0
T BLOCKER	2	10	1	.212	198	0.5	0.7	0.2	−1.3	0.1	0
S ABNER	2	5	0	.181	83	0.5	0.3	0.0	−0.9	−0.1	0
C GWYNN	0	0	0	.182	11	0.0	0.0	0.0	−0.1	−0.1	0
E MILNER	0	2	2	.176	51	0.0	0.1	0.3	−0.6	−0.1	0
S JEFFERSON	1	4	5	.144	111	0.3	0.3	0.8	−1.8	−0.4	−1
J MUMPHREY	0	9	0	.136	66	0.0	0.6	0.0	−1.1	−0.5	−1
G GROSS	0	5	0	.203	133	0.0	0.3	0.0	−1.0	−0.7	−1

NL PITCHERS

	W	S	ERA	RATIO	IP	W+	S+	ERA+	RATIO+	POINTS	$
J FRANCO	6	39	1.57	9.10	86	2.0	15.6	2.7	1.9	22.2	45
R MYERS	7	26	1.72	8.21	68	2.3	10.4	2.0	2.2	16.9	35
O HERSHISER	23	1	2.26	9.47	267	7.7	0.4	4.3	4.0	16.4	34
M DAVIS	5	28	2.01	10.25	98	1.7	11.2	2.2	0.9	16.0	33
J GOTT	6	34	3.49	10.47	77	2.0	13.6	−0.2	0.6	15.9	33

CONTINUED ON NEXT PAGE

	W	S	ERA	RATIO	IP	W+	S+	ERA+	RATIO+	POINTS	S
T WORRELL	5	32	3.00	10.30	90	1.7	12.8	0.5	0.8	15.8	32
D JACKSON	23	0	2.73	9.56	261	7.7	0.0	2.3	3.7	13.7	28
J HOWELL	5	21	2.08	9.00	65	1.7	8.4	1.5	1.6	13.1	27
D CONE	20	0	2.22	10.04	231	6.7	0.0	4.0	2.3	12.9	26
D SMITH	4	27	2.67	12.40	57	1.3	10.8	0.7	−0.8	12.0	25
S BEDROSIAN	6	28	3.75	12.35	74	2.0	11.2	−0.6	−1.0	11.6	24
P PEREZ	12	0	2.44	8.47	188	4.0	0.0	2.7	4.9	11.6	24
M SCOTT	14	0	2.92	8.85	219	4.7	0.0	1.4	4.8	10.8	22
A PENA	6	12	1.91	9.73	94	2.0	4.8	2.3	1.4	10.6	22
D ROBINSON	10	6	2.45	10.24	177	3.3	2.4	2.5	1.5	9.7	20
T BELCHER	12	4	2.91	9.72	180	4.0	1.6	1.2	2.5	9.3	19
T LEARY	17	0	2.91	10.12	229	5.7	0.0	1.4	2.1	9.2	19
R MCDOWELL	5	16	2.63	11.22	89	1.7	6.4	1.1	−0.1	9.0	19
T BROWNING	18	0	3.41	9.66	251	6.0	0.0	−0.4	3.4	9.0	18
D MARTINEZ	15	0	2.72	10.33	235	5.0	0.0	2.2	1.7	8.9	18
B OJEDA	10	0	2.88	9.03	190	3.3	0.0	1.3	3.9	8.6	18
E SHOW	16	0	3.26	9.74	235	5.3	0.0	0.2	3.0	8.6	18
R REUSCHEL	19	0	3.12	10.43	245	6.3	0.0	0.7	1.5	8.6	17
J RIJO	13	0	2.39	10.17	162	4.3	0.0	2.5	1.5	8.3	17
D DRABEK	15	0	3.08	10.01	219	5.0	0.0	0.8	2.3	8.1	17
B SMITH	12	0	3.00	9.59	198	4.0	0.0	1.0	2.9	7.9	16
S FERNANDEZ	12	0	3.03	9.48	187	4.0	0.0	0.9	3.0	7.9	16
C LEFFERTS	3	11	2.92	9.45	92	1.0	4.4	0.6	1.7	7.7	16
J PARRETT	12	6	2.65	10.90	92	4.0	2.4	1.1	0.2	7.7	16
J TUDOR	10	0	2.32	10.47	198	3.3	0.0	3.2	1.2	7.7	16
J AGOSTO	10	4	2.26	10.21	92	3.3	1.6	1.7	0.9	7.6	15
R DARLING	17	0	3.25	10.40	241	5.7	0.0	0.2	1.6	7.5	15
T BURKE	3	18	3.40	11.96	82	1.0	7.2	−0.1	−0.8	7.3	15
B WALK	12	0	2.71	10.50	213	4.0	0.0	2.1	1.2	7.2	15
D GOODEN	18	0	3.19	10.84	248	6.0	0.0	0.5	0.5	7.0	14

CONTINUED ON NEXT PAGE

	W	S	ERA	RATIO	IP	W+	S+	ERA+	RATIO+	POINTS	$
J MAGRANE	5	0	2.18	10.02	165	1.7	0.0	3.1	1.8	6.6	13
J SMILEY	13	0	3.25	10.14	205	4.3	0.0	0.2	1.9	6.4	13
J DESHAIES	11	0	3.00	10.26	207	3.7	0.0	1.0	1.7	6.4	13
K DOWNS	13	0	3.32	10.02	168	4.3	0.0	0.0	1.8	6.1	13
B HOLTON	7	1	1.70	10.10	85	2.3	0.4	2.4	1.0	6.1	13
G MADDUX	18	0	3.18	11.24	249	6.0	0.0	0.5	−0.4	6.1	12
L MCCULLERS	3	10	2.49	11.52	98	1.0	4.0	1.4	−0.4	6.0	12
S GARRELTS	5	13	3.58	11.57	98	1.7	5.2	−0.4	−0.5	5.9	12
S TERRY	9	3	2.92	10.65	129	3.0	1.2	0.9	0.6	5.7	12
J HESKETH	4	9	2.85	12.14	73	1.3	3.6	0.6	−0.8	4.7	10
J OROSCO	3	9	2.72	12.06	53	1.0	3.6	0.6	−0.5	4.7	10
G GOSSAGE	4	13	4.33	13.40	44	1.3	5.2	−0.8	−1.1	4.7	10
D RASMUSSEN	16	0	3.43	11.30	205	5.3	0.0	−0.4	−0.5	4.5	9
B KNEPPER	14	0	3.14	11.47	175	4.7	0.0	0.5	−0.7	4.5	9
P ASSENMACHER	8	5	3.06	11.80	79	2.7	2.0	0.4	−0.6	4.4	9
J ROBINSON	11	0	3.03	10.97	125	3.7	0.0	0.6	0.2	4.4	9
B SUTTER	1	14	4.77	11.91	45	0.3	5.6	−1.2	−0.4	4.4	9
T LEACH	7	3	2.54	11.64	92	2.3	1.2	1.3	−0.5	4.3	9
A HAWKINS	14	0	3.35	11.25	218	4.7	0.0	−0.1	−0.4	4.2	9
A HAMMAKER	9	5	3.73	11.01	145	3.0	2.0	−1.0	0.1	4.1	8
A MCGAFFIGAN	6	4	2.76	11.63	91	2.0	1.6	0.9	−0.5	4.0	8
G HARRIS (PHI)	4	1	2.36	11.10	107	1.3	0.4	1.8	0.0	3.5	7
K DAYLEY	2	5	2.77	10.90	55	0.7	2.0	0.6	0.2	3.4	7
D LEIPER	3	1	2.17	9.83	54	1.0	0.4	1.1	0.8	3.4	7
E WHITSON	13	0	3.77	10.83	205	4.3	0.0	−1.5	0.5	3.3	7
L ANDERSEN	2	5	2.94	11.11	83	0.7	2.0	0.6	0.0	3.2	7
N RYAN	12	0	3.52	11.17	220	4.0	0.0	−0.7	−0.2	3.1	6
M KRUKOW	7	0	3.54	10.25	125	2.3	0.0	−0.5	1.1	3.0	6
R DIBBLE	1	0	1.82	9.71	59	0.3	0.0	1.6	1.0	2.9	6
J COSTELLO	5	1	1.81	12.50	50	1.7	0.4	1.4	−0.7	2.7	6

CONTINUED ON NEXT PAGE

	W	S	ERA	RATIO	IP	W+	S+	ERA+	RATIO+	POINTS	$
J DELEON	13	0	3.67	11.34	225	4.3	0.0	−1.3	−0.6	2.5	5
J BOEVER	0	1	1.77	5.76	20	0.0	0.4	0.6	1.3	2.4	5
D DARWIN	8	3	3.84	11.11	192	2.7	1.2	−1.6	−0.1	2.2	4
G HARRIS (SD)	2	0	1.50	8.00	18	0.7	0.0	0.6	0.7	2.0	4
J ALVAREZ	5	3	2.99	12.40	102	1.7	1.2	0.6	−1.4	2.0	4
D LAPOINT	4	0	2.77	11.08	52	1.3	0.0	0.5	0.1	1.9	4
R JOHNSON	3	0	2.42	10.38	26	1.0	0.0	0.5	0.3	1.7	4
J DOPSON	3	0	3.04	11.10	169	1.0	0.0	0.8	0.0	1.7	4
M COOK	2	0	2.86	8.18	22	0.7	0.0	0.2	0.8	1.7	3
K GROSS	12	0	3.69	11.58	232	4.0	0.0	−1.4	−1.2	1.5	3
D DRAVECKY	2	0	3.16	9.97	37	0.7	0.0	0.1	0.5	1.3	3
R MURPHY	0	3	3.08	11.37	85	0.0	1.2	0.4	−0.2	1.3	3
M LACOSS	7	0	3.62	11.49	114	2.3	0.0	−0.6	−0.5	1.3	3
K TEKULVE	3	4	3.60	12.26	80	1.0	1.6	−0.4	−1.0	1.2	2
K BROWN	2	0	2.76	9.92	16	0.7	0.0	0.2	0.3	1.2	2
T CREWS	4	0	3.14	11.68	72	1.3	0.0	0.2	−0.4	1.1	2
F YOUMANS	3	0	3.21	11.25	84	1.0	0.0	0.2	−0.1	1.0	2
D MEADS	3	0	3.18	11.57	40	1.0	0.0	0.1	−0.2	1.0	2
L LANCASTER	4	5	3.78	12.92	86	1.3	2.0	−0.7	−1.7	0.9	2
R SAMUELS	1	0	3.47	9.26	23	0.3	0.0	0.0	0.6	0.9	2
J MOYER	9	0	3.48	11.90	202	3.0	0.0	−0.5	−1.7	0.8	2
A NIPPER	2	1	3.04	11.93	80	0.7	0.4	0.4	−0.7	0.8	2
B MEYER	0	0	1.46	9.49	12	0.0	0.0	0.5	0.3	0.8	2
B JONES	1	2	3.04	12.46	56	0.3	0.8	0.3	−0.8	0.6	1
F WILLIAMS	3	1	2.59	13.50	63	1.0	0.4	0.8	−1.7	0.6	1
Average, top 90	8	5	2.98	10.57	128	2.7	1.9	0.7	0.7	6.1	12.47
A MADRID	1	0	2.76	11.57	16	0.3	0.0	0.2	0.0	0.5	1
S MEDVIN	3	0	4.88	10.41	28	1.0	0.0	−0.8	0.3	0.5	1
R ST. CLAIRE	1	0	2.64	11.86	14	0.3	0.0	0.2	0.0	0.5	1
P PERRY	4	1	4.14	11.81	59	1.3	0.4	−0.9	−0.4	0.4	1
B HOLMAN	4	0	3.23	12.11	100	1.3	0.0	0.2	−1.1	0.4	1

CONTINUED ON NEXT PAGE

	W	S	ERA	RATIO	IP	W+	S+	ERA+	RATIO+	POINTS	S
T MULHOLLAND	2	0	3.72	11.15	46	0.7	0.0	−0.3	0.0	0.4	1
L MCWILLIAMS	6	1	3.90	11.58	136	2.0	0.4	−1.3	−0.7	0.4	1
J PRICE	1	4	3.94	12.55	62	0.3	1.6	−0.7	−1.0	0.3	1
R MAHLER	9	0	3.69	11.60	249	3.0	0.0	−1.4	−1.3	0.3	1
R SUTCLIFFE	13	0	3.86	12.03	226	4.3	0.0	−1.9	−2.1	0.3	1
B KIPPER	2	0	3.74	11.08	65	0.7	0.0	−0.5	0.0	0.2	0
N CHARLTON	4	0	3.96	11.74	61	1.3	0.0	−0.7	−0.4	0.2	0
J PICO	6	1	4.15	11.58	113	2.0	0.4	−1.6	−0.6	0.2	0
S SANDERSON	1	0	5.28	9.39	15	0.3	0.0	−0.5	0.4	0.2	0
B MCCLURE	2	3	5.40	12.90	30	0.7	1.2	−1.1	−0.6	0.2	0
C PULEO	5	1	3.47	12.53	106	1.7	0.4	−0.3	−1.6	0.2	0
S HILLEGAS	3	0	4.13	11.28	57	1.0	0.0	−0.8	−0.1	0.1	0
R DAVIS	1	0	4.67	10.91	17	0.3	0.0	−0.4	0.1	0.0	0
M HARKEY	0	0	2.60	12.46	35	0.0	0.0	0.5	−0.5	0.0	0
R HORTON	1	0	5.00	13.00	9	0.3	0.0	−0.3	−0.1	0.0	0
G BOOKER	2	0	3.39	12.30	64	0.7	0.0	−0.1	−0.8	−0.2	0
K BLANKENSHIP	1	0	4.60	12.64	16	0.3	0.0	−0.4	−0.2	−0.2	0
L SORENSEN	0	2	4.86	14.58	17	0.0	0.8	−0.5	−0.6	−0.3	−1
R MARTINEZ	1	0	3.79	12.37	36	0.3	0.0	−0.3	−0.5	−0.4	−1
J EICHELBERGER	2	0	3.86	13.02	37	0.7	0.0	−0.3	−0.8	−0.4	−1
M BIELECKI	2	0	3.35	13.22	48	0.7	0.0	0.0	−1.1	−0.5	−1
E NUNEZ	1	0	4.50	15.43	14	0.3	0.0	−0.3	−0.6	−0.6	−1
R O'NEAL	2	0	4.58	11.38	53	0.7	0.0	−1.2	−0.1	−0.7	−1
D COX	3	0	3.98	11.93	86	1.0	0.0	−1.0	−0.8	−0.8	−2
G MATHEWS	4	0	4.24	12.44	68	1.3	0.0	−1.1	−1.0	−0.8	−2
J JONES	9	0	4.12	11.87	179	3.0	0.0	−2.3	−1.4	−0.8	−2
T WILSON	0	0	4.09	13.50	22	0.0	0.0	−0.3	−0.5	−0.8	−2
M MADDUX	4	0	3.76	12.69	89	1.3	0.0	−0.7	−1.5	−0.9	−2
E OLWINE	0	1	6.75	12.54	19	0.0	0.4	−1.2	−0.2	−1.0	−2
J BRANTLEY	0	0	5.66	12.19	21	0.0	0.0	−0.9	−0.2	−1.1	−2
K HOWELL	0	0	6.40	14.21	13	0.0	0.0	−0.7	−0.4	−1.1	−2

CONTINUED ON NEXT PAGE

	W	S	ERA	RATIO	IP	W+	S+	ERA+	RATIO+	POINTS	S
C CARPENTER	2	0	4.72	12.27	48	0.7	0.0	−1.2	−0.6	−1.1	−2
S BAROJAS	0	0	8.31	15.58	9	0.0	0.0	−0.8	−0.4	−1.2	−2
M GRANT	2	0	3.69	12.26	98	0.7	0.0	−0.6	−1.2	−1.2	−2
T BIRTSAS	1	0	4.20	11.89	64	0.3	0.0	−1.0	−0.5	−1.2	−2
D SUTTON	3	0	3.92	12.47	87	1.0	0.0	−0.9	−1.3	−1.2	−2
M CAPEL	2	0	4.91	14.42	29	0.7	0.0	−0.8	−1.1	−1.2	−3
R BOCKUS	1	0	4.78	13.50	32	0.3	0.0	−0.8	−0.8	−1.3	−3
R CHILDRESS	1	0	6.17	13.50	23	0.3	0.0	−1.2	−0.6	−1.5	−3
P SMITH	7	0	3.69	12.49	195	2.3	0.0	−1.2	−2.8	−1.6	−3
B FORSCH	10	0	4.29	13.01	136	3.3	0.0	−2.2	−2.8	−1.7	−3
B SEBRA	1	0	7.94	19.86	11	0.3	0.0	−1.0	−1.1	−1.7	−4
J ACKER	0	0	4.71	12.64	42	0.0	0.0	−1.1	−0.7	−1.7	−4
C SCHIRALDI	9	1	4.38	12.39	166	3.0	0.4	−2.9	−2.2	−1.8	−4
D HALL	1	1	7.66	14.11	22	0.3	0.4	−1.8	−0.7	−1.8	−4
R ROBINSON	3	0	4.12	13.04	79	1.0	0.0	−1.1	−1.7	−1.8	−4
F DIPINO	2	6	4.98	13.35	90	0.7	2.4	−2.6	−2.2	−1.8	−4
M SOTO	3	0	4.66	12.00	87	1.0	0.0	−2.0	−0.8	−1.9	−4
D PALMER	7	0	4.47	12.35	129	2.3	0.0	−2.5	−1.7	−1.9	−4
D RUCKER	0	0	4.76	15.25	28	0.0	0.0	−0.7	−1.3	−2.0	−4
J ANDUJAR	2	0	4.00	13.16	79	0.7	0.0	−0.9	−1.8	−2.0	−4
G JIMENEZ	1	0	5.01	12.45	56	0.3	0.0	−1.7	−0.8	−2.2	−4
V PALACIOS	1	0	6.66	15.91	24	0.3	0.0	−1.5	−1.3	−2.4	−5
J HEATHCOCK	0	0	5.81	14.23	31	0.0	0.0	−1.4	−1.1	−2.5	−5
R AGUILERA	0	0	6.93	14.23	25	0.0	0.0	−1.6	−0.8	−2.5	−5
B DAWLEY	0	0	13.50	20.77	9	0.0	0.0	−1.6	−0.9	−2.5	−5
D QUISENBERRY	2	0	6.16	14.21	38	0.7	0.0	−2.0	−1.3	−2.6	−5
D CARMAN	10	0	4.29	12.56	201	3.3	0.0	−3.1	−3.0	−2.8	−6
N HEATON	3	2	4.99	13.04	97	1.0	0.8	−2.8	−2.0	−3.1	−6
M DUNNE	7	0	3.92	13.29	170	2.3	0.0	−1.7	−3.9	−3.2	−7
Z SMITH	5	0	4.30	13.02	140	1.7	0.0	−2.3	−2.9	−3.5	−7

CONTINUED ON NEXT PAGE

	W	S	ERA	RATIO	IP	W+	S+	ERA+	RATIO+	POINTS	S
J ARMSTRONG	4	0	5.79	13.91	65	1.3	0.0	−2.9	−2.0	−3.6	−7
B FISHER	8	0	4.61	13.16	146	2.7	0.0	−3.2	−3.2	−3.7	−8
T GLAVINE	7	0	4.56	12.16	195	2.3	0.0	−3.9	−2.1	−3.7	−8
S PETERS	3	0	6.40	15.80	45	1.0	0.0	−2.5	−2.4	−3.9	−8
F VALENZUELA	5	1	4.24	13.78	142	1.7	0.4	−2.2	−4.0	−4.2	−8
B RUFFIN	6	3	4.43	14.40	144	2.0	1.2	−2.7	−5.0	−4.5	−9
J SMOLTZ	2	0	5.48	15.05	64	0.7	0.0	−2.5	−2.8	−4.6	−9
C CARY	0	0	6.48	56.16	8	0.0	0.0	−0.5	−4.4	−4.8	−10
S RAWLEY	8	0	4.18	13.55	198	2.7	0.0	−2.7	−4.9	−5.0	−10
M FREEMAN	2	0	6.10	17.07	52	0.7	0.0	−2.6	−3.5	−5.4	−11
K COFFMAN	2	0	5.78	15.58	67	0.7	0.0	−2.9	−3.3	−5.6	−11

AL CATCHERS

	HR	RBI	SB	BA	AB	HR+	RBI+	SB+	BA+	POINTS	$
E WHITT	16	70	4	.251	398	3.2	4.0	0.9	−0.6	7.5	15
C FISK	19	50	0	.277	253	3.8	2.8	0.0	0.5	7.1	15
B SURHOFF (3B)	5	38	21	.245	493	1.0	2.1	4.7	−1.0	6.8	14
M NOKES	16	53	0	.251	382	3.2	3.0	0.0	−0.5	5.7	12
T STEINBACH	9	51	3	.265	351	1.8	2.9	0.7	0.1	5.5	11
D SLAUGHT	9	43	1	.283	322	1.8	2.4	0.2	0.8	5.3	11
B BOONE	5	39	2	.295	352	1.0	2.2	0.4	1.5	5.1	11
T LAUDNER	13	54	0	.251	375	2.6	3.1	0.0	−0.5	5.1	10
A ALLANSON	5	50	5	.263	434	1.0	2.8	1.1	0.0	5.0	10
G PETRALLI	7	36	0	.282	351	1.4	2.0	0.0	0.9	4.3	9
M TETTLETON	11	37	0	.261	283	2.2	2.1	0.0	0.0	4.3	9
R HASSEY	7	45	2	.257	323	1.4	2.5	0.4	−0.2	4.2	9
D VALLE	10	50	0	.231	290	2.0	2.8	0.0	−1.2	3.7	8
R CERONE	3	27	0	.280	254	0.6	1.5	0.0	0.6	2.7	6
J QUIRK	8	25	1	.240	196	1.6	1.4	0.2	−0.6	2.7	5
S BRADLEY	4	33	1	.257	335	0.8	1.9	0.2	−0.2	2.7	5
B HARPER	3	20	0	.295	166	0.6	1.1	0.0	0.7	2.5	5
P BORDERS	5	21	0	.273	154	1.0	1.2	0.0	0.2	2.4	5
M MACFARLANE	4	26	0	.265	211	0.8	1.5	0.0	0.1	2.4	5
J SUNDBERG	4	13	0	.286	91	0.8	0.7	0.0	0.3	1.9	4
M HEATH	5	18	1	.247	219	1.0	1.0	0.2	−0.4	1.8	4
R GEDMAN	9	39	0	.197	299	1.8	2.2	0.0	−2.5	1.5	3
M STANLEY	3	27	0	.229	249	0.6	1.5	0.0	−1.1	1.1	2
J SKINNER	4	23	0	.227	251	0.8	1.3	0.0	−1.1	1.0	2
Average, top 24	8	37	2	.260	293	1.5	2.1	0.4	−0.1	3.9	8.05
M SALAS	3	9	0	.250	196	0.6	0.5	0.0	−0.3	0.8	2
R KARKOVICE	3	9	4	.174	115	0.6	0.5	0.9	−1.3	0.7	1
B WYNEGAR	1	8	0	.255	55	0.2	0.5	0.0	0.0	0.6	1
C KREUTER	1	5	0	.275	51	0.2	0.3	0.0	0.1	0.6	1
D MILLER	2	7	2	.221	140	0.4	0.4	0.4	−0.7	0.5	1

CONTINUED ON NEXT PAGE

	HR	RBI	SB	BA	AB	HR+	RBI+	SB+	BA+	POINTS	$
S BUTERA	1	6	0	.233	60	0.2	0.3	0.0	−0.2	0.3	1
T KENNEDY	3	16	0	.226	265	0.6	0.9	0.0	−1.2	0.3	1
C O'BRIEN	2	9	0	.220	118	0.4	0.5	0.0	−0.6	0.3	1
R TINGLEY	1	2	0	.167	24	0.2	0.1	0.0	−0.3	0.0	0
B SCHROEDER	5	10	0	.156	122	1.0	0.6	0.0	−1.7	−0.1	0
L OWEN	1	3	0	.210	81	0.2	0.2	0.0	−0.5	−0.2	0
C NICHOLS	0	1	0	.191	47	0.0	0.1	0.0	−0.4	−0.4	−1

AL FIRST BASEMEN

	HR	RBI	SB	BA	AB	HR+	RBI+	SB+	BA+	POINTS	$
G BRETT	24	103	14	.306	589	4.8	5.8	3.1	3.1	16.8	34
F MCGRIFF	34	82	6	.282	536	6.8	4.6	1.3	1.3	14.0	29
E MURRAY	28	84	5	.284	603	5.6	4.7	1.1	1.5	13.0	27
K HRBEK	25	76	0	.312	510	5.0	4.3	0.0	3.1	12.4	25
D MATTINGLY	18	88	1	.311	599	3.6	5.0	0.2	3.5	12.3	25
M MCGWIRE	32	99	0	.260	550	6.4	5.6	0.0	−0.2	11.8	24
W JOYNER	13	85	8	.295	597	2.6	4.8	1.8	2.3	11.5	24
J CLARK	27	93	3	.242	496	5.4	5.3	0.7	−1.3	10.1	21
A DAVIS	18	69	1	.295	478	3.6	3.9	0.2	1.9	9.7	20
P O'BRIEN	16	71	1	.272	547	3.2	4.0	0.2	0.7	8.1	17
S BALBONI	23	66	0	.235	413	4.6	3.7	0.0	−1.4	6.9	14
W UPSHAW	11	50	12	.245	493	2.2	2.8	2.7	−1.0	6.7	14
T BENZINGER (OF)	13	70	2	.254	405	2.6	4.0	0.4	−0.4	6.6	13
G LARKIN	8	70	3	.267	505	1.6	4.0	0.7	0.3	6.5	13
DA EVANS	22	64	1	.208	437	4.4	3.6	0.2	−3.0	5.3	11

CONTINUED ON NEXT PAGE

	HR	RBI	SB	BA	AB	HR+	RBI+	SB+	BA+	POINTS	$
J MEYER	11	45	0	.263	327	2.2	2.5	0.0	0.0	4.8	10
D BERGMAN	5	35	0	.294	289	1.0	2.0	0.0	1.2	4.2	9
B BUCKNER	3	43	5	.249	285	0.6	2.4	1.1	−0.5	3.7	8
Average, top 18	18	72	3	.273	481	3.7	4.1	0.8	0.6	9.1	18.70
L PARRISH	14	52	0	.217	406	2.8	2.9	0.0	−2.3	3.4	7
G WALKER	8	42	0	.247	377	1.6	2.4	0.0	−0.7	3.2	7
G BROCK	6	50	6	.212	364	1.2	2.8	1.3	−2.3	3.0	6
J TRABER	10	45	1	.222	352	2.0	2.5	0.2	−1.8	3.0	6
L MEDINA	6	8	0	.255	51	1.2	0.5	0.0	0.0	1.6	3
R KNIGHT	3	33	1	.217	299	0.6	1.9	0.2	−1.7	1.0	2
MI DIAZ	3	12	0	.237	152	0.6	0.7	0.0	−0.5	0.8	2
R MORMAN	0	3	0	.240	75	0.0	0.2	0.0	−0.2	0.0	0

AL SECOND BASEMEN

	HR	RBI	SB	BA	AB	HR+	RBI+	SB+	BA+	POINTS	$
J FRANCO	10	54	25	.303	613	2.0	3.1	5.6	3.0	13.6	28
H REYNOLDS	4	41	35	.283	598	0.8	2.3	7.8	1.5	12.4	25
J RAY (OF)	6	83	4	.306	602	1.2	4.7	0.9	3.1	9.9	20
J GANTNER	0	47	20	.276	539	0.0	2.7	4.4	0.9	8.0	16
M BARRETT	1	65	7	.283	612	0.2	3.7	1.6	1.5	6.9	14
L WHITAKER	12	55	2	.275	403	2.4	3.1	0.4	0.7	6.6	14
C WILKERSON (SS)	0	28	9	.293	338	0.0	1.6	2.0	1.3	4.9	10
N LIRIANO	3	23	12	.264	276	0.6	1.3	2.7	0.1	4.7	10
M LEE (SS)	2	38	3	.291	381	0.4	2.1	0.7	1.4	4.6	9
F WHITE	8	58	7	.235	537	1.6	3.3	1.6	−1.8	4.6	9

CONTINUED ON NEXT PAGE

	HR	RBI	SB	BA	AB	HR+	RBI+	SB+	BA+	POINTS	$
T HERR	1	21	10	.263	304	0.2	1.2	2.2	0.0	3.7	7
M MCLEMORE	2	16	13	.240	233	0.4	0.9	2.9	−0.6	3.5	7
F MANRIQUE	5	37	6	.235	345	1.0	2.1	1.3	−1.2	3.2	7
W RANDOLPH	2	34	8	.230	404	0.4	1.9	1.8	−1.6	2.5	5
G HUBBARD	3	33	1	.255	294	0.6	1.9	0.2	−0.3	2.4	5
J BROWNE	1	17	7	.229	214	0.2	1.0	1.6	−0.9	1.8	4
J WALEWANDER	0	6	11	.211	175	0.0	0.3	2.4	−1.1	1.6	3
D HILL	2	20	3	.217	221	0.4	1.1	0.7	−1.3	0.9	2
Average, top 18	3	38	10	.268	394	0.7	2.1	2.3	0.3	5.4	10.96
B WELLMAN	1	6	1	.271	107	0.2	0.3	0.2	0.2	0.9	2
M LOVULLO	1	2	0	.381	21	0.2	0.1	0.0	0.4	0.7	1
S LOMBARDOZZI	3	27	2	.209	287	0.6	1.5	0.4	−2.0	0.6	1
B RIPKEN	2	34	8	.207	512	0.4	1.9	1.8	−3.5	0.6	1
J KUNKEL	2	15	0	.227	154	0.4	0.8	0.0	−0.7	0.6	1
W TOLLESON	0	5	1	.254	59	0.0	0.3	0.2	0.0	0.5	1
M GALLEGO (SS)	2	20	2	.209	277	0.4	1.1	0.4	−1.9	0.1	0
T PHILLIPS (OF)	2	17	0	.203	212	0.4	1.0	0.0	−1.6	−0.3	−1
M WOODARD	0	4	1	.133	45	0.0	0.2	0.2	−0.7	−0.3	−1

AL SHORTSTOPS

	HR	RBI	SB	BA	AB	HR+	RBI+	SB+	BA+	POINTS	$
A TRAMMELL	15	69	7	.311	466	3.0	3.9	1.6	2.8	11.3	23
T FERNANDEZ	5	70	15	.287	648	1.0	4.0	3.3	1.9	10.2	21
C RIPKEN	23	81	2	.264	575	4.6	4.6	0.4	0.1	9.8	20
O GUILLEN	0	39	25	.261	566	0.0	2.2	5.6	−0.1	7.7	16
L SALAZAR (3B, OF)	12	62	6	.270	452	2.4	3.5	1.3	0.4	7.7	16

CONTINUED ON NEXT PAGE

	HR	RBI	SB	BA	AB	HR+	RBI+	SB+	BA+	POINTS	$
G GAGNE	14	48	15	.236	461	2.8	2.7	3.3	−1.5	7.4	15
D SCHOFIELD	6	34	20	.239	527	1.2	1.9	4.4	−1.5	6.1	12
K STILLWELL	10	53	6	.251	459	2.0	3.0	1.3	−0.7	5.7	12
S FLETCHER	0	47	8	.276	515	0.0	2.7	1.8	0.8	5.3	11
R QUINONES	12	52	0	.248	499	2.4	2.9	0.0	−0.9	4.5	9
D SVEUM	9	51	1	.242	467	1.8	2.9	0.2	−1.2	3.7	8
J REED	1	28	1	.293	338	0.2	1.6	0.2	1.3	3.3	7
W WEISS	3	39	4	.250	452	0.6	2.2	0.9	−0.7	3.0	6
A NEWMAN (2B)	0	19	12	.223	260	0.0	1.1	2.7	−1.3	2.4	5
R WASHINGTON	2	21	3	.256	223	0.4	1.2	0.7	−0.2	2.1	4
G SHEFFIELD	4	12	3	.238	80	0.8	0.7	0.7	−0.2	1.9	4
R SANTANA	4	38	1	.240	480	0.8	2.1	0.2	−1.4	1.8	4
S OWEN	5	18	0	.249	257	1.0	1.0	0.0	−0.4	1.6	3
Average, top 18	7	43	7	.260	429	1.4	2.5	1.6	−0.1	5.3	10.84
B PECOTA	1	15	7	.208	178	0.2	0.8	1.6	−1.2	1.4	3
B MEACHAM	0	7	7	.217	115	0.0	0.4	1.6	−0.7	1.3	3
J BELL	2	21	4	.218	211	0.4	1.2	0.9	−1.2	1.3	3
MA DIAZ	0	9	0	.306	72	0.0	0.5	0.0	0.5	1.0	2
R VELARDE	5	12	1	.174	115	1.0	0.7	0.2	−1.3	0.6	1
R RENTERIA	0	6	1	.205	88	0.0	0.3	0.2	−0.6	−0.1	0
P ZUVELLA	0	7	0	.231	130	0.0	0.4	0.0	−0.5	−0.1	0
G POLIDOR	0	4	0	.148	81	0.0	0.2	0.0	−1.2	−1.0	−2

AL THIRD BASEMEN

	HR	RBI	SB	BA	AB	HR+	RBI+	SB+	BA+	POINTS	$
P MOLITOR	13	60	41	.312	609	2.6	3.4	9.1	3.6	18.7	38
G GAETTI	28	88	7	.301	468	5.6	5.0	1.6	2.3	14.4	29
K GRUBER	16	81	23	.278	569	3.2	4.6	5.1	1.1	13.9	29
C LANSFORD	7	57	29	.279	556	1.4	3.2	6.4	1.1	12.2	25
W BOGGS	5	58	2	.366	584	1.0	3.3	0.4	7.4	12.1	25
K SEITZER	5	60	10	.304	559	1.0	3.4	2.2	2.8	9.5	19
J HOWELL	16	63	2	.254	500	3.2	3.6	0.4	−0.5	6.7	14
S BUECHELE	16	58	2	.250	503	3.2	3.3	0.4	−0.7	6.2	13
J PRESLEY	14	62	3	.230	544	2.8	3.5	0.7	−2.2	4.8	10
M PAGLIARULO	15	67	1	.216	444	3.0	3.8	0.2	−2.6	4.5	9
S LYONS	5	45	1	.269	472	1.0	2.5	0.2	0.4	4.2	9
B JACOBY	9	49	2	.241	552	1.8	2.8	0.4	−1.5	3.6	7
R SCHU	4	20	6	.256	270	0.8	1.1	1.3	−0.2	3.0	6
T BROOKENS	5	38	4	.243	441	1.0	2.1	0.9	−1.1	3.0	6
K WILLIAMS	8	28	6	.159	220	1.6	1.6	1.3	−2.9	1.6	3
E RILES	1	9	2	.252	127	0.2	0.5	0.4	−0.1	1.0	2
K PARIS	3	6	0	.250	44	0.6	0.3	0.0	0.0	0.9	2
L AGUAYO	3	8	0	.250	140	0.6	0.5	0.0	−0.2	0.9	2
Average, top 18	10	48	8	.270	422	1.9	2.7	1.7	0.4	6.8	13.81
E MARTINEZ	0	5	0	.281	32	0.0	0.3	0.0	0.1	0.4	1
R GONZALES	2	15	2	.215	237	0.4	0.8	0.4	−1.4	0.3	1
J CASTILLO	0	2	2	.222	90	0.0	0.1	0.4	−0.5	0.1	0
E ROMERO	0	5	0	.240	75	0.0	0.3	0.0	−0.2	0.1	0
D RAMOS	0	5	0	.230	61	0.0	0.3	0.0	−0.2	0.0	0
C WORTHINGTON	2	4	1	.185	81	0.4	0.2	0.2	−0.8	0.0	0
E WILLIAMS	0	1	0	.190	21	0.0	0.1	0.0	−0.2	−0.1	0
C MARTINEZ	0	0	1	.164	55	0.0	0.0	0.2	−0.7	−0.5	−1

AL OUTFIELDERS

	HR	RBI	SB	BA	AB	HR+	RBI+	SB+	BA+	POINTS	$
R HENDERSON	6	50	93	.305	554	1.2	2.8	20.7	2.9	27.6	56.41
J CANSECO	42	124	40	.307	610	8.4	7.0	8.9	3.3	27.5	56.35
K PUCKETT	24	121	6	.356	657	4.8	6.8	1.3	7.4	20.3	42
M GREENWELL	22	119	16	.325	590	4.4	6.7	3.6	4.5	19.2	39
J CARTER	27	98	27	.271	621	5.4	5.5	6.0	0.6	17.5	36
D WINFIELD	25	107	9	.322	559	5.0	6.0	2.0	4.1	17.1	35
E BURKS	18	92	25	.294	540	3.6	5.2	5.6	2.1	16.5	34
R YOUNT	13	91	22	.306	621	2.6	5.1	4.9	3.3	15.9	33
B JACKSON	25	68	27	.246	439	5.0	3.8	6.0	−0.9	13.9	29
DW EVANS (1B)	21	111	5	.293	559	4.2	6.3	1.1	2.1	13.7	28
D TARTABULL	26	102	8	.274	507	5.2	5.8	1.8	0.7	13.5	28
D HENDERSON	24	94	2	.304	507	4.8	5.3	0.4	2.6	13.1	27
R SIERRA	23	91	18	.254	615	4.6	5.1	4.0	−0.7	13.1	27
D GLADDEN	11	62	28	.269	576	2.2	3.5	6.2	0.5	12.4	25
C DAVIS	21	93	9	.268	600	4.2	5.3	2.0	0.4	11.9	24
C WASHINGTON	11	64	15	.308	455	2.2	3.6	3.3	2.6	11.7	24
G BELL	24	97	4	.269	614	4.8	5.5	0.9	0.5	11.6	24
C SNYDER	26	75	5	.272	511	5.2	4.2	1.1	0.6	11.2	23
R DEER	23	85	9	.252	492	4.6	4.8	2.0	−0.6	10.8	22
M BRANTLEY	15	56	18	.263	577	3.0	3.2	4.0	0.1	10.2	21
W WILSON	1	37	35	.262	591	0.2	2.1	7.8	0.0	10.1	21
L MOSEBY	10	42	31	.239	472	2.0	2.4	6.9	−1.3	9.9	20
O MCDOWELL	6	37	33	.247	437	1.2	2.1	7.3	−0.8	9.8	20
G PETTIS	3	36	44	.210	458	0.6	2.0	9.8	−3.0	9.4	19
H COTTO	8	33	27	.259	386	1.6	1.9	6.0	−0.2	9.3	19
C ESPY	2	39	33	.248	347	0.4	2.2	7.3	−0.6	9.3	19
G REDUS	6	34	26	.263	262	1.2	1.9	5.8	0.1	8.9	18
D WHITE	11	51	17	.259	455	2.2	2.9	3.8	−0.2	8.7	18
L POLONIA	2	27	24	.292	288	0.4	1.5	5.3	1.1	8.4	17
P INCAVIGLIA	22	54	6	.249	418	4.4	3.1	1.3	−0.7	8.1	17

CONTINUED ON NEXT PAGE

216

	HR	RBI	SB	BA	AB	HR+	RBI+	SB+	BA+	POINTS	$
M HALL	6	71	7	.280	515	1.2	4.0	1.6	1.1	7.9	16
F LYNN	25	56	2	.246	391	5.0	3.2	0.4	−0.8	7.8	16
C LEMON	17	64	1	.266	512	3.4	3.6	0.2	0.2	7.4	15
R BUSH	14	51	8	.261	394	2.8	2.9	1.8	0.0	7.4	15
J RICE	15	72	1	.264	485	3.0	4.1	0.2	0.1	7.4	15
J BARFIELD	18	56	7	.244	468	3.6	3.2	1.6	−1.1	7.2	15
S JAVIER	2	35	20	.257	397	0.4	2.0	4.4	−0.3	6.6	13
J ORSULAK	8	27	9	.288	379	1.6	1.5	2.0	1.2	6.3	13
P SHERIDAN	11	47	8	.254	347	2.2	2.7	1.8	−0.4	6.3	13
T ARMAS	13	49	1	.272	368	2.6	2.8	0.2	0.4	6.0	12
P TABLER	2	66	3	.282	444	0.4	3.7	0.7	1.1	5.9	12
G BRAGGS	10	42	6	.261	272	2.0	2.4	1.3	0.0	5.7	12
D GALLAGHER	5	31	5	.303	347	1.0	1.8	1.1	1.8	5.6	12
D COLES	10	34	3	.292	195	2.0	1.9	0.7	0.8	5.4	11
D PARKER	12	55	0	.257	377	2.4	3.1	0.0	−0.2	5.3	11
D PASQUA	20	50	1	.227	422	4.0	2.8	0.2	−1.8	5.2	11
D BOSTON	15	31	9	.217	281	3.0	1.8	2.0	−1.6	5.1	10
J LEONARD	8	44	10	.235	374	1.6	2.5	2.2	−1.3	5.0	10
J MOSES	2	12	11	.316	206	0.4	0.7	2.4	1.5	5.0	10
I CALDERON	14	35	4	.212	264	2.8	2.0	0.9	−1.7	4.0	8
J BUHNER	13	38	1	.215	261	2.6	2.1	0.2	−1.6	3.4	7
P STANICEK	4	17	12	.230	261	0.8	1.0	2.7	−1.1	3.3	7
C CASTILLO	4	14	6	.273	176	0.8	0.8	1.3	0.3	3.2	7
L SHEETS	10	47	1	.230	452	2.0	2.7	0.2	−1.8	3.1	6
K GERHART	9	23	7	.195	262	1.8	1.3	1.6	−2.3	2.4	5
J EISENREICH	1	19	9	.218	202	0.2	1.1	2.0	−1.2	2.1	4
B BROWER	1	11	10	.224	201	0.2	0.6	2.2	−1.0	2.1	4
DW MURPHY	4	19	1	.250	144	0.8	1.1	0.2	−0.2	1.9	4
R LEACH	0	23	0	.276	199	0.0	1.3	0.0	0.4	1.7	3
D CLARK	3	18	0	.263	156	0.6	1.0	0.0	0.0	1.7	3
Average, top 60	13	56	14	.269	418	2.6	3.2	3.1	0.4	9.2	18.72

CONTINUED ON NEXT PAGE

	HR	RBI	SB	BA	AB	HR+	RBI+	SB+	BA+	POINTS	s
R KELLY	1	7	5	.247	77	0.2	0.4	1.1	−0.1	1.6	3
B ANDERSON	1	21	10	.212	325	0.2	1.2	2.2	−2.1	1.5	3
G HENDRICK	3	19	0	.244	127	0.6	1.1	0.0	−0.3	1.4	3
G WILSON	3	17	1	.250	284	0.6	1.0	0.2	−0.4	1.3	3
D HAMILTON	1	11	7	.184	103	0.2	0.6	1.6	−1.0	1.3	3
J EPPARD	0	14	0	.283	113	0.0	0.8	0.0	0.3	1.1	2
J ADDUCI	1	15	0	.266	94	0.2	0.8	0.0	0.1	1.1	2
M FELDER	0	5	8	.173	81	0.0	0.3	1.8	−0.9	1.1	2
L HERNDON	4	20	0	.224	174	0.8	1.1	0.0	−0.8	1.1	2
G WARD	4	24	0	.225	231	0.8	1.4	0.0	−1.1	1.1	2
R DUCEY	0	6	1	.315	54	0.0	0.3	0.2	0.4	1.0	2
M DAVIDSON	1	10	3	.217	106	0.2	0.6	0.7	−0.6	0.8	2
T BOSLEY	0	9	1	.260	96	0.0	0.5	0.2	0.0	0.7	2
B FIELDS	1	5	0	.269	67	0.2	0.3	0.0	0.1	0.6	1
E BULLOCK	0	3	1	.294	17	0.0	0.2	0.2	0.1	0.5	1
D BICHETTE	0	8	0	.261	46	0.0	0.5	0.0	0.0	0.5	1
K HUGHES	2	14	1	.194	108	0.4	0.8	0.2	−0.9	0.5	1
M KINGERY	1	9	3	.203	123	0.2	0.5	0.7	−0.9	0.4	1
L JOHNSON	0	6	6	.185	124	0.0	0.3	1.3	−1.2	0.4	1
G THURMAN	0	2	5	.167	66	0.0	0.1	1.1	−0.8	0.4	1
D JENNINGS	1	15	0	.208	101	0.2	0.8	0.0	−0.7	0.3	1
K ROMINE	1	6	2	.192	78	0.2	0.3	0.4	−0.7	0.3	1
S CAMPUSANO	2	12	0	.218	142	0.4	0.7	0.0	−0.8	0.3	1
T BRUNANSKY	1	6	1	.184	49	0.2	0.3	0.2	−0.5	0.3	1
R WILLIAMS	1	3	0	.323	31	0.2	0.2	0.0	0.3	0.7	1
B DAVIS	0	0	1	.240	25	0.0	0.0	0.2	0.0	0.2	0
J STONE	0	1	4	.164	61	0.0	0.1	0.9	−0.8	0.2	0

DESIGNATED HITTERS

	HR	RBI	SB	BA	AB	HR+	RBI+	SB+	BA+	POINTS	$
H BAINES	13	81	0	.277	599	2.6	4.6	0.0	1.1	8.2	17
K PHELPS	24	54	1	.263	297	4.8	3.1	0.2	0.0	8.1	17
B DOWNING	25	64	3	.242	484	5.0	3.6	0.7	−1.2	8.0	16
R MULLINIKS	12	48	1	.300	337	2.4	2.7	0.2	1.6	6.9	14
R KITTLE	18	43	0	.258	225	3.6	2.4	0.0	−0.1	5.9	12
C FIELDER	9	23	0	.230	174	1.8	1.3	0.0	−0.7	2.4	5
T FRANCONA	1	12	0	.311	212	0.2	0.7	0.0	1.4	2.3	5
D BAYLOR	7	34	0	.220	264	1.4	1.9	0.0	−1.4	1.9	4
J DWYER	2	18	0	.255	94	0.4	1.0	0.0	−0.1	1.4	3
J BENIQUEZ	1	8	0	.293	58	0.2	0.5	0.0	0.3	0.9	2
J CRUZ	1	7	0	.200	80	0.2	0.4	0.0	−0.6	0.0	0
S HORN	2	8	0	.148	61	0.4	0.5	0.0	−0.9	−0.1	0
Average, top 12	10	33	0	.260	240	1.9	1.9	0.1	−0.1	3.8	7.85

AL PITCHERS

	W	S	ERA	RATIO	IP	W+	S+	ERA+	RATIO+	POINTS	$
D ECKERSLEY	4	45	2.35	7.80	73	1.3	18.0	2.0	3.3	24.6	50
D JONES	3	37	2.27	9.18	83	1.0	14.8	2.4	2.5	20.6	42
J REARDON	2	42	2.47	10.23	73	0.7	16.8	1.8	1.3	20.6	42
M HENNEMAN	9	22	1.87	9.46	91	3.0	8.8	3.2	2.4	17.4	36
F VIOLA	24	0	2.64	10.22	255	8.0	0.0	4.7	4.0	16.8	34
T HIGUERA	16	0	2.45	8.99	227	5.3	0.0	5.0	6.4	16.7	34
R CLEMENS	18	0	2.93	9.51	264	6.0	0.0	3.7	5.9	15.6	32
B THIGPEN	5	34	3.30	12.90	90	1.7	13.6	0.9	−1.0	15.1	31
D PLESAC	1	30	2.41	9.98	52	0.3	12.0	1.4	1.1	14.8	30
L SMITH	4	29	2.80	11.73	84	1.3	11.6	1.6	0.1	14.6	30

CONTINUED ON NEXT PAGE

	W	S	ERA	RATIO	IP	W+	S+	ERA+	RATIO+	POINTS	S
M GUBICZA	20	0	2.70	10.68	270	6.7	0.0	4.7	3.0	14.4	29
B HARVEY	7	17	2.13	9.36	76	2.3	6.8	2.3	2.1	13.6	28
T HENKE	4	25	2.91	11.12	68	1.3	10.0	1.2	0.6	13.1	27
A ANDERSON	16	0	2.45	10.50	202	5.3	0.0	4.6	2.8	12.6	26
S FARR	5	20	2.50	11.32	83	1.7	8.0	2.0	0.5	12.1	25
G SWINDELL	18	0	3.20	10.38	242	6.0	0.0	2.5	3.5	11.9	24
D RIGHETTI	5	25	3.52	12.72	87	1.7	10.0	0.5	−0.8	11.4	23
D STEIB	16	0	3.04	10.24	207	5.3	0.0	2.7	3.3	11.4	23
D STEWART	21	0	3.23	11.43	276	7.0	0.0	2.6	1.1	10.7	22
J ROBINSON	13	0	2.98	10.10	172	4.3	0.0	2.5	3.1	9.9	20
C CRIM	7	9	2.91	10.54	105	2.3	3.6	1.7	1.5	9.2	19
J CANDELARIA	13	1	3.38	9.92	157	4.3	0.4	1.2	3.2	9.1	19
C GUANTE	5	12	2.82	10.51	80	1.7	4.8	1.5	1.2	9.1	19
D WARD	9	15	3.30	12.98	112	3.0	6.0	1.1	−1.3	8.7	18
T NIEDENFUER	3	18	3.51	11.90	59	1.0	7.2	0.4	0.0	8.6	18
M LANGSTON	15	0	3.34	11.43	261	5.0	0.0	2.1	1.1	8.1	17
C LEIBRANDT	13	0	3.19	11.33	243	4.3	0.0	2.5	1.2	8.1	17
W HERNANDEZ	6	10	3.06	10.77	68	2.0	4.0	1.0	0.8	7.8	16
C HOUGH	15	0	3.32	11.71	252	5.0	0.0	2.1	0.4	7.4	15
M SCHOOLER	5	15	3.54	12.85	48	1.7	6.0	0.3	−0.6	7.4	15
M MOORE	9	1	3.78	10.19	229	3.0	0.4	0.3	3.7	7.4	15
T CANDIOTTI	14	0	3.28	11.55	217	4.7	0.0	2.0	0.7	7.3	15
G NELSON	9	3	3.06	10.56	112	3.0	1.2	1.5	1.6	7.3	15
C BOSIO	7	6	3.36	11.27	182	2.3	2.4	1.5	1.1	7.3	15
D AUGUST	13	0	3.09	11.22	148	4.3	0.0	1.9	1.0	7.2	15
M JACKSON	6	4	2.63	10.60	99	2.0	1.6	2.1	1.4	7.1	15
J REUSS	13	0	3.44	11.11	183	4.3	0.0	1.2	1.4	7.0	14
B WELCH	17	0	3.64	11.70	245	5.7	0.0	0.8	0.4	6.9	14
J KEY	12	0	3.29	10.76	131	4.0	0.0	1.3	1.5	6.8	14
B STANLEY	6	5	3.19	10.54	102	2.0	2.0	1.2	1.5	6.7	14

CONTINUED ON NEXT PAGE

	W	S	ERA	RATIO	IP	W+	S+	ERA+	RATIO+	POINTS	$
B HURST	18	0	3.66	11.92	217	6.0	0.0	0.7	−0.1	6.6	13
S BANKHEAD	7	0	3.07	10.20	135	2.3	0.0	1.8	2.4	6.5	13
M WILLIAMS	2	18	4.63	12.57	68	0.7	7.2	−0.9	−0.6	6.4	13
P MIRABELLA	2	4	1.65	9.75	60	0.7	1.6	2.4	1.4	6.1	12
B SABERHAGEN	14	0	3.80	11.39	261	4.7	0.0	0.2	1.2	6.1	12
M BODDICKER	13	0	3.39	11.86	236	4.3	0.0	1.7	0.0	6.0	12
D LAPOINT	10	0	3.40	11.05	161	3.3	0.0	1.2	1.4	5.9	12
G MINTON	4	7	2.85	11.51	79	1.3	2.8	1.4	0.3	5.9	12
C MCMURTRY	3	3	2.25	9.15	60	1.0	1.2	1.8	1.8	5.8	12
E PLUNK	7	5	3.00	11.65	78	2.3	2.0	1.2	0.2	5.7	12
W GARDNER	8	2	3.50	11.05	149	2.7	0.8	0.9	1.3	5.6	11
K ATHERTON	7	3	3.41	10.58	74	2.3	1.2	0.6	1.0	5.2	11
T BURNS	8	1	3.16	11.13	103	2.7	0.4	1.3	0.8	5.1	11
J GUZMAN	11	0	3.70	11.41	207	3.7	0.0	0.5	0.9	5.1	10
R HONEYCUTT	3	7	3.50	11.18	80	1.0	2.8	0.5	0.6	4.9	10
J MORRIS	15	0	3.94	11.80	235	5.0	0.0	−0.3	0.2	4.8	10
M PEREZ	12	0	3.79	11.79	197	4.0	0.0	0.2	0.1	4.4	9
J CERUTTI	6	1	3.13	11.79	124	2.0	0.4	1.5	0.1	4.0	8
B WEGMAN	13	0	4.12	11.62	199	4.3	0.0	−0.8	0.5	4.0	8
G CADARET	5	3	2.89	12.06	72	1.7	1.2	1.3	−0.2	4.0	8
J MUSSELMAN	8	0	3.18	11.65	85	2.7	0.0	1.0	0.2	3.9	8
B MILACKI	2	0	0.72	6.48	25	0.7	0.0	1.5	1.5	3.7	8
P KILGUS	12	0	4.16	11.55	203	4.0	0.0	−1.0	0.6	3.6	7
D SCHMIDT	8	2	4.03	11.59	130	2.7	0.8	−0.4	0.4	3.5	7
J RUSSELL	10	0	3.82	11.88	189	3.3	0.0	0.1	0.0	3.4	7
J NIEVES	7	1	4.08	10.93	110	2.3	0.4	−0.4	1.1	3.4	7
P GIBSON	4	0	2.93	11.45	92	1.3	0.0	1.5	0.4	3.2	7
J MONTGOMERY	7	1	3.45	12.06	63	2.3	0.4	0.5	−0.2	3.1	6
J BERENGUER	8	2	3.96	12.15	100	2.7	0.8	−0.2	−0.3	3.0	6
B LONG	8	2	4.03	11.90	174	2.7	0.8	−0.5	−0.1	2.9	6

CONTINUED ON NEXT PAGE

	W	S	ERA	RATIO	IP	W+	S+	ERA+	RATIO+	POINTS	S
J FARRELL	14	0	4.24	12.11	210	4.7	0.0	−1.3	−0.5	2.9	6
E KING	4	3	3.41	12.32	69	1.3	1.2	0.6	−0.4	2.7	6
C HUDSON	6	2	4.49	10.92	106	2.0	0.8	−1.1	1.1	2.7	6
R RHODEN	12	0	4.20	11.97	197	4.0	0.0	−1.1	−0.2	2.7	6
G GARBER	0	6	3.58	11.57	33	0.0	2.4	0.2	0.1	2.7	5
D LAMP	7	0	3.48	12.09	83	2.3	0.0	0.6	−0.2	2.7	5
F TANANA	14	0	4.21	12.28	203	4.7	0.0	−1.1	−0.8	2.7	5
D ALEXANDER	14	0	4.32	12.03	229	4.7	0.0	−1.7	−0.4	2.6	5
R SMITH	3	0	2.68	9.97	37	1.0	0.0	0.8	0.8	2.6	5
S DAVIS	16	0	3.70	13.48	202	5.3	0.0	0.5	−3.3	2.6	5
F BANNISTER	12	0	4.33	11.88	189	4.0	0.0	−1.4	0.0	2.5	5
J CLANCY	11	1	4.49	11.64	196	3.7	0.4	−2.0	0.4	2.5	5
C YOUNG	11	0	4.15	12.20	156	3.7	0.0	−0.7	−0.6	2.4	5
T MCCARTHY	2	1	1.38	7.62	13	0.7	0.4	0.6	0.6	2.3	5
S HILLEGAS	3	0	3.15	10.80	40	1.0	0.0	0.5	0.5	2.0	4
B JONES	2	1	2.42	11.08	26	0.7	0.4	0.7	0.2	2.0	4
B WITT	8	0	3.92	12.13	174	2.7	0.0	−0.2	−0.5	2.0	4
E HANSON	2	0	3.24	10.15	42	0.7	0.0	0.5	0.8	2.0	4
D MOHORCIC	4	6	4.22	13.50	75	1.3	2.4	−0.5	−1.4	1.9	4
J BAUTISTA	6	0	4.30	11.32	172	2.0	0.0	−1.2	0.9	1.7	3
O JONES	5	1	4.35	11.60	81	1.7	0.4	−0.7	0.2	1.6	3
W TERRELL	7	0	3.97	12.08	206	2.3	0.0	−0.4	−0.5	1.5	3
B HAVENS	2	1	3.14	12.40	57	0.7	0.4	0.8	−0.4	1.5	3
B WILKINSON	2	2	3.48	12.48	31	0.7	0.8	0.2	−0.2	1.5	3
J GLEATON	0	3	3.55	11.84	38	0.0	1.2	0.2	0.0	1.4	3
M WITT	13	0	4.15	12.62	250	4.3	0.0	−1.1	−1.8	1.4	3
M PORTUGAL	3	3	4.53	12.02	58	1.0	1.2	−0.7	−0.1	1.4	3
T CASTILLO	1	0	3.00	7.20	15	0.3	0.0	0.3	0.8	1.4	3
N ALLEN	5	0	3.84	12.12	117	1.7	0.0	0.1	−0.3	1.4	3
D MOORE	5	4	4.91	15.27	33	1.7	1.6	−0.6	−1.3	1.3	3

CONTINUED ON NEXT PAGE

	W	S	ERA	RATIO	IP	W+	S+	ERA+	RATIO+	POINTS	S
M FLANAGAN	13	0	4.18	12.80	211	4.3	0.0	−1.1	−2.0	1.3	3
M KNUDSON	0	0	1.13	10.69	16	0.0	0.0	0.8	0.2	1.1	2
D HEINKEL	0	1	3.96	10.40	36	0.0	0.4	0.0	0.6	0.9	2
J MCDOWELL	5	0	3.97	12.20	159	1.7	0.0	−0.3	−0.6	0.8	2
L STRAKER	2	1	3.92	12.08	83	0.7	0.4	−0.1	−0.2	0.8	2
H PENA	1	0	2.51	11.93	14	0.3	0.0	0.4	0.0	0.7	1
E VANDE BERG	2	2	4.14	13.38	37	0.7	0.8	−0.2	−0.7	0.6	1
J BALLARD	8	0	4.40	12.27	153	2.7	0.0	−1.4	−0.6	0.6	1
AVERAGE, TOP 108	8.1	4.1	3.50	11.38	131	2.7	1.7	0.8	0.7	5.9	12.01
A LEITER	4	0	3.92	12.87	57	1.3	0.0	−0.1	−0.7	0.6	1
G GONZALES	0	1	3.38	11.81	21	0.0	0.4	0.2	0.0	0.6	1
D WELLS	3	4	4.62	13.43	64	1.0	1.6	−0.9	−1.1	0.6	1
S CLIBURN	4	0	4.07	12.32	84	1.3	0.0	−0.3	−0.4	0.6	1
J SOLANO	0	3	4.09	13.91	22	0.0	1.2	−0.1	−0.5	0.6	1
R GUIDRY	2	0	4.18	11.57	56	0.7	0.0	−0.3	0.2	0.5	1
C FINLEY	9	0	4.17	12.64	194	3.0	0.0	−1.0	−1.5	0.5	1
J REED	1	1	3.96	11.99	86	0.3	0.4	−0.1	−0.1	0.5	1
M CLEAR	1	0	2.79	13.66	29	0.3	0.0	0.6	−0.6	0.3	1
D GORDON	3	1	4.40	12.74	59	1.0	0.4	−0.6	−0.6	0.2	0
I SANCHEZ	3	1	4.54	13.63	36	1.0	0.4	−0.4	−0.7	0.2	0
D OTTO	0	0	1.80	13.50	10	0.0	0.0	0.4	−0.2	0.2	0
D QUISENBERRY	0	1	3.55	13.15	25	0.0	0.4	0.2	−0.4	0.2	0
M BIRKBECK	10	0	4.72	12.92	124	33	0.0	−1.8	−1.4	0.1	0
S BAILES	9	0	4.90	12.10	145	3.0	0.0	−2.5	−0.4	0.1	0
J LAZORKO	0	0	3.35	12.67	38	0.0	0.0	0.4	−0.4	0.0	0
T FILER	5	0	4.43	12.48	102	1.7	0.0	−1.0	−0.7	0.0	0
F TOLIVER	7	0	4.24	13.19	115	2.3	0.0	−0.7	−1.6	0.0	0
R ANDERSON	2	0	4.24	13.24	34	0.7	0.0	−0.2	−0.6	−0.1	0
G OLSON	1	0	3.27	16.36	11	0.3	0.0	0.1	−0.6	−0.1	0

CONTINUED ON NEXT PAGE

	W	S	ERA	RATIO	IP	W+	S+	ERA+	RATIO+	POINTS	S
R SCURRY	0	2	4.02	14.36	31	0.0	0.8	−0.1	−0.9	−0.2	0
J NUNEZ	0	0	3.07	13.81	29	0.0	0.0	0.5	−0.7	−0.2	0
S CORBETT	2	1	4.17	13.90	45	0.7	0.4	−0.2	−1.1	−0.2	0
M THURMOND	1	3	4.58	12.90	75	0.3	1.2	−0.9	−0.9	−0.3	−1
L AQUINO	1	0	2.79	15.52	29	0.3	0.0	0.6	−1.2	−0.3	−1
S ONTIVEROS	3	0	4.61	12.84	55	1.0	0.0	−0.7	−0.6	−0.3	−1
S SEARCY	0	0	5.63	13.50	8	0.0	0.0	−0.2	−0.2	−0.4	−1
G WALTER	1	0	5.13	12.31	26	0.3	0.0	−0.6	−0.2	−0.4	−1
J BITTIGER	2	0	4.23	12.84	62	0.7	0.0	−0.4	−0.7	−0.4	−1
K PATTERSON	0	1	4.79	13.94	21	0.0	0.4	−0.3	−0.5	−0.5	−1
M WILLIAMSON	5	2	4.90	12.62	118	1.7	0.8	−2.1	−1.0	−0.6	−1
K MCCASKILL	8	0	4.31	13.29	146	2.7	0.0	−1.1	−2.2	−0.6	−1
T GORDON	0	0	5.17	13.22	16	0.0	0.0	−0.4	−0.3	−0.6	−1
T BOLTON	1	1	4.75	14.54	30	0.3	0.4	−0.5	−1.0	−0.7	−1
D SCHATZEDER	0	3	6.49	14.01	26	0.0	1.2	−1.3	−0.7	−0.7	−2
S SHIELDS	5	0	4.37	13.77	82	1.7	0.0	−0.7	−1.7	−0.8	−2
B BLACK	4	1	5.00	12.89	81	1.3	0.4	−1.6	−0.9	−0.8	−2
D EILAND	0	0	6.40	13.50	13	0.0	0.0	−0.6	−0.3	−0.8	−2
J DEDMON	1	1	4.55	14.97	34	0.3	0.4	−0.4	−1.2	−0.9	−2
K BROWN	1	0	4.24	15.82	23	0.3	0.0	−0.1	−1.1	−0.9	−2
J CECENA	0	1	4.79	14.70	26	0.0	0.4	−0.4	−0.9	−0.9	−2
P HARNISCH	0	0	5.54	15.23	13	0.0	0.0	−0.4	−0.5	−0.9	−2
R YETT	9	0	4.62	13.47	134	3.0	0.0	−1.7	−2.3	−1.0	−2
S ROSENBERG	0	1	4.30	14.09	46	0.0	0.4	−0.4	−1.2	−1.1	−2
M MORGAN	1	1	5.43	11.73	71	0.3	0.4	−2.0	0.1	−1.2	−2
L GUETTERMAN	1	0	4.65	13.94	41	0.3	0.0	−0.6	−1.0	−1.2	−2
R DOTSON	12	0	5.00	13.16	171	4.0	0.0	−3.2	−2.3	−1.5	−3
D PETRY	3	0	4.38	12.76	140	1.0	0.0	−1.2	−1.3	−1.5	−3
D BUICE	2	3	5.88	15.90	41	0.7	1.2	−1.5	−1.9	−1.6	−3
R NICHOLS	1	0	5.06	12.46	69	0.3	0.0	−1.5	−0.5	−1.6	−3

CONTINUED ON NEXT PAGE

	W	S	ERA	RATIO	IP	W+	S+	ERA+	RATIO+	POINTS	$
J PERLMAN	0	0	5.49	16.48	20	0.0	0.0	−0.6	−1.1	−1.7	−3
D STAPLETON	0	0	5.93	19.10	14	0.0	0.0	−0.5	−1.2	−1.7	−3
D SISK	3	0	3.72	14.69	94	1.0	0.0	0.2	−2.9	−1.7	−3
T TAYLOR	0	0	6.26	14.48	23	0.0	0.0	−1.0	−0.7	−1.7	−4
D AASE	0	0	4.05	14.85	47	0.0	0.0	−0.1	−1.6	−1.7	−4
M EICHHORN	0	1	4.19	14.31	67	0.0	0.4	−0.4	−1.8	−1.8	−4
O BOYD	9	0	5.34	13.05	130	3.0	0.0	−3.3	−1.6	−1.9	−4
D VAUGHN	0	0	7.63	16.44	15	0.0	0.0	−1.1	−0.8	−1.9	−4
T JOHN	9	0	4.49	13.63	176	3.0	0.0	−1.8	−3.2	−2.0	−4
R HAYWARD	4	0	5.46	14.08	63	1.3	0.0	−1.8	−1.6	−2.0	−4
J NIEKRO	1	0	10.03	19.29	12	0.3	0.0	−1.3	−1.0	−2.0	−4
J DEJESUS	0	0	27.07	43.98	3	0.0	0.0	−1.1	−1.0	−2.2	−4
S NIELSEN	1	0	6.86	18.31	20	0.3	0.0	−1.1	−1.5	−2.2	−5
T STODDARD	2	3	6.38	14.56	55	0.7	1.2	−2.5	−1.7	−2.3	−5
S CURRY	0	0	8.18	23.73	11	0.0	0.0	−0.9	−1.6	−2.4	−5
B SWIFT	8	0	4.59	13.60	175	2.7	0.0	−2.1	−3.1	−2.5	−5
T CLARK	6	0	5.07	14.46	94	2.0	0.0	−2.0	−2.7	−2.7	−5
S MCGREGOR	0	0	8.83	17.66	17	0.0	0.0	−1.6	−1.2	−2.8	−6
C SCHILLING	0	0	9.82	19.64	15	0.0	0.0	−1.6	−1.4	−3.0	−6
J TRAUTWEIN	0	0	9.00	19.69	16	0.0	0.0	−1.5	−1.5	−3.0	−6
O PERAZA	5	0	5.55	14.13	86	1.7	0.0	−2.5	−2.2	−3.0	−6
C LEA	7	0	4.85	14.26	130	2.3	0.0	−2.2	−3.3	−3.1	−6
S ELLSWORTH	1	0	6.75	15.75	36	0.3	0.0	−1.9	−1.6	−3.2	−7
W FRASER	12	0	5.41	13.08	195	4.0	0.0	−4.9	−2.4	−3.2	−7
M SMITHSON	9	0	5.97	13.15	127	3.0	0.0	−4.5	−1.7	−3.3	−7
R RODRIGUEZ	1	0	7.09	16.36	33	0.3	0.0	−1.9	−1.7	−3.3	−7
B BLYLEVEN	10	0	5.43	12.63	207	3.3	0.0	−5.2	−1.6	−3.4	−7
S CARLTON	0	0	16.76	23.28	10	0.0	0.0	−2.3	−1.3	−3.6	−7
M CAMPBELL	6	0	5.89	13.42	115	2.0	0.0	−4.0	−1.9	−3.9	−8
E NUNEZ	1	0	7.98	18.10	29	0.3	0.0	−2.2	−2.1	−4.0	−8

CONTINUED ON NEXT PAGE

	W	S	ERA	RATIO	IP	W+	S+	ERA+	RATIO+	POINTS	$
J SELLERS	1	0	4.83	15.23	86	0.3	0.0	−1.5	−3.2	−4.3	−9
T POWER	6	0	5.91	14.45	99	2.0	0.0	−3.5	−2.8	−4.3	−9
T STOTTLEMYRE	4	0	5.69	14.23	98	1.3	0.0	−3.1	−2.5	−4.3	−9
J TIBBS	4	0	5.39	14.01	159	1.3	0.0	−4.0	−3.5	−6.2	−13
JN DAVIS	2	1	6.64	17.95	64	0.7	0.4	−3.2	−4.4	−6.5	−13
S TROUT	4	0	7.83	18.69	56	1.3	0.0	−4.0	−4.4	−7.1	−14

In a book like this, there should be something useful on each page. Did you find that there was? Was there anything important left out?

This is an open invitation to the peanut gallery. While you're at it, please send information on your leagues. Judging by this year, the odds of that information appearing in *Patton's 1990 Price Guide* are low, but they will get much higher if Jerry Heath either retires or asks for a piece of Gulf and Western. The information I find most useful, and hardest to get, is the round-by-round record of the auctions.

But feel free to send any and all missiles and missives to:

Alex Patton
Village Consulting
5th floor
177 Prince Street
New York, NY 10012

I'd be more insulted by silence than insults.